THE COATS BOOK OF
Embroidery

THE COATS BOOK OF
Embroidery
Mary Gostelow

With over 800 line illustrations by the author
Colour photographs by Martin F. Gostelow

David&Charles Newton Abbot·London·Vancouver

British Library Cataloguing in Publication Data

Gostelow, Mary
  The Coats book of embroidery.
  1. Embroidery
  I. Title
  746.4′4   TT770

  ISBN 0-7153-7614-4

Typeset and Printed in Great Britain
by Redwood Burn Limited Trowbridge & Esher
for David & Charles (Publishers) Limited
Brunel House Newton Abbot Devon

Published in Canada
by Douglas David & Charles Limited
1875 Welch Street North Vancouver BC

Contents

Acknowledgements

The author would like to thank, for their help in so many ways, Chottie Alderson; The Magazine *Antiques*, Wendell Garrett and A Hyatt Mayor, for information on 'fishing lady' needlepoints; Mrs JC Brenton; Elizabeth Catheray; Pamela Clabburn; J & P Coats (UK) Ltd, Peter Williams, Jim Clarke, Jean Kinmond and Elizabeth Bellamy; Fleur Cowles; Pamela Dubreil; Jacqueline Enthoven, for giving permission to use her copyrighted material on the forbidden stitch; Julie Fallowfield; Jane Galloway; Anne Harrel; Nancy Hodgkin; Donald King; The Needlewoman Shop, D Macleod, Miss Wood, Miss Chalmers and Miss Thomas; Anna and Patrick Pearson; Selectus Ltd; Stephanie Teychenné; Jean Van Wagenen; Sheila Watson; and Martin Gostelow, without whom the book would not have been possible.

Picture Acknowledgements

Thanks are given to the following owners of items illustrated:

Chottie Alderson, pp175, 190; The Duke of Atholl (photographs Martin Gostelow), p235; Christie's South Kensington Ltd, pp100, 134, 158 (right), 219, 220; Daughters of the American Revolution Museum, Washington DC, p83 (No 3632); Nancy Dent, p27; Dorset Natural History and Archaeological Society, p228; Virginia Felker and Felker Art-Needlework, p79; Fitzwilliam Museum, Cambridge, p229; Audrey Francini, p66; Dorrit Gutterson, p127; Polly Hope, p195; Caroline Jubb, p66; Posy McMillen, p128; Metropolitan Museum of Art, p54 (right, No 38.157, Gift of Katharine Keyes in memory of her father Homer Eaton Keyes, 1938); Museum of Fine Arts, Boston, pp50 (right, No 43.222), 173 (No 21.2233); Museum für Kunst und Gewebe, Hamburg, p147; Museum of London, pp34 (left), 158 (left, No 42.51), 171 (No 4340); Needlewoman Shop, pp112, 117, 119, 121; Sir John Paget, Bart, p166; from the collection at Parham Park, Sussex, by kind permission of Mrs P A Tritton, pp34 (right), 65, 165, 194; Anna Pearson, p175; Philadelphia Museum of Art, p50 (left, No 69-288-204); Barbara Price, p35; Royal Ontario Museum, pp8 (No 932.15), 77 (No 959.60.2); Pat Russell, p153 (right); Diana Springall and Mr D D A Piesold (photograph John Hunnex), p18; Mrs L H Steadman, p222; Gigs Stevens, p32; Mr Peter Maxwell Stuart, p84; Textile Conservation Centre, Mrs Karen Finch, OBE, and Mr A R Dufty, CBE, FSA, p62; Textile Museum, Washington DC, p7 (No 91.192); Victoria and Albert Museum, Crown Copyright, pp17 (on loan to Oxburgh Hall, No T30-1955), 53 (No Ch.00450-2), 68 (left, No 673-1864; right, No 761-1868), 91 (No 288.1906), 98 (No 1861-1921), 174 (No T333-1910), 209 (No T27-1940), 216 (No T99-1961); Welsh Folk Museum, p200; Mrs Christopher Wharton, p90; Henry Francis du Pont Winterthur Museum, p54 (left, No 69.1345).

Introduction

This is primarily a book for embroiderers who want clear, precise details of techniques. Those who do not themselves embroider can admire those methods and the beauty of finished items and they may be tempted to begin work themselves. There is a special section in chapter one showing how to thread a needle and start embroidery.

Generally, professional work can be recognized by regularity of stitches and even tension. In the past most professional embroiderers were men, though at certain times in history, especially in western Europe from the sixteenth century, some types of embroidery were popular as ladies' pastimes. In North America, embroidery in the colonial period was a more practical matter.

Embroidery is not an isolated textile art. From the beginning, lost in antiquity, it is almost certain that embroidery followed whenever weaving became commonplace. Embroidery has been closely related to other textile embellishments used for

Detail from a mantle, Nasca I style, probably worked in southern Peru in the fourth century BC, is decorated with stem stitch, a technique still popular with embroiderers everywhere (wool embroidered with wools and cottons, 117.5 × 219cm [46¼ × 86¼in] overall)

Some techniques can be combined. Here a mid-seventeenth-century picture incorporates couched work, metal thread embroidery and stump, or raised, work as well as surface embroidery. The intricate detailing of strawberries and other devices on the figures' clothing illustrates how embroidery has often been employed for costume decoration (white satin embroidered with silks, linen, metal thread and chenille in a variety of stitches including back stitch, buttonhole stitch, long-and-short stitch and satin stitch 25.4 × 34.9cm [10 × 13¾in])

costume, household and other decoration, the first definite evidence of which comes from Asia and South America. Surviving fragments indicate that appliqué, chain stitch and stem stitch were as popular then as they are today.

The oldest extant English embroideries, worked in the middle of the ninth century, consist of four linen strips decorated with couching and satin stitch in silk, linen and gold metal strips wound round brown animal hair. The earliest dated American embroidery is a stumpwork picture finished by Rebekah Wheeler in 'ye month of May, 1664'.

But this is intended less as a history of embroidery than as a guide to embroidery practised today. Without wishing to offend scholars, embroidery is here taken to include all forms of stitched decoration including canvas work, referred to by the popular name needlepoint. Other frequently used generic terms here employed include counted-thread, comprising Assisi work, blackwork, cross stitches and other techniques in which warp and weft of the ground fabric must be counted, and surface embroidery, in which the stitches are made regardless of alignment of fabric threads beneath. Similarly, to aid the practising embroiderer, all measurements within this book are recorded in metric and imperial counts, apart from thread counts (numbers of warp and weft threads within a stated area of fabric), which are given in centimetres only.

As well as introductory details, the first chapter gives general hints that may be of interest to all embroiderers, beginners and advanced. Thereafter there are thirty-five chapters arranged alphabetically. Some concentrate on aspects of knots and loop stitches and straight or other groups of stitches. Most sections concentrate on one technique, opening with a definition and the basic evolution of the technique covered and followed by notes on material requirements and methods of working. Such techniques as appliqué and simple needlepoint are less demanding than others, and it is possible to combine more than one technique. Other chapters relate to blocking and mounting and other practical matters. Following these thirty-five chapters is a comprehensive list of general reference books and specialized works for further reading.

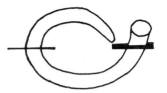

The main key to the book is the index at the back. Stitch entries refer to the explanatory diagram of that stitch. Stem stitch, for example, is listed within the index by the page on which it is illustrated but it will also be found under alternative names, all referring the reader back to the main diagram. There is no page cross-referencing within the main text so if something is not explained within one section, reference to the index will quickly lead to where a full explanation is set out.

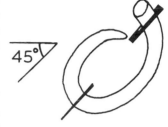

Black and white photographs and line drawings relate directly to the text. The latter have in some instances been worked on a grid of $\frac{1}{10}$ in squares. A piece of tracing paper with the same grid laid over these designs will aid transposition of charted diagrams. When illustrating stitch instructions, line drawings are intentionally stylized. Shading is used to indicate the reverse of fabrics, empty spaces and sometimes to distinguish one stage of forming a stitch from the next. In this last instance a change of diagram shade does not require a change of embroidery thread colour.

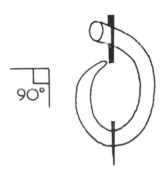

The direction of working a stitch is not unalterable. If it is easier to work chain stitch going upwards rather than, say, to the left, then the book can simply be turned through any angle as required. As long as the same finished stitch results, the embroiderer should work in whichever direction is most handy. Left-handed embroiderers can hold the book in front of a mirror to see a reverse image.

A stitch can be executed at whatever angle is most handy. Left-handed embroiderers should hold the diagram in front of a mirror

Apart from many designs that can be copied from photographs and line drawings in the book, there are such useful projects as embroidered uppers for a pair of wooden-soled sandals, a cross-stitch cushion cover using traditional Middle Eastern motifs and a patchwork board for the game of pachisi. In some instances the materials required for these projects are inexpensive and handy and in each case the directions are geared to the embroiderer who as yet is primarily equipped with enthusiasm.

And so to embroidery . . . a stimulation and addiction that can attract *anyone*!

1. Preparing to embroider

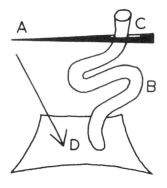

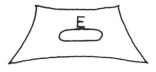

Embroidery is ornamental stitchery, usually worked with a hand-held needle with thread through its eye, or hole, on a ground (base) material. Many embroiderers like the feel of a soft, limp woven fabric in their hands as they work. Others prefer the stiffness of meshed canvas, held in their hands or supported on a frame, and occasionally felt or paper are preferred. Although some techniques demand specific fabrics, the ground material chosen is often up to the embroiderer (see chapter 18 Fabrics and Threads).

Before starting to embroider, it is a good idea to bind the edges of the chosen fabric to prevent them fraying. The ground can also be marked into quarters or eighths to help balance or centre a finished design. This can be done as shown by using a non-solvent fibre pen, which should be thoroughly tested to make sure that it will not run (bleed) on either the fabric or the embroidery thread to be employed (see p 11).

Needle (A) with thread (B) passing through its eye (C) and working from the ground, or base, material (D), form a stitch (E)

The needle is held at the thickest, eyed, end, between the embroiderer's thumb and forefinger

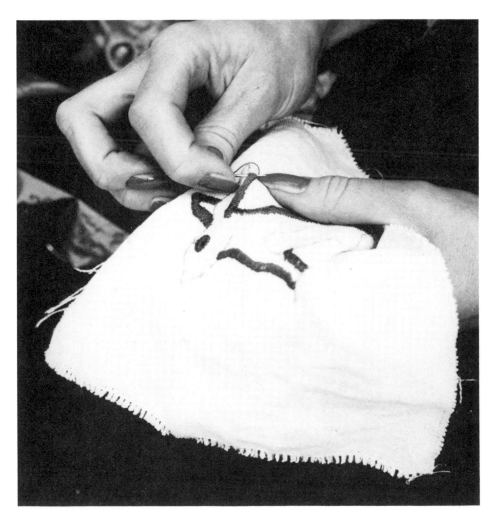

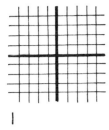

1

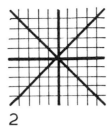

2

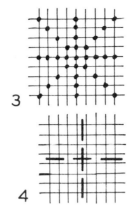

3

4

To balance or centre a design, it is a good idea to mark the ground fabric into quarters (1) or eighths (2). Dots can be made at relevant cross-overs of warp and weft threads. This marks *threads* of the ground fabric (3). Alternatively, long sewn stitches can be worked. This method marks the *holes* between the threads (4)

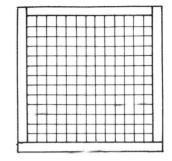

(*Below, left*) The edges of this piece of Glenshee linen have been bound with machine stitching to prevent them from fraying.

(*Below*) Stiff canvas, here held in place in a 'fanny' frame. The edges of the canvas are bound with cotton tape doubled over and machine-stitched in place. Loose ends of worked lengths of woollen thread are left on the front of the canvas and will later be cut off

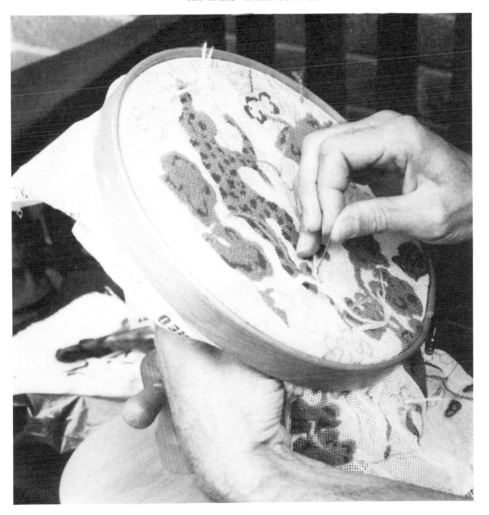

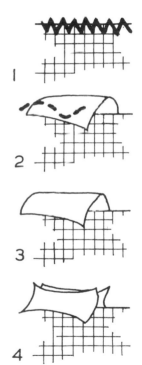

1

2

3

4

Methods of binding the edges of fabric include: **1** Machine stitching direct on to the material. **2** Cotton tape folded over and secured with machine stitching. **3** A length of wide masking tape folded over. **4** Two lengths of masking tape put one either side of the ground fabric, sticky sides together. The last two methods can be ironed for greater bonding

11

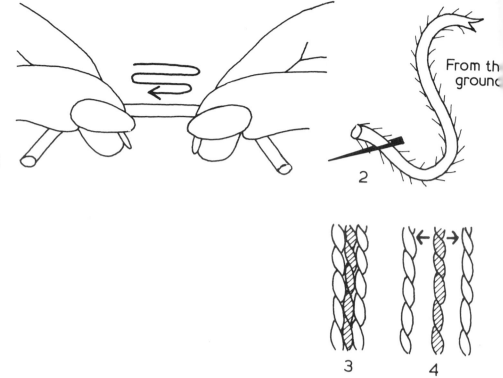

(Right) **1** An easy way to find the nap of woollen thread is to pull a short length back and forth close to the skin of one's upper lip. **2** All wool should be threaded through the needle with the hairs running smoothly back to the ground fabric. **3** Some wools have three strands of plied thread. **4** After the nap direction is determined, the strands should be separated to give a fluffier embroidery

From the ground

(Below) **1** After three strands of Persian or other woollen thread are separated, they can be worked singly or put together again as required to work with two, three or more strands. **2** Sometimes woollen thread has strands of different thicknesses. **3** A thick and a thin strand equals the combination of two medium strands and therefore when working with two strands at one time two lengths of thread should be separated and put back together in the manner illustrated

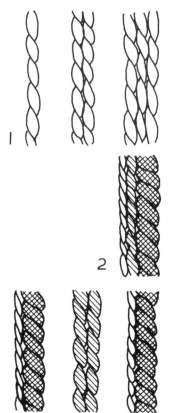

As with the ground fabric, there is a wide variety of threads available. Wool threads sometimes have a noticeable nap which can be found by passing a length of thread close to the skin of a particularly sensitive area, such as above the upper lip. To get a fluffier embroidery, the strands can be separated and put back together before attempting to thread the needle. Thread lengths longer than 46cm (18in) may knot and become unmanageable.

One end of a length of thread is passed, 'threaded', through the eye of a needle, a challenge that, as in any kind of sewing, sometimes presents problems to the beginner; embroiderers quickly develop a method that suits them, and calyx-eyed or self-threading needles and a variety of needle-threaders are now available. Once the eye has been successfully penetrated the thread is pulled through so that there is one short end which remains loose during work and one long end along which embroidery stitches are formed.

This long end must be attached to the ground before any stitches are worked and two securing methods are illustrated on p13. When most of the length of thread has been worked, or if a new colour is required, the old thread must also be secured (see p 14).

There are literally thousands of different stitches that can be worked, and indeed some that are set out here may be recognized by another name. Stitches are either sewn or stabbed and since the latter method requires two hands it is imperative to work with a frame. (Other useful pieces of equipment are listed in chapter 17.) Although some equipment can prove expensive, embroidery need not entail a large outlay. The card embroidery illustrated in chapter 7 shows a frog worked with four left-over skeins of stranded cotton on a scrap of brown manilla envelope.

Once the beginner knows something of what simple embroidery is all about he or she can progress with the aid of general hints which recur again and again throughout the book.

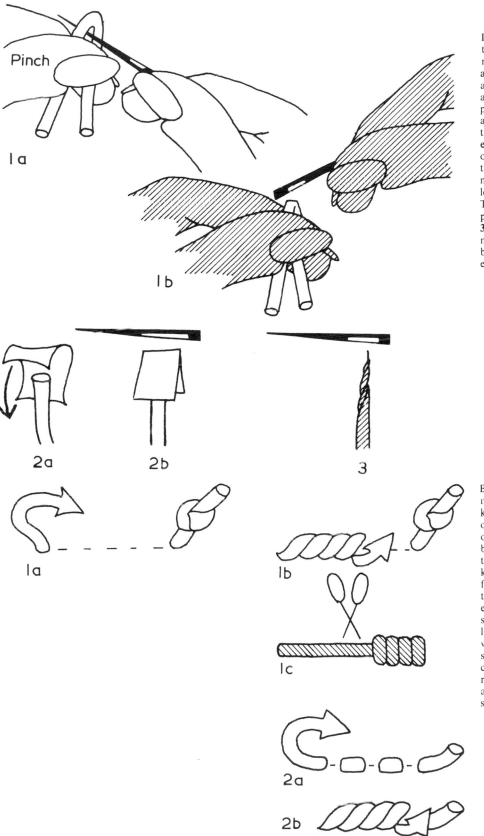

Pinch

1a

1b

2a

2b

3

It is sometimes difficult to get a thick thread through the eye of a needle. Three possible solutions are: **1** The thread should be folded around the point end of a needle and pinched hard as close as possible to the needle (a) before attempting to pass the tight fold that results through the needle's eye (b). **2** The cut end of a length of thread should be placed inside the fold of a piece of paper (a) narrow enough to fit within the length of the needle's eye (b). The paper with thread then passes easily through the eye. **3** The end of the thread can be moistened or twisted firmly before being pushed through the eye

1a

1b

1c

2a

2b

Beginning a new thread should never be done with a permanent knot. Two solutions, both originating away from the start of the embroidery and worked back towards it, are: **1** The end to be secured is temporarily knotted. From the front of the fabric, a long stitch is taken towards the beginning of the embroidered design (a), then sewn normally, catching in the long retaining thread on the wrong side (b). After a few stitches the retaining thread is cut from the reverse (c). **2** Tiny running stitches are worked (a) and then covered by embroidery stitches (b)

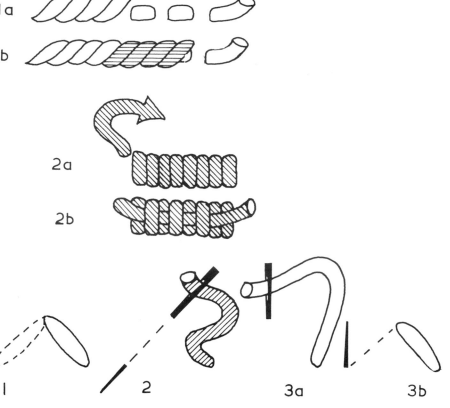

1a

1b

2a

2b

When most of a thread has been worked or a new colour is required, the loose end can be secured in several ways. Two methods are: **1** Tiny running stitches are worked within the confines of ground area shortly to be covered by area shortly to be covered by embroidery (a). The next length of thread (shaded) therefore covers those stitches (b) **2** From the reverse, the loose end of thread (a) is carefully woven in and out of existing stitches (b)

A stitch (1) can be formed by *sewing* (2), which makes an entrance to and exit from the ground with each movement of the needle, or by *stabbing* (3), which makes two separate movements (a and b). When stabbing, the needle passes from one hand to the other, down through the fabric (c) and back up again (d). It is a matter of personal preference which hand is held uppermost

1   2   3a   3b

An indication of how simple embroidery can be is this trio of letters worked in big cross stitches. Stranded cotton is here combined with Binca canvas on which each stitch is worked over one clearly-defined block of warp and weft threads. The uppermost diagonals of cross stitches should always face the same way, ideally uppermost to the right

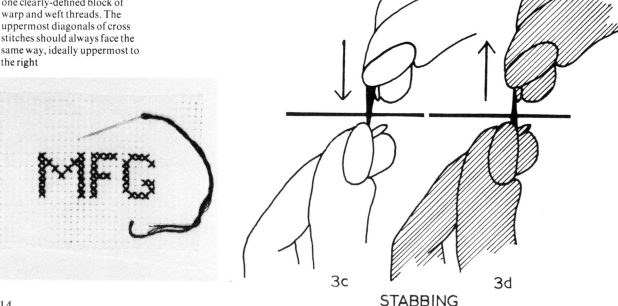

3c   3d

STABBING

14

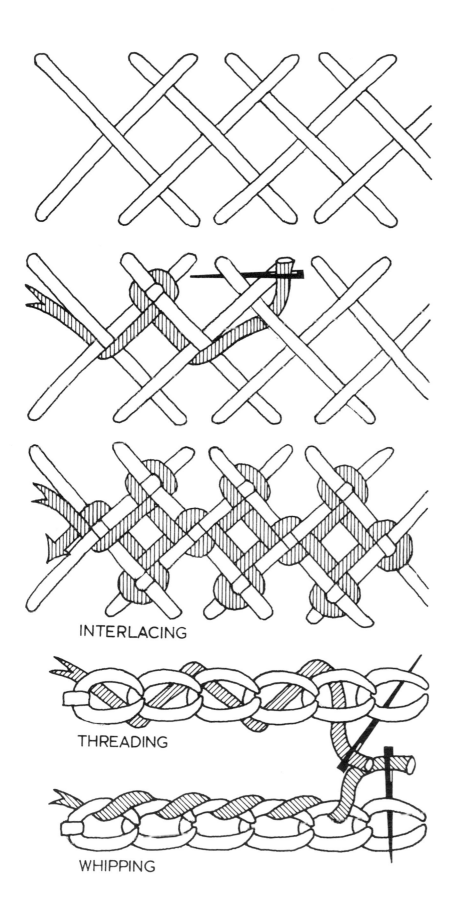

Among the many ways to augment basic stitches once they have been worked are superficial techniques which, apart from the beginning and end of each thread, *do not enter the ground fabric*. Three superficial techniques are interlacing, threading and whipping

INTERLACING

THREADING

WHIPPING

Tacking, or basting, temporarily holds fabric in place while it is being embroidered and these stitches are subsequently withdrawn. A compensation stitch (shaded) fills a small ground area in a style as close as possible to those stitches covering the main ground

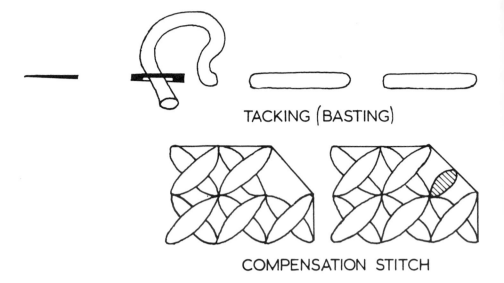

TACKING (BASTING)

COMPENSATION STITCH

Tacking, or basting, implies long loose stitches providing temporary markers or retainers to hold fabric until it is permanently secured with embroidery, at which point the temporary stitches can be removed; or the stitches may simply mark out an area of fabric. Although technically basting, the more usual American term, is worked only through one thickness of fabric, and tacking, a word more generally employed in England, refers to stitches sewn through two or more layers of fabric, the two words are often taken as synonymous.

Equally useful are compensation stitches. Sometimes a block of, for instance, cross stitches will not exactly fit into a required area of ground fabric. The excess space is therefore covered with small stitches as similar as possible to the main stitches. Interlacing, threading and whipping, extras employed subsequent to basic embroidery, are three other general techniques that should be understood. One version of each is illustrated.

2. Appliqué

Appliqué, or applied work, signifies that at least one different piece of fabric has been placed over or under another and is held in place with embroidery stitches.

The term appliqué, from the French verb *appliquer*, to put on, usually refers to onlay work in which layers of fabric are added to the surface of the main ground. Other forms of appliqué, extensively covered later in this chapter, include inlay work and reverse and mola techniques. Net embroidery (see chapter 27), padded work (chapter 28) and shadow work (chapter 33) also include application.

Historically the lineage of appliqué can be traced to finds at Pazyryk in Siberia dating from about the fourth century BC. In the Hermitage in Leningrad there is a reconstruction of a wall-hanging from an Altaian-Scythian chieftain's burial chamber, the hanging being decorated with three bands of coloured felts hemmed to a ground of beige felt in a design showing seated goddesses and horsemen. Greeks

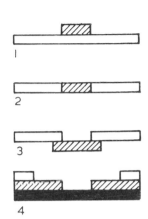

Appliqué implies layers of fabric laid over or under the main ground. Here, seen in cross section, with the main ground left white, are: **1** Overlaid, onlay, appliqué, generally known simply as appliqué. **2** Inlay appliqué. **3** Reverse appliqué. **4** Mola appliqué

The Cavendish Hanging, embroidered in the late sixteenth century, partially by Mary, Queen of Scots (1542–87). The main central panel, 56 × 58.5cm (22 × 23in), and smaller cruciform and octagonal medallions were worked in fine tent stitch in silks on canvas and subsequently applied, each in its own padded tailored frame of damask or brocade, on to a ground of green velvet.

and the Copts of Ancient Egypt are also known to have used appliqué, and the art was possibly introduced to western Europe by crusaders who brought back from the eastern Mediterranean surcoats, banners and other costume items decorated with applied motifs.

In England, appliqué became especially popular in the sixteenth century. Since it was difficult to embroider directly on to the sumptuous velvet fabric that was then in use, needlepoint devices worked on canvas were cut out and hemmed to a velvet ground. Application stitches were sometimes subsequently covered with laid and couched cord.

In America, appliqué has been extensively used in conjunction with quilting. Particularly during the nineteenth century, broderie perse, alternatively known as cretonne appliqué, was sometimes preferred. Motifs were cut out of printed chintz fabric and attached to a plain ground, possibly with hemming or buttonhole stitch.

Appliqué remains popular with modern creative embroiderers as well as those who prefer traditional designs, and various characteristic forms are still worked by peoples in North, Central and South America, by the Fon of Benin, several northern Thai tribes and in Hawaii.

Malachite IV, an abstract appliqué panel with felt hand-stitched on to a dark blue velvet ground fabric, designed and worked by Diana Springall

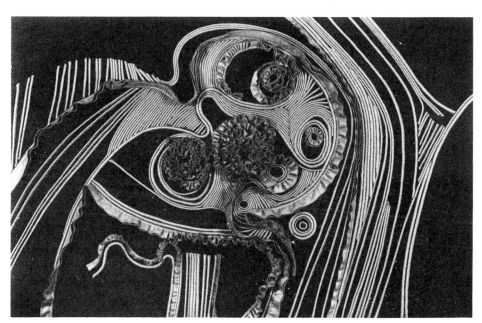

Materials

It is obviously preferable to cut motifs from fabrics that do not fray excessively (matted felt is convenient). Cut-outs that are likely to fray can be made more manageable by backing them with an iron-on bonding. Any fabric can be used for the base material, although it is advisable to use a heavier fabric than is used for the applied motifs. Ideally, hemming and other stitching should be worked with one strand of stranded cotton matching the colour of the fabric being applied; sewing cotton, which is sometimes preferred, has a round, hard appearance which is more visible. Alternatively thread and colour can be planned intentionally to show. Pointed, chenille or crewel needles should be used and it is not essential to work on a frame.

Typical appliqué design from a Fon wall-hanging from western Africa. Men design and execute colourful pictures, attaching cotton motifs with back stitch, chain stitch, running stitch or hemming to a black cotton ground fabric

Mola appliqué panel worked by Cuna Indian women in Colombia. The design has been cut down through orange to black cotton fabric. All cut edges have been, albeit roughly, turned under and hemmed. Small running stitches and scraps of other fabric have been used for facial details (29.2 × 43cm [11½ × 17in])

Methods of working

The following instructions are all concerned with hand embroidery although machine stitching can also be employed (see chapter 23).

Onlay appliqué

The outline of the design should be marked on to the base ground fabric. Shapes to be applied are then marked on another piece of fabric, usually of contrasting colour.

There are two main methods of attaching onlay appliqué. If the edges of the motif are to be turned under, the fabric is cut 8mm (⅛in) outside the marked lines and the excess is turned under, small scissor snips being made where necessary to

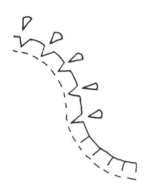

When excess fabric has to be turned under to form a rounded line (dotted), small snips are made to within 1mm of that line. V-shaped cuts are made when a convex line is required and single slits when a concave edge is planned

accommodate curves. With the warp and weft threads aligned with those of the ground fabric, the motif is temporarily held in place with large tacking stitches. The device is permanently secured with buttonhole stitch, chain stitch, cross stitch, stem stitch or hemming. When hemming appliqué, the needle should always be brought *up* through the fabric on the *outside* of the motif and taken *down through* the applied shape.

Alternatively, the motif can be cut out exactly on the marked lines. It is temporarily held with tacking stitches and then the raw edges are sewn permanently to the ground fabric. Laid and couched cord can be worked to cover both the raw edges and the application stitching.

Inlay appliqué

Often worked for church embroideries, this has the design set *into*, rather than on to, the ground fabric. As with onlay appliqué, the outline of the required design is marked both on the ground fabric and on the piece from which the applied motifs will be cut; but in the inlay form the design is also cut out of the ground fabric and a matching piece of contrasting colour fitted into the resulting jigsaw hole. It is helpful to lay the ground fabric, with the hole already cut, on a lining fabric such as muslin to prevent distortion while the motif is being inlaid, and stitching is worked from the edge of the ground to the edge of the applied motif with hemming, herringbone stitch or another suitable technique.

Reverse appliqué

Known sometimes as découpé, this consists of a motif cut out from the main ground to reveal another fabric underneath. A piece of fabric somewhat larger than the eventual motif is placed underneath the ground fabric and tacked outside the

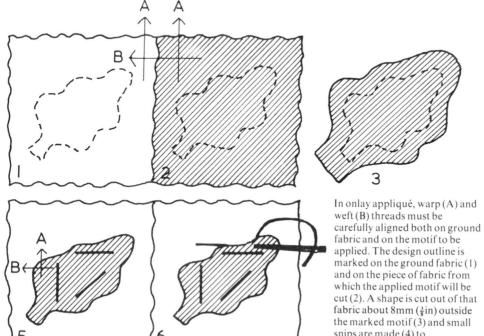

In onlay appliqué, warp (A) and weft (B) threads must be carefully aligned both on ground fabric and on the motif to be applied. The design outline is marked on the ground fabric (1) and on the piece of fabric from which the applied motif will be cut (2). A shape is cut out of that fabric about 8mm (⅜in) outside the marked motif (3) and small snips are made (4) to accommodate curves before the

8mm excess is turned under and held with tacking to the ground fabric (5). The motif can then be permanently secured with hemming (6) or other stitching

APPLIQUÉ

marked outline of the device. The ground fabric is then carefully cut, about 8mm ($\frac{1}{8}$in) inside the marked outline. Small cuts are made to accommodate curves and then the excess is turned under before the shape is applied to the underlaid fabric.

Mola or 'San Blas' appliqué

The mola technique, especially associated with the Cuna women of Panama and Colombia, is related to the standard reverse appliqué form. Two or more layers of fabric, the same size, are held together with tacking. A design is cut down from the uppermost to the bottom layers in steps forming a 'contour map' design. The bottom layer of fabric is not cut at any time.

After applying motifs with onlay, inlay, reverse or mola methods, the design can be embellished with surface stitching and miscellaneous beads, buttons or spangles.

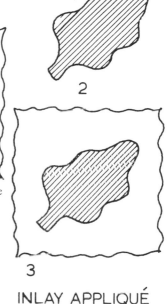

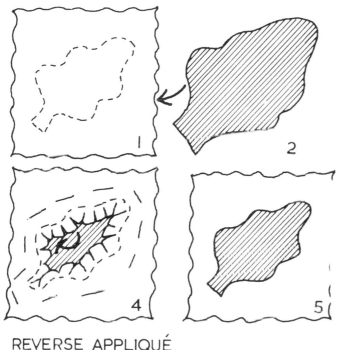

Reverse appliqué: after the outline of a required design is marked on the ground fabric (1), a piece of fabric bigger than the marked design (2) is laid under the ground fabric and temporarily held in place with tacking stitches worked around the outside of the design. An area is then cut out of the ground fabric about 8mm inside the original marked line (3). Small cuts are made to accommodate curves (4) and the surplus fabric is carefully turned under and attached permanently, possibly with hemming, to the fabric applied beneath. The tacking stitches are then removed (5)

REVERSE APPLIQUÉ

INLAY APPLIQUÉ

Inlay appliqué: into a cut hole (1), a motif of the same shape and size (2) is laid and held in place, possibly with hemming or herringbone stitch (3)

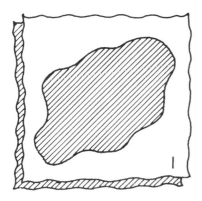

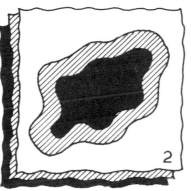

MOLA APPLIQUÉ

Mola appliqué: a design is cut down in step formation through one layer of fabric (1) or through two or more layers of fabric (2), always leaving the bottom layer of fabric uncut. Steps thus formed are turned under, and usually attached with hemming, as in reverse appliqué

3. Assisi work

Assisi work is a counted-thread embroidery in which stitches are worked over a precise number of warp and weft ground threads. Usually, borders of an item are decorated, with the main design left unworked except for a few motif details and the reserves, the background of the design, densely embroidered. Generally today a ground of evenweave linen is used, with the main outline of a border design executed in back stitch or double-running stitch, the latter also known as Holbein stitch and, in Assisi work, as Chiara stitch. This is usually worked in black and the reserves are infilled with cross stitch or long-armed cross stitch worked in one colour thread. Outside the border there is often a repeating scrolled pattern, worked in black, which helps to soften the otherwise rather solid appearance of some Assisi examples.

It is possible that nuns in the Convent of St Francis, founded in 1128 in Assisi, Umbria, central Italy, evolved the counted-thread embroidery that is now named after their home. Records suggest that by the late fourteenth century this embroidery was being executed with designs similar to the local wood carvings and other decorative art forms.

Some examples still in existence date from the sixteenth and seventeenth centuries. Cushion covers and border fragments were at that time sometimes embroidered with the outline of the design worked in the same colour thread that was later used for the reserves. The most popular outline stitches were back, running and double-running forms and, for the reserves, Italian and long-armed cross stitches. Many of the designs, on bands about 23cm (9in) in height, had patterns which were

Assisi design, the main outline and details worked in back stitch and double-running stitch over two threads and the reserves, or background, infilled with cross stitch over four threads (linen, 23 threads per 2.5cm [1in] embroidered with black coton à broder and two strands of orange stranded cotton, panel 10.7 × 14.6cm [4¼ × 5¾in] overall)

the same when inverted, with motifs of scrolled leaves, vines with trellis surrounds or birds, dragons, lions and other mythical beasts. Designs, which were sometimes skilfully adapted to pass through a corner of 90°, seldom had outer scrolls subsequently worked.

There was a revival of interest in embroidery in Assisi at the beginning of the twentieth century. Encouraged by Maria Bartocci Rossi and her daughter Chiara, some items made in the town itself can be distinguished by a Franciscan cross, often with a lion rampant and a cross embroidered in one corner.

Earlier examples such as this seventeenth-century Italian panel have one colour thread used both for outlining motifs and for infilling the reserves (linen embroidered with red silk in back stitch and long-armed cross stitch, 15.2 × 52cm [6 × 20¼in])

A basic motif (1) can be repeated in reverse (2) and the whole reversed again (3)

Lions rampant are popular themes in Assisi work

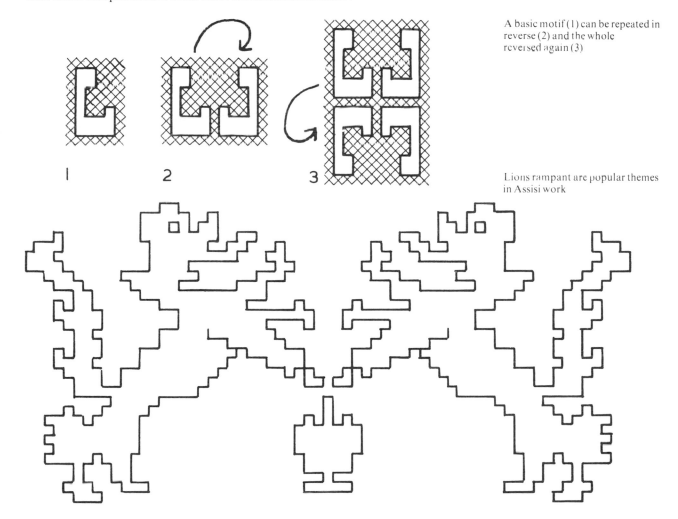

Materials

Assisi work should be executed on a loosely woven fabric with even warp and weft. Recommended fabrics include linens and cottons with a thread count of 25 to 29 per 2.5cm (1in) and wool with a thread count of about 18 per 2.5cm (1in). Although white or natural fabric is generally used, Assisi work can be formed on a coloured ground as long as the fabric and thread colour combination provides ample contrast to show the design to advantage. It can be worked with stranded or other cotton, silk or wool thread and often only one strand is used at a time. Different threads can, however, be worked into one design. Pearl cotton No 5 could be used for the outlining of a motif and the reserves (background) subsequently worked in cross stitch in pearl cotton No 8. To avoid splitting the ground fabric a tapestry needle should be used, and Assisi work need not be worked on a frame.

Assisi embroidery: to achieve a required pattern (as at 5), the outline of a motif is worked in black double-running stitch (1, 2). The reserves are then infilled with coloured cross stitch (3, 4) and edging and scrolls worked in black double-running stitch (5) to achieve a required pattern

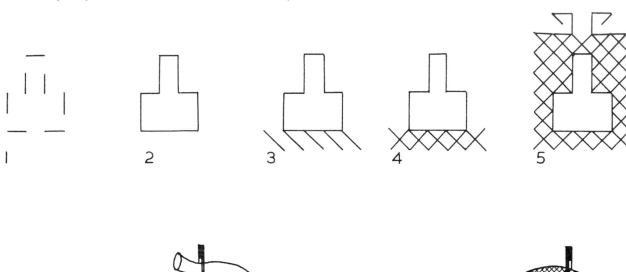

To make sure that all the uppermost diagonals of cross stitches face the same direction, it is advisable to work each line of stitches in two journeys

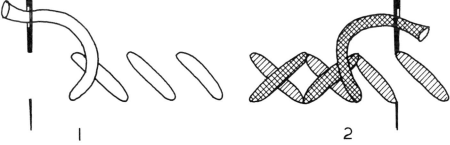

Small repeating patterns, worked in back or double-running stitch, are often executed as finishing touches to Assisi work

Methods of working

If a band of embroidery is to be worked round all four sides of an item, it is advisable to start embroidering in the middle of each side, the same number of threads in each direction from the centre of the item.

Assisi embroidery is then worked in three stages:

a The outline of the main border design is worked in back or double-running stitches, generally in black thread. Any details within the motif can also be worked, in back, cross or double-running stitches.

b The reserves are embroidered in another colour thread in cross stitch or long-armed cross stitch. As it is important that all the upper diagonals of the stitch face the same direction, it is advisable to work a line of crosses in two journeys.

c Black back or double-running stitches are employed for working the finishing touches of ornamental scrolls or other repeating motifs outside the main border.

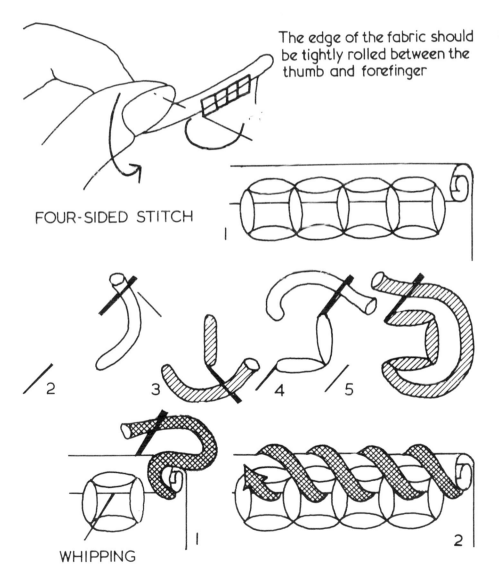

The edge of the fabric should be tightly rolled between the thumb and forefinger

Finishing Assisi work: four-sided stitch is worked through the main fabric and the hem. Whipping can then be executed

FOUR-SIDED STITCH

WHIPPING

25

Finishing

Assisi work is generally finished with a narrow hem rolled over tightly between the forefinger and thumb and worked in four-sided stitch in thread the same colour as the ground fabric. This rolled hem can then be whipped in the same colour thread as that of the main embroidery in the reserves. Corners are sometimes decorated with three small tassels.

A tassel can be made by passing a threaded needle from a corner of the finished item around the forefinger of the left hand (1), into the fabric and back round the finger (2), continuing this process up to ten or more times. These threads are then bound (3) with another thread, fastened off by stitching into the fabric, and the tassel is cut (4)

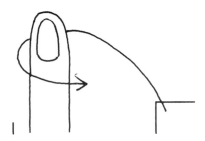
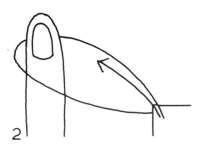
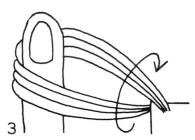
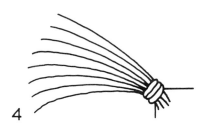

4. Bargello

Bargello, also known as Florentine embroidery or, variously, as Byzantine, flame, Hungarian point or Irish work, is characterized by parallel rows of differently coloured stitches worked in zigzag, wave or flame shapes to cover the entire ground fabric. The ground can be turned successively through 90°, 180° and 270° to form four-way or mitred Bargello. Another variant, free-form Bargello, is more loosely aligned to the proportions of the ground fabric.

The name Bargello comes from a set of seventeenth-century chairs in the National Museum in Florence. Built in 1255, the Palazzo del Podesta was converted into a prison and assigned to the head of the police, the Bargelli, in 1574. It was restored and opened as a museum in the middle of the nineteenth century. The chairs, furnished with silks worked in what is now known as Bargello style, are supposed to have been purchased from a Señor Menicetti in 1886.

One theory is that the embroidery technique originated in a workshop established in the eleventh century by Gisela, Bavarian-born queen of Stephen I of

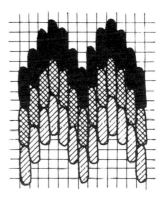

Bargello is characterized by parallel rows of differently coloured stitches. Usually at least three colours are employed

Bargello coat designed and worked by Nancy Dent. Using three strands of Persian yarn on canvas with 20 threads per 5cm (2in) (colloquially known as '10 mesh', or 10 threads per inch), she reckons the coat took 400 hours to complete

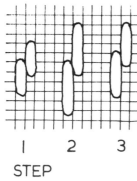

I 2 3

STEP

Step: two numbers denoting the length of stitches and the riser between one stitch and the next. These three examples are (1) 4.2 (one stitch over four threads is two threads higher than its neighbour) (2) 6.4 (3) 5.3

Repeat: a basic shape (1) may be repeated in reverse (2) and this again reversed (3)

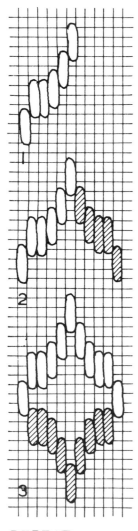

REPEAT

Hungary. The title Florentine which is sometimes given to this embroidery, is possibly associated with a later Hungarian princess who married into the Medici family in Italy, and brought in her trousseau several items embroidered with this type of stitching.

Some of the earliest surviving examples of English Bargello are early seventeenth-century wall-hangings and bed curtains, sometimes worked on narrow strips of canvas embroidered and then joined selvedge to selvedge. Other popular uses for Bargello in the past, especially in the eighteenth century in America, included decoration for pocket-books, handy envelopes with or without end gussets. These were liberally embroidered with Bargello, generally known as Irish stitch, in a carnation, flame or other jagged design. During the eighteenth century, too, four-way or mitred Bargello was sometimes worked in England and America. This variant lost popularity until it was revived with great enthusiasm in the twentieth century, but the more standard one-way Bargello has remained in favour, particularly during the 1820–70 era when it was sometimes used in Berlin woolwork samplers (see chapter 26), in bright, contrasting and often garish colours.

Materials

Partly to facilitate counting, Bargello is generally worked on single-weave, mono, canvas with a thread count of 20 to 36 per 5cm (2in), with 28 a good compromise for beginners. Alternatively, rug canvas can be employed. If a non-canvas ground is preferred, Hardanger cloth or an evenweave linen can be used.

Nowadays such wools as Persian, crewel or tapestry are most popular, although cotton or silk threads are also permissible. Different threads used on one item need not be of the same thickness. Varying, but complementary, thicknesses may indeed add texture to the finished work, although it is essential when working embroidery stitches parallel to the threads of the ground fabric to make sure that all embroidery threads employed spread out to cover the ground and it is therefore necessary to use more strands of Persian yarn than, say, when working ordinary tent stitch. For the same reason, it is a good idea not to pull the embroidery thread too tight but to keep a relaxed tension throughout. At least three differently coloured threads are generally used. If some shades are similar to others it may be a help to write down the order in which they will be used in case a mistake is made when working under artificial light.

Terminology

Bargello has its own terminology:

Step: two numbers, signifying the length of stitch and the number of threads by which its neighbour rises or descends from it. For instance, '4.2' implies a stitch worked over four threads and the second stitch is two threads vertically removed from it.

Repeat: when a basic pattern is worked again, be it in reverse or upside-down order to the last time of working.

Pivot stitch: a stitch on which the direction of a design changes.

Unbroken pattern: a repeating pattern with each stitch and step the same as those of its neighbours.

A

B

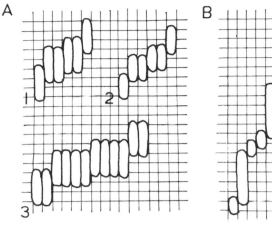

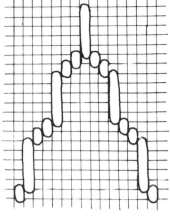

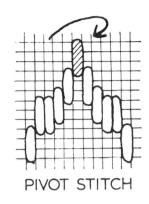

PIVOT STITCH

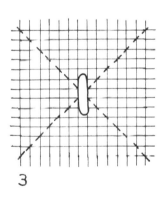

1   2

A The proportions and scale of a
basic design (1) can be changed
by altering the length of stitches
(2) or by doubling the number of
stitches at each level (3).
B Hungarian point: a pattern with
long stitches, usually over six
threads, and short stitches,
generally over two threads

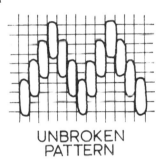

UNBROKEN
PATTERN

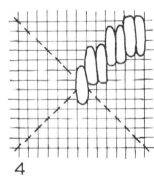

3   4

Working always in the same
direction (1) produces a
corduroy, ribbed, effect on the
reverse. Alternating directions
of working (2) gives a more even
backing. It is a good idea to
begin any Bargello design in the
centre of the fabric (3) and work
towards the edges (4)

Pivot stitch: the stitch (shaded) on
which a design reverses. It is not
itself repeated.
Unbroken pattern: a zigzag or
curvilinear pattern with simple
repeats.
Interval: a zigzag interruption
(shaded) in what would
otherwise be an unbroken
pattern

Interval: a zigzag crest, with a predetermined number of points, separating repeats
of a design.
Proportion: by altering the step count, a pattern can be distorted as required.
Hungarian point: long and short stitches are worked in repeating order to a predetermined design.

Methods of working

The basic Bargello stitch—up and down, up and down—can be worked in various
ways to give a different type of backing. To avoid an uneven ribbed effect on the
back it is a good idea to work rows alternately from the left and then from the right
side of the front of the fabric.

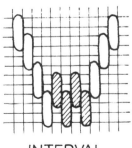

INTERVAL

Before printed patterns were available embroiderers copied worked samples of Bargello designs. Since it is imperative to work the base, or main structural, line of a repeating Bargello design with absolute accuracy, it is a good idea to copy this first line of stitching from a paper graph or chart.

One-way Bargello

It is helpful to mark the canvas and work from a central point along the main vertical or horizontal axes of the entire design. Stitching is begun in the middle of one motif and an entire row of base stitches is worked in the required pattern. This base line is the key to all subsequent rows of stitching, which are then executed according to:

  a The required pattern (stitch length and step count) and
  b The predetermined colour sequence.

In some Bargello patterns each stitch is the same length as the one in the line before (1). In others, especially Hungarian point variations, the length of each stitch varies from line to line

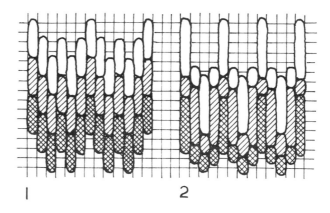

It will be noticed that in some Bargello patterns each stitch is the same length as its predecessor in the previous line. In other patterns, especially Hungarian point, stitch lengths vary from line to line.

Although in true Bargello all the ground fabric is covered, sometimes only part of that ground is embroidered in Bargello. Other areas can be worked in tent stitch or another needlepoint technique.

A Bargello design, of which only the base line is shown here, can be worked as a border. Corners should be worked on the mitre principle used in four-way Bargello

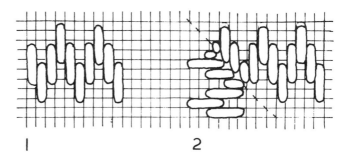

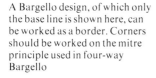

Once Bargello terminology is mastered, an embroiderer can understand many patterns such as this popular traditional pomegranate shape. Here each vertical stitch is worked over four threads and the amount of the 'rise' is two threads. The numbers on the diagram indicate how many stitches are worked to each 'block'. Bargello motifs are fitted together to produce finished patterns such as that illustrated beneath

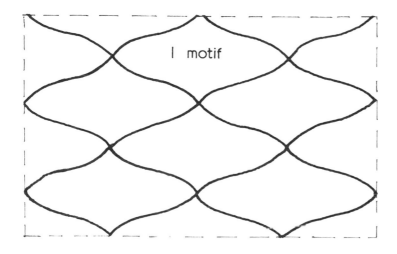

1 motif

In four-way Bargello a square (1) or a rectangular ground (2) can be used. In either case it should be divided into eighths before any embroidery is worked (3). After the canvas is marked, the first base line is worked, starting from the centre and continuing until a diagonal is reached (4). Then the base line is worked in the other seven segments, the canvas being turned as required so that all stitches radiate from the centre. Especially in Hungarian point variations, four-way Bargello may produce colour blocks isolated from the main lines of stitching. Subsequent lines of stitches co-ordinate the design

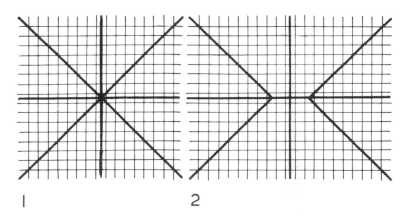

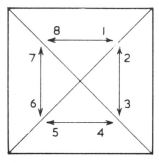

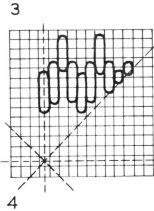

Free-form Bargello is an individual variation in which a basic design 'moves' in waves of colour as different shades of thread are employed. The shell picture was designed and worked by Gigs Stevens

Four-way Bargello

A basic design is continued through all quadrants of a marked ground, either mitred to the centre or to either side of the centre to produce a rectangular design. The first base line of the motif is worked in one half-quadrant, starting from the centre and progressing to the diagonal. If a design begins to curve outwards as that diagonal line is reached, it is a good idea to adjust the last few stitches and turn the design in towards the centre. Sometimes one line of stitches produces isolated blocks as the diagonal is reached but these stitches will be co-ordinated by subsequent rows of stitches. When the first half-quadrant of the base line is finished, the other seven sections are similarly worked, each starting from the vertical or horizontal end, the same number of threads out from the centre, and worked towards

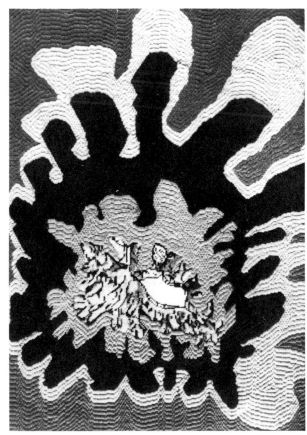

the diagonal. After the entire base line has been finished the rest of the ground is filled according to the required pattern. The mesh right in the centre of the item can be covered with a large cross stitch.

Free-form and other experimental styles of Bargello are now becoming increasingly popular, especially in America.

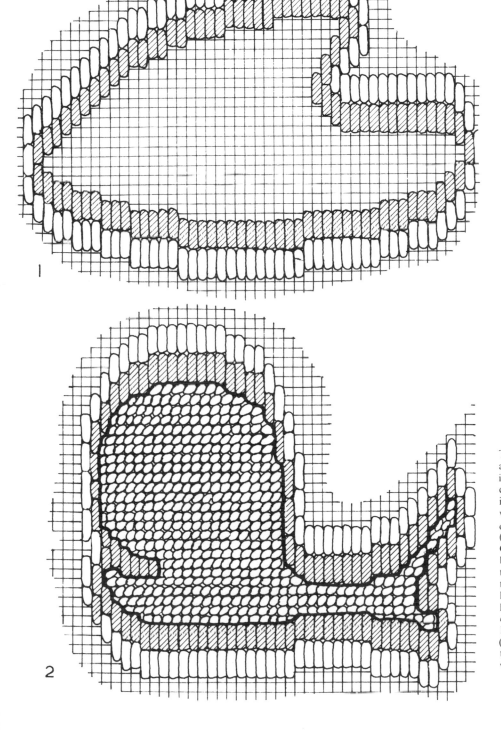

To work free-form Bargello, a simple outline is worked in the first colour (drawing 1, dark stitches), and the areas inside and around it are worked in formation, as in ordinary two-way Bargello (drawing 1, light stitches). Compensation stitches should be worked over two or four threads rather than one thread to avoid a small stitch that may look like a 'mistake'. Free-form Bargello can also be cleverly co-ordinated with needlepoint. Here (drawing 2) a basic motif (outlined) has been worked in tent stitch and then surrounded with Bargello

5. Blackwork

(*Below, left*) In the sixteenth and seventeenth centuries blackwork, monochrome embroidery on a white ground fabric, was popular as costume decoration. This bodice is dated 1605–15 and the matching skirt was probably made shortly afterwards (white linen embroidered with black silk, stem stitch and darning)

(*Below, right*) Blackwork can be seen on the collar, cuffs and through the panes of the sleeves on this portrait, painted by a follower of Holbein *c* 1545. (oil on two boards joined vertically, 76.2 × 55.9cm [30 × 22in])

Blackwork, sometimes known as Spanish work, is a counted-thread monochrome embroidery with high contrast between the colour of embroidery thread and the ground fabric on which it is worked. Stitches, executed parallel with the warp and weft threads or diagonally to them, are usually worked in black thread on a white or natural evenweave linen fabric. In earlier times, however, dark blue, green, brown or red silk was sometimes preferred, with or without subsequent highlighting from metal thread or spangles.

Such monochrome embroidery probably derived from Moorish art brought to Spain and thence to the rest of Europe by settlers who crossed from northern Africa from AD 711. One of the first mentions of blackwork in England is in Chaucer's *Canterbury Tales*, written in the last decade of the fourteenth century, and it was to reach its heyday at the beginning of the sixteenth century. The main uses of blackwork in England until the beginning of the eighteenth century, when it was superseded by polychrome styles, were as decorations for household items or clothing.

During the sixteenth century printed books began to appear with woodcut illustrations of herbs, birds, flowers and animals, real and mythical. These pictures

obviously inspired embroiderers, and other designs were formed from box-shaped, intertwined strapwork and other repeating motifs.

Blackwork today can in turn be inspired by many of the designs worked by sixteenth- and seventeenth-century embroiderers and sometimes recorded by contemporary artists who depicted their subjects wearing robes with fine blackwork embellishment. Double-running stitch is, indeed, sometimes called Holbein stitch because of its frequent appearance in that artist's works.

Blackwork remains essentially an embroidered *art* form. The dramatic effect of black on white, and the geometry of much of the design, has a certain fascination for non-embroiderers.

Materials

Blackwork is generally executed with such thread and ground combinations as:

a one strand of stranded cotton worked over two threads of evenweave linen, thread count 30 per 2.5cm (1in), worked with tapestry needle No 24.
b one strand pearl cotton No 5 worked over three threads of acrylic cloth, thread count 16 per 2.5cm (1in), worked with tapestry needle No 22.

It is usual to work with one, two or three strands of a stranded thread at any one time, although threads of varying thicknesses may be used throughout a design.

(*Below, left*) Pieces of newsprint can be cut and pieced together to form the pattern for a blackwork design

(*Below, right*) This can then be interpreted with stitches (linen embroidered with black cotton, back stitch, buttonhole stitch, satin stitch, straight stitch and with couched lurex outlining the wing, 31.7 × 25.4cm [12¼ × 10in])

Double-running stitch: after a line of ordinary running stitches (1) a second line, here shaded, is worked, making sure that the needle enters one side of the stitch already worked and exits the other side (2) to avoid what would otherwise be an uneven line (as at 3)

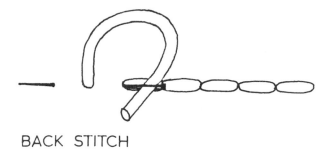

BACK STITCH

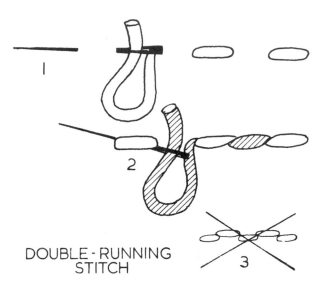

DOUBLE - RUNNING STITCH

Density can be altered by working a design (1) in thicker thread (2) or by executing more stitches (3)

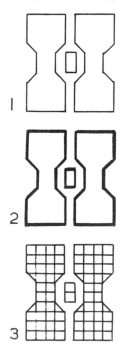

Partly to avoid splitting the ground fabric, tapestry needles are often used, although sometimes a crewel needle might be preferred for working outlines in double-running stitch. Having the ground fabric stretched taut facilitates counting threads and many embroiderers use a frame when working blackwork.

Methods of working

It is possible to envisage how a piece of blackwork will look when finished by using the newspaper cut-out method. Newsprint is formed with some areas having greater density of inked dots than others and one page can often provide enough variety to afford a palette for the blackwork embroiderer. Pieces of newsprint can therefore be cut into required shapes and fitted together as a collage impression of how an embroidery could look. The darkest pieces of newsprint in the paper pattern will require a greater density of embroidery. This density can be produced either by working with a thicker embroidery thread or by executing more stitches.

The main stitches of blackwork embroidery are back stitch and double-running or Holbein stitch. Others used extensively include braid, buttonhole, chain, coral, herringbone and stem stitches and a variety of filling stitches, including seeding. The stitches can be combined as required, and in order to add highlight, controlled use of metal thread and spangles can be made once the main embroidery is finished.

BRAID STITCH

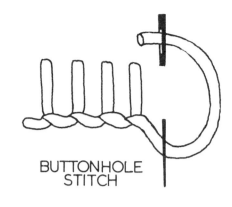

BUTTONHOLE
STITCH

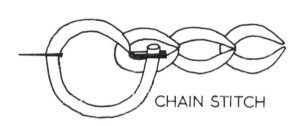

CHAIN STITCH

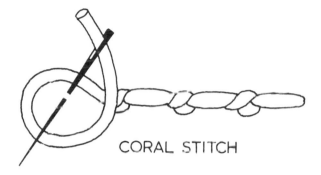

CORAL STITCH

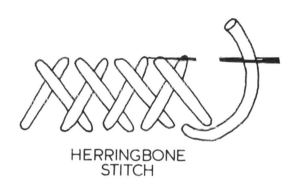

HERRINGBONE
STITCH

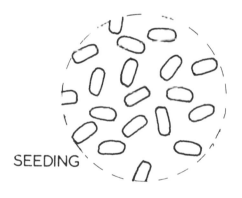

SEEDING

Among other popular blackwork
stitches are braid stitch,
buttonhole or blanket stitch,
chain stitch, coral or knot stitch,
herringbone stitch and seeding
or speckling, tiny stitches dotted
at random over the ground
fabric

6. Blocking and mounting

The way in which an embroidery is finished and presented can make or mar its effect. Professional blocking, or coaxing an embroidery into its original shape, and mounting, or framing, are becoming expensive and embroiderers who possess these skills are finding them increasingly useful. This section therefore offers basic practical guides to blocking and pressing, hemming and mitreing corners, decorative insertion stitches and seams, and mounting for display.

Blocking and pressing

When a piece of embroidery is completed it may, even if worked on a frame, have suffered shape distortion. This is eradicated, it is to be hoped completely, by blocking.

It is essential to test for colour fastness before attempting to block embroidery. A small section of damp cotton wool should be applied to the back of the work, testing each differently coloured embroidery thread. If any colour runs (bleeds) into the cotton wool, dry blocking must be used. If there is no discoloration, ordinary blocking can proceed.

Materials necessary for blocking are:

1 A blocking board, carefully marked with a centimetre or inch-square grid or covered with such fabric as gingham, which has exactly evenweave squares. Insulating wall board, known in the trade as white board, or another fibre board are suitable as long as they are covered with fabric or blotting paper, to avoid any of the board's finish running on to the embroidery
2 Clean towels
3 Supply of paper towels and tissues
4 Ruler and T-square
5 Hammer and upholsterers' tacks
6 T-pins or other stainless pins(alternatively a staple gun can be employed but it should be remembered that staples can split ground threads, and also rust)
7 Upholsterers' stretching pliers are also handy

If the embroidery contains no metal thread or other addendum that is likely to tarnish, and *if* it has been thoroughly tested for colour fastness, then the item can either be rolled in a damp—not wet—towel for half an hour at most or left in a steamy atmosphere such as in a bathroom for a short while. It is then laid on to the blocking board. Most needlepoints and other embroideries with raised surfaces are laid right side up to maintain textural effect, although if there is any doubt about discoloration of pens or paints used originally to mark a design on the ground, the embroidery should be laid wrong side up. Wool in particular tends to draw pen dyes to the top of its surface. Other embroideries such as blackwork are generally laid out wrong side up to prevent the front of the item from getting dirty.

The item is gently stretched on to the board with tacks or pins placed at 1.25cm ($\frac{1}{2}$in) intervals in the excess fabric, as close as possible to the limit of the embroid-

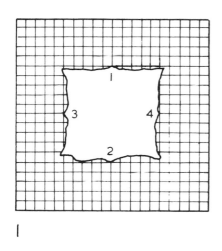

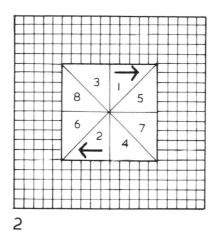

1

2

Stretching a distorted embroidery:
1 The item is placed on a gridded board and the centre of each of the four edges securely held with a staple gun or strong tacks.
2 The eight half-quadrants of the cloth are then pulled gently into shape and each section is pinned working *from the centre of the side towards the corner*. The sections should be worked in the order indicated

ered area of the ground. If there is no excess outside the embroidered area careful blocking has to be executed just within the embroidered limit. Tacks or pins are placed leaning slightly outwards from the item.

Some people, when stretching an embroidery to its original limit, begin by securing the corners, but it is often easier to start by stretching first the centre vertical and then the centre horizontal points. Each half-quadrant should then be secured, working from the centre towards the diagonal line in each case. The sections should be worked in the order illustrated in the diagram above.

Edges of a square or rectangular embroidery must lie in straight lines on the blocking board and this is why it is advisable to work with a gridded board and to have a ruler and T-square handy. Upholsterers' pliers are useful if a great deal of pulling is required to achieve the item's former shape. A steam iron held close to a difficult corner can also aid re-shaping. When all the edges have been secured the item should be left on the board until at least twenty-four hours after it is com-

To mitre a corner of a hem: **1** Excess fabric, the same width as the desired hem plus 8mm (⅜in), is left outside what will eventually be the edge of the item (A marking the desired corner point). **2** To guide subsequent sewing, a crease is made across that corner, passing through A at 45°, **3** Working from the wrong side of the fabric, here shaded, a neat seam is sewn, by hand or machine, from A to within 8mm of B. **4** Excess corner fabric is cut away and the sewn corner is turned inside out. **5** The outer 8mm is turned under. **6** This produces a neat, mitred, corner

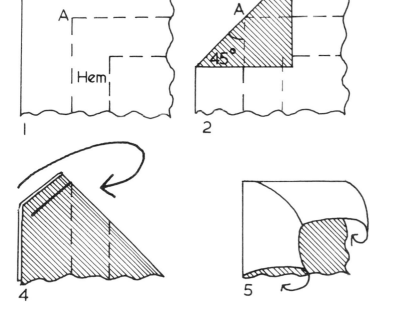

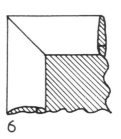

pletely dry. It should be kept out of sunlight and away from artificial heat. Some techniques can then be pressed while the item is still on the board. A hot iron should never be applied to the front of an embroidery. Blackwork and other items being blocked wrong sides up can be gently pressed with a cool iron. Any pressing of the front of an embroidery should only be done with a steam iron carefully passed over a layer of substantial material protecting the surface and in this instance the item must once again be left to dry completely.

When the dry item is taken off the blocking board, original shaping should have been achieved. If there is still distortion a second blocking can be undertaken.

As its name implies, dry blocking, undertaken when any constituent of the embroidery might run or tarnish, is done exactly as above but without using any water or steam.

Hemming and mitreing corners

The edge of a piece of cloth may need to be secured permanently in order to stop it fraying. Sometimes this is achieved by turning under a small section of the fabric to produce a hem. Another way of preventing fraying is to attach the cloth to an edging. Corners of a square or rectangular cloth can be mitred before a hem is permanently held in place.

The technique of hemming or felling is also employed in appliqué and many other embroidery forms. The stitches should be diagonal parallels and look the same on both sides. Alternatively, a narrow width of turned-under hem that requires attachment can be worked with rolled hemming, worked in either single or double form. There are also more complicated hemming techniques including Italian, napery and Portuguese variants.

Hemming should not be confused with hemstitch, which is a drawn and pulled thread technique, although it is extensively used to finish items worked on woven

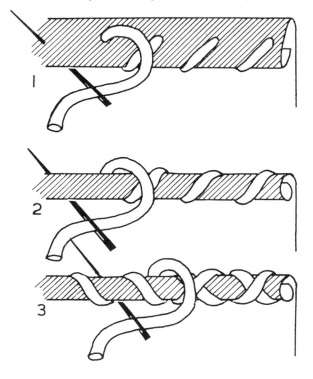

Hemming: **1** The needle passes into the main ground fabric and exits via that fabric and the turned up hem. **2** Ordinary hemming can also be rolled, in which case the needle passes only once through the ground fabric and is brought forward above the rolled hem. **3** The hem can also be double-rolled

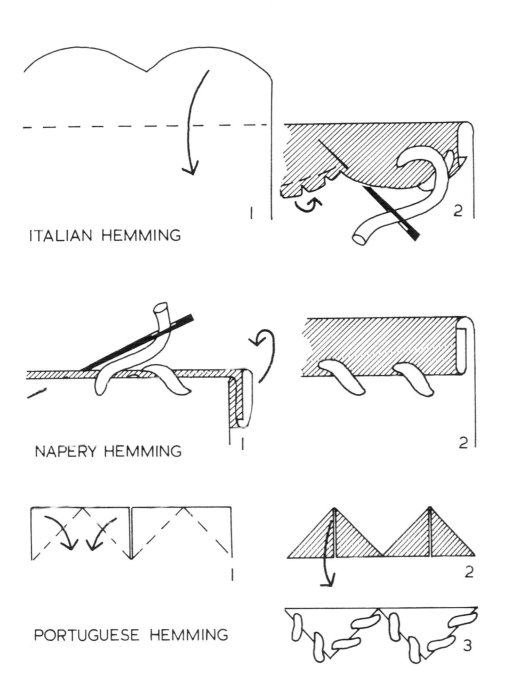

ITALIAN HEMMING

NAPERY HEMMING

PORTUGUESE HEMMING

grounds other than canvas. Threads are withdrawn and after mitreing the corners and turning up the hem to the bottom of the resulting vertical fence trellis and temporarily tacking it in place, permanent stitching is worked through the hem, main fabric and the vertical bars. Variants on basic hemstitch include antique hemstitch, which does not go through both layers of fabric, double, also known as Italian or Romanian hemstitch, interlaced hemstitch, ladder hemstitch or ladder stitch and zigzag hemstitch.

Sometimes other stitches such as satin stitch can be used as hem retainers without withdrawing any threads of the ground fabric.

Threads of fabric are withdrawn, a hem is turned up (1) and tacked in place (2)

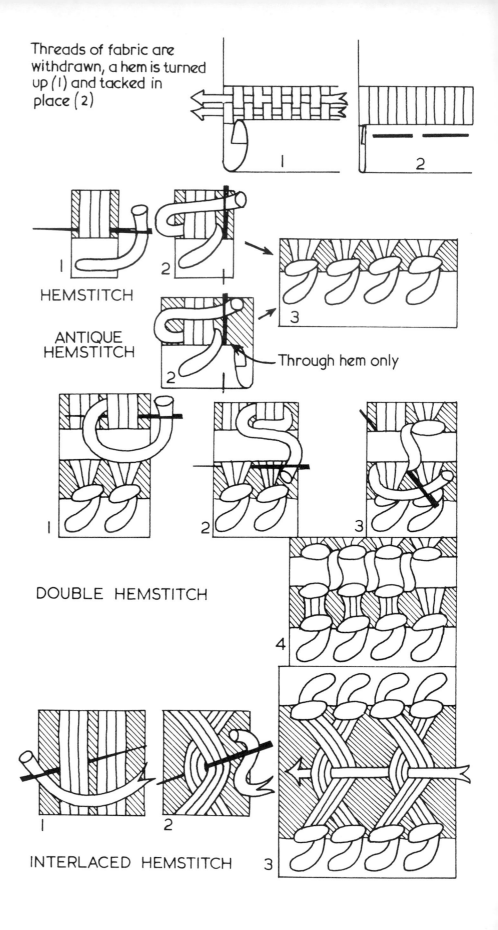

HEMSTITCH

ANTIQUE HEMSTITCH

Through hem only

DOUBLE HEMSTITCH

INTERLACED HEMSTITCH

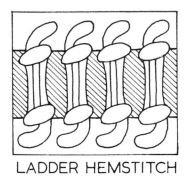

LADDER HEMSTITCH

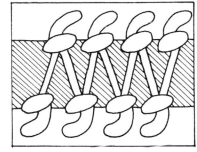

ZIGZAG LADDER HEMSTITCH

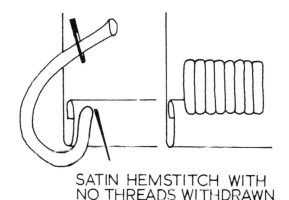

SATIN HEMSTITCH WITH
NO THREADS WITHDRAWN

Decorative insertion stitches and seams

Technically, an insertion is a length of lace, fabric, ribbon or other material which is let in to make a decorative join between two pieces of, for instance, a baby's christening robe. Openwork stitches are sometimes employed instead of a let-in piece. These insertion stitches include faggoting (also known as twisted insertion stitch), buttonhole, knotted, laced and plaited insertion stitches.

Alternatively, close joins between two pieces of fabric can be achieved with simple decorative seams formed from overcast stitching worked from the right or wrong sides of the fabric. Closely worked overcasting on the right side is known as cord stitch.

Mounting for display

Square or rectangular embroideries can be mounted for framing by leaving at least 5cm (2in) of excess fabric around all edges of a blocked item with all corners exactly 90°. The edges should be securely bound with tape, and the item is placed, right side up, on a piece of board exactly the same size as, or smaller than, the embroidered area. The size of board used will depend upon the type of design, and care should be taken to ensure that none of the design is lost, and that there is sufficient area for a margin. The excess fabric is taken over to the back of the board and two opposite sides are laced together with two strong lengths of thread or tape, passed through the bindings and working from the centre towards the corners. The other two edges are similarly laced and all four lacing threads are pulled taut and secured. Excess corners should be neatly folded under and held with stay stitches (large overcast stitches pulled tight).

Two methods of insertion stitching, decoration bridging a void between two edges of fabric, are faggoting and buttonhole insertion stitch. It is a good idea to back both pieces of fabric temporarily to a piece of paper or muslin to maintain tension while decorating the void

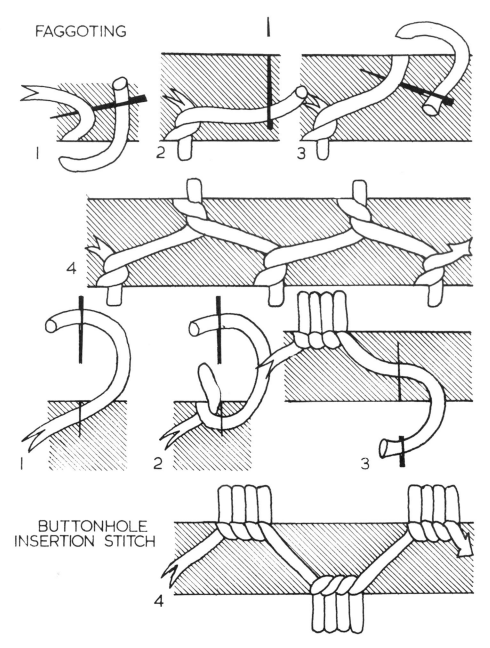

FAGGOTING

BUTTONHOLE
INSERTION STITCH

Round or oval embroideries can similarly be mounted by working a line of tacking stitches within the 5cm (2in) excess fabric. As before, the item is laid on a board the same size as the embroidered area or slightly smaller, the excess is folded over the board and tacking stitches are pulled taut and secured. A piece of waste fabric smaller than the embroidery is placed on the back of the board and temporarily held to the excess 5cm either with stay stitches or safety pins, and the excess is then laced permanently to the waste fabric in the manner illustrated on p 47.

A mounted embroidery can then be framed as required. A wide variety of lucite and other framing devices is now available from needlework and art suppliers as well as more generally. Glazing is a matter of taste and although some people prefer non-reflecting glass it does detract from the textural effect of a finished item.

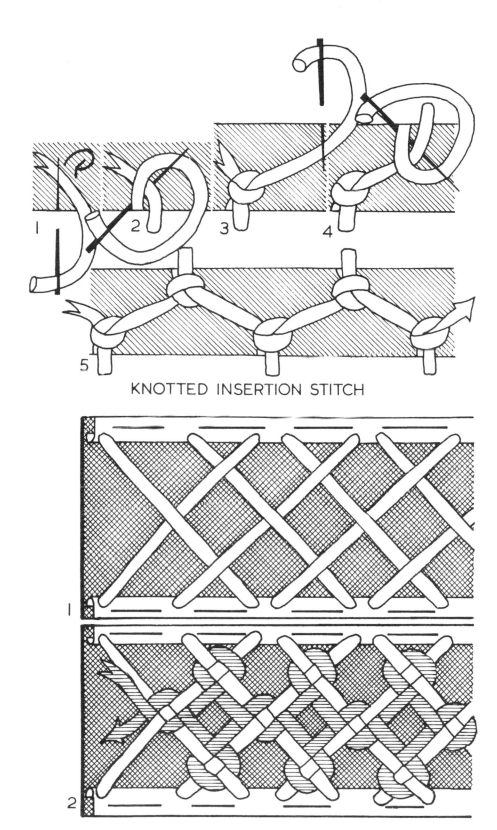

KNOTTED INSERTION STITCH

LACED INSERTION STITCH – INTERLACING
OVER HERRINGBONE STITCH

45

Many insertion stitches look rather complicated. Plaited insertion stitch (1) can be mastered by remembering that with each stitch (2) the needle weaves in and out of any threads en route to the next. The order of stitches is set out at (3)

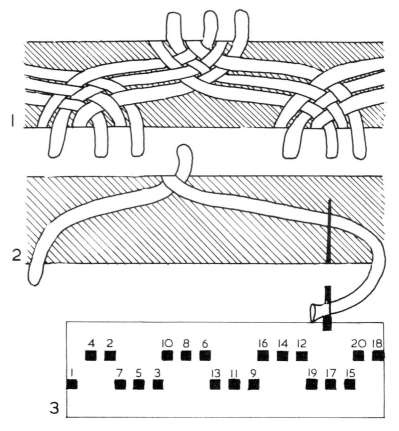

PLAITED INSERTION STITCH

OVERCAST STITCH

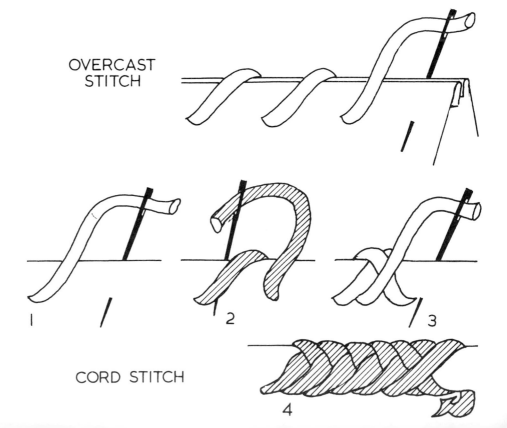

CORD STITCH

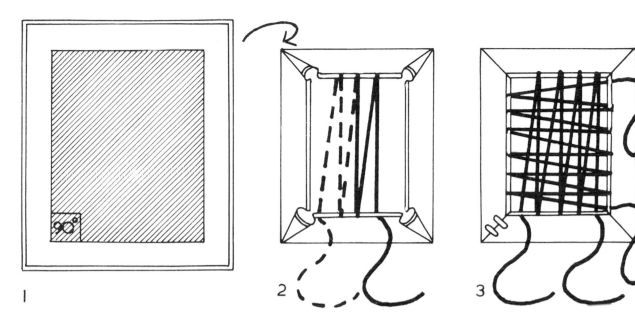

Square or rectangular mounting:
1 A finished embroidery which has been blocked leaving 5cm (2in) excess fabric. **2** The excess is folded over a board (here seen from the reverse), the same size as the worked embroidery. Two opposite sides of the excess are pulled together with lacing. Starting from the centre, two threads, one here dotted, are laced in zigzag formation. **3** The other two sides are similarly laced and secured. The excess corner fabric is turned under and stitched

Circular or oval mounting: **1** As with square mounting, about 5cm (2in) excess is left around a worked embroidery (here shaded). Long tacking stitches are executed around this excess fabric. **2** The excess is folded over a mounting board (here seen from the reverse), the tacking stitches are pulled taut and the ends secured. A small scrap of muslin or other fabric (A) is placed within the central space and lacing is worked from the excess to the central fabric

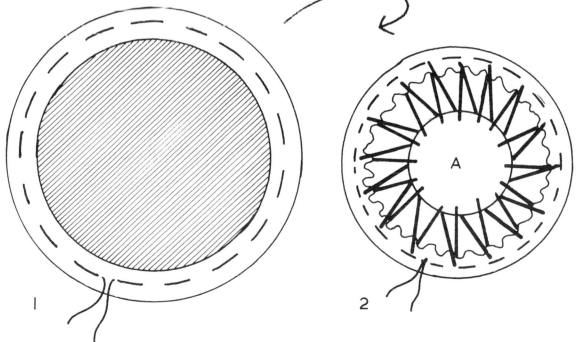

How to embroider and attach a pair of uppers for wooden sandals

Materials

1 pair wooden-soled sandals with simple slip-on uppers attached with screws.
1 small screwdriver.
2 pieces canvas, interlock if possible, 24 threads per 5cm, each piece 22 × 10cm
    (8½ × 4in).
2 pieces lining 22 × 10cm (8½ × 4in) (sample used grey ultrasuede).
3 colours woollen thread (sample used Persian yarn, 1 skein—4g or ⅛oz—each of
    black, green and grey).
Tapestry needle No 24.
Grey sewing thread and needle.

Instructions (see diagram opposite)
1 The uppers are unscrewed and the screws carefully kept to one side.
2 The removed uppers are used as templates. Two similar shapes but with *an excess 2cm all round* are cut from the canvas, and two also from the lining fabric.

The sample was worked with the Bargello design illustrated but embroiderers may prefer to work their own design. Both pieces of canvas should be completely

Embroidered mule project: using the wooden soles of a bought pair of sandals as a foundation, individual and decorative uppers can easily be embroidered

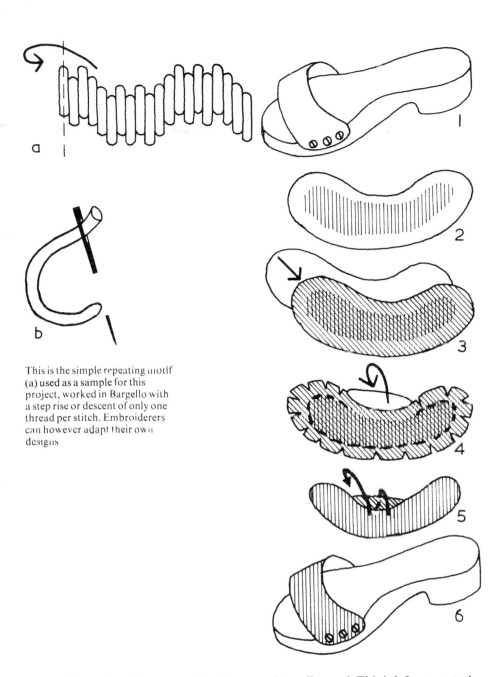

a

b

This is the simple repeating motif (a) used as a sample for this project, worked in Bargello with a step rise or descent of only one thread per stitch. Embroiderers can however adapt their own designs

1

2

3

4

5

6

covered by embroidery except for the excess 2cm all round. This is left unworked.

3 When both pieces are embroidered according to the required design, each is put next to a piece of lining, wrong sides out.

4 The canvas is sewn, by hand or machine, around the edge of the embroidered area, leaving a gap of about 6cm (2¼in) to one side. The excess is carefully snipped to accommodate curves and the item is turned the right way out through the 6cm gap.

5 The gap is then closed with overcast stitching.

6 If necessary, the new uppers can be blocked and then, using the original screws and taking care that they are eased between canvas and wool threads rather than splitting them, the new uppers are attached to the wooden soles.

7. Card embroidery

(*Below, left*) Card used as a ground for a centennial sampler worked in blue, brown, tan, yellow, grey and green silk, satin and tent stitches (35.6 × 27.3cm [14 × 10¼in])

(*Below, right*) A page from *A Devotional Miscellany*, the only surviving complete volume of bound colifichets, embroideries on fine paper. Worked in Spain, possibly in a convent *c* 1662, this detail shows the Archangel Raphael commanding Tobias to draw a fish from the Tigris (paper embroidered in silks with metal picot looped edging, 14.6 × 11.6cm [5¼ × 4⅝in])

This is here defined as stitching worked on and through a paper base. Card also enters the realm of embroidery because of its use as a padding material (see chapter 28).

The most usual form of stitching worked on a paper-based ground is card work, known in America as perforated or punctured card work, and especially popular during the nineteenth century. Stitches are executed through round holes set in regular lines on a card base, sometimes called Bristol Board, usually white, silvered or golden. During the main lifetime of Berlin woolwork, designs copied from paper patterns were mostly executed in silk and wool cross, satin and tent stitches. If the perforations were large enough to allow it to show through, a sheet of foil was sometimes placed as backing behind a card work embroidery.

Passing thread through holes in card calls for dexterity but no great skill. The making of colifichets, another form of paper-based embroidery, does on the other hand require extremely delicate working.

Colifichets are double-faced embroideries, usually with satin stitch executed in shaded silks and metal thread on paper such as good-quality writing paper. The name comes from French convent slang for 'trifle' or 'bagatelle' and the art, possibly brought from China by missionaries during the sixteenth and seventeenth centuries, seems in Europe to have been primarily convent-inspired.

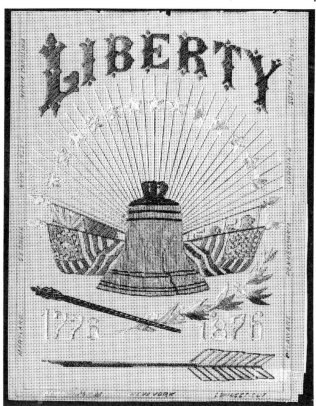

The outline of a design is pricked with a needle on to paper, possibly protected by a sandwich of thicker card, each side of which has a hole cut in it. The sandwich is gently moved round during subsequent embroidery through the pricked holes in the paper so that only one section of the 'ground' is visible at a time.

The few surviving colifichets have been protected by sheets of glass or preserved as book marks within a volume. Only one complete bound volume, possibly worked in a Spanish convent c1662, exists. Its twenty pages are embroidered with religious themes partly taken from sixteenth-century woodcuts by Bernard Salomon (c1508–1601).

Four other well-known colifichets are thought to have been worked by two young daughters of the fourth Earl of Traquair during the year 1713–14 when they were at the Convent of St Jacques in Paris belonging to the Ursulines, an Order especially famous for its embroidery. Two of the Traquair pictures show altars and the others have bunches of flowers in rounded vases.

The delicate art of colifichet embroidery is not now generally practised. On a somewhat cruder scale, paper embroideries can be fun to work. A piece of brown manilla envelope or other strong paper should be reinforced from the back with a sheet of self-adhesive transparent vinyl and can be stapled to a lightweight frame fashioned from a piece of stronger card with the middle removed. To keep paper plus frame easily manageable it is easiest to work on a fairly small scale, say 25cm (10in) square maximum.

A design is drawn in outline on the paper. Embroidery is then worked, with a fine pointed needle threaded with, say, three strands of stranded cotton. If satin stitch is employed it is advisable not to work the economy version which is likely to tear the paper, although if any accidental tears do result during working immediate first aid

Embroidery worked on a brown manilla envelope backed with self-adhesive vinyl for greater strength (paper embroidered in three strands of stranded cottons, white, dark rose and two greens, motif size 11 × 12cm [4½ × 4¾in])

can be carried out by sticking a small patch of vinyl over the lesion on the reverse of the paper. Before finishing each stitch and taking the needle through the paper from right to wrong sides, a small prick should be made marking the entry for the next stitch. The needle is then taken down through the paper in the usual way and the whole frame can easily be turned over to locate the small hole through which the next stitch begins.

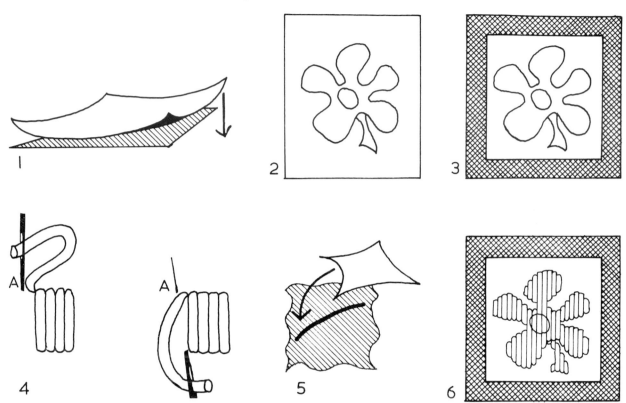

Method of working embroidery on paper: **1** Self-adhesive transparent vinyl is placed on the reverse side (shaded) of the required ground paper. **2** The design is lightly outlined in pencil on the front of the paper **3** The paper can be supported by stapling it to an outer frame of thick card. **4** The design is worked in stab fashion in neat parallel satin or other stitching. Before stabbing the needle down through the paper at the end of a stitch, a simple 'pattern prick' (A) should be made to indicate the beginning of the next stitch. The previous stitch having been finished in the ordinary way, the needle is then stabbed upwards, from the reverse, through the prepared pattern prick. **5** Any tear in the paper can be supported with a vinyl patch put on the reverse (shaded) of the paper. **6** The finished paper embroidery

8. Chain stitches

Chain stitch is characterized as a continuous line of interlocking stitches. It has many forms, for it can be used as a single line stitch, filling stitch, or each link can form a separate stitch. It can be worked on most ground fabrics, including canvas. Although a needle is often used, chain stitch can be formed with a tambour or ari hook or on a Cornely or other sewing machine. From the front of an item it is sometimes difficult to distinguish how chain stitches have been executed, although hooked or machine-made links are generally more regular than those fashioned with a needle.

Chain stitch is one of the most universal forms of embroidery and it has a long and international history. The earliest surviving fragment was found in the Pazyryk excavations and other old examples, dated *c*180 BC, have been discovered in a tomb at Mawangtui, near Changsha in Hunan. Chain-stitch fragments have also been noted by Sir Aurel Stein at Loulan in Chinese Central Asia, by an expedition in Noin-Ula, Northern Mongolia, and by travellers in the Crimea. By the tenth century the technique had long been popular with the Copts of Egypt and it was being used by Islamic embroiderers in many areas.

According to the memoirs of the official embroiderer to the French court, hooked chain stitch worked on a frame was introduced into Europe around 1760 and it soon gained popularity. Professional embroiderers used silk tambour stitching to embellish such costume items as silk waistcoats and coats and tambouring at home became the ladylike pastime of devotees who included Marie Antoinette.

The earliest known reference to the term tambouring in England dates from

Chain stitch fragment showing Buddha's face, worked in Eastern Asia, eighth to eleventh century AD. (linen embroidered in silk, 3.2 × 3.8cm [1¼ × 1½in])

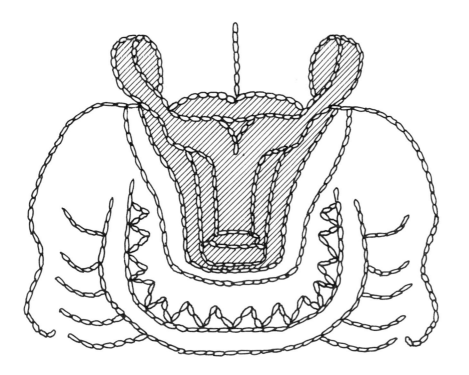

Design of a fragment, now in the Hermitage in Leningrad, found in excavations in Noin-Ula, Northern Mongolia, and thought to date from the second century BC. The outline of the design was originally worked in wools on a wool ground. Shaded areas of this drawing could be infilled if required with Cretan stitch

53

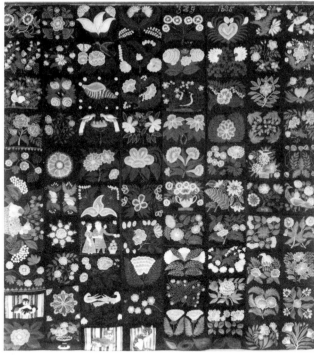

(*Above, left*) Tamboured chain stitch is worked with a tambour hook. This example, which combines tamboured stitching with pulled thread techniques, was executed on cotton fabric woven between 1790–1820

(*Above, right*) The Caswell Carpet was embroidered in tamboured chain stitch in wools on a checked, twill weave wool. Mostly worked by Zeruah Higley Guernsey in 1835, at least two of the designs are thought to have been embroidered by Potawatami Indians studying at the Castle Medical College in Vermont (3.6 × 4m, 12 × 13⅓ft)

1774, and the high point of English hooked chain stitch was 1780 to 1850, the period of large-scale production of many whitework muslin forms. (In Scotland, 'tamboured muslin' is confusingly applied not only to hooked chain stitch but to any needle chain stitching executed on a ground fabric stretched between two rollers on a large horizontal frame. Scottish 'tamboured muslin' was produced in large quantities, for commercial purposes, especially from 1782 to the 1830s.)

One of the most famous North American tamboured items is the Caswell carpet, also known as the bluecat or Guernsey rug, worked by Zeruah Higley Guernsey, later Mrs Caswell, in 1835, with the help of at least two Potawatami Indians. Tambouring had long been taught in North American schools. As early as the 1770s newspapers carried advertisements by teachers offering to instruct students in 'Tambour . . . and all kinds of needlework'.

In some other parts of the world, notably the Indian sub-continent, chain stitching today is sometimes worked with another form of hook known as an ari in a process similar to tambouring except that no frame is required.

Materials

Needle chain stitch can be worked on any fabric, including felt, and most embroidery threads are suitable. Except in needlepoint, chain stitch is usually worked with a crewel or chenille needle, and a frame is desirable, especially if large stitches are to be executed.

Methods of working

Needle chain stitch

As well as chain stitch, there are its variants, including broken chain stitch, cable chain or cable stitch, with knotted and zigzag forms, crested chain stitch, detached

Before making an ordinary chain stitch, the needle snakes under and over the thread. It is a good idea to hold the thread at 'a' with the thumb.

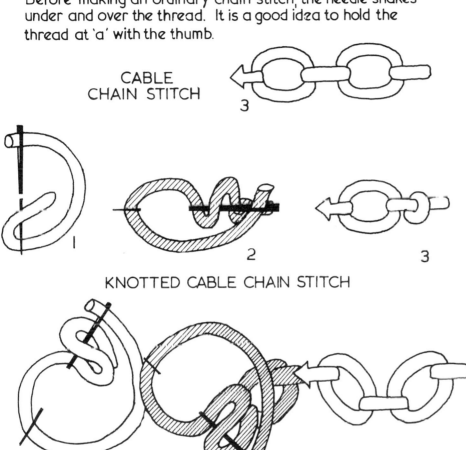

CABLE CHAIN STITCH

KNOTTED CABLE CHAIN STITCH

ZIGZAG CABLE CHAIN STITCH

chain stitch, also known as chain stitch tail, daisy stitch, knotted knot stitch and lazy daisy stitch, and long-tailed detached chain stitch. Other forms include double chain stitch or zigzag cable stitch, heavy chain stitch, Hungarian braided chain stitch and knotted chain stitch, alternatively called link stitch. Magic chain stitch is also known as chequered chain stitch, open chain stitch as square chain stitch or ladder stitch, and reverse chain stitch as broad chain stitch. Rosette chain stitch or bead edging stitch, Russian chain stitch, Singhalese chain stitch, twisted and zigzag variations complete the selection of chain stitches. After a line of stitches has been worked it can be given surface decoration as desired, and two more variations of threading and whipping are illustrated on p60.

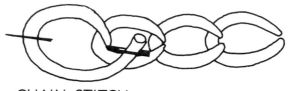

CHAIN STITCH

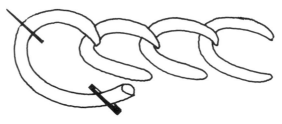

BROKEN CHAIN STITCH

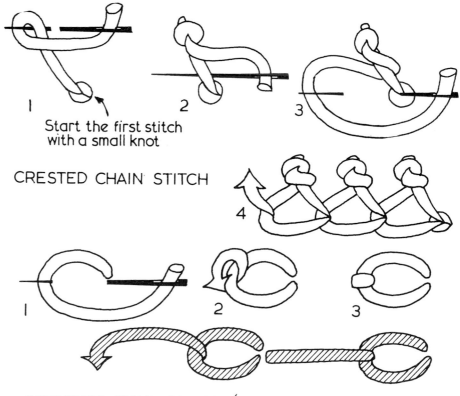

1

Start the first stitch
with a small knot

CRESTED CHAIN STITCH

4

1   2   3

DETACHED CHAIN STITCH (LONG-TAILED VERSION
SHADED)

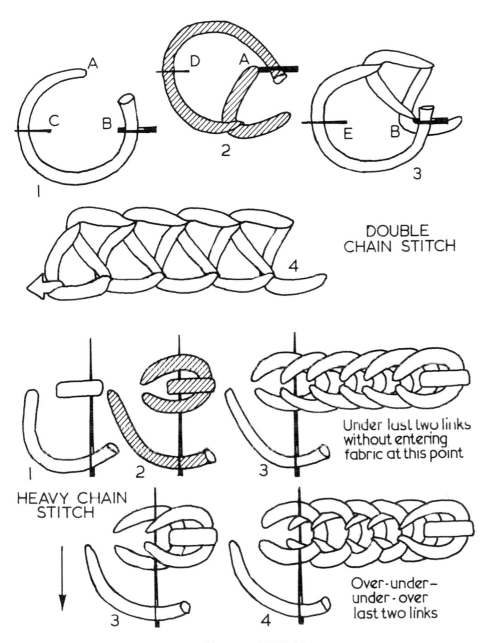

DOUBLE
CHAIN STITCH

Under last two links
without entering
fabric at this point

HEAVY CHAIN
STITCH

Over-under-
under-over
last two links

HUNGARIAN BRAIDED CHAIN STITCH

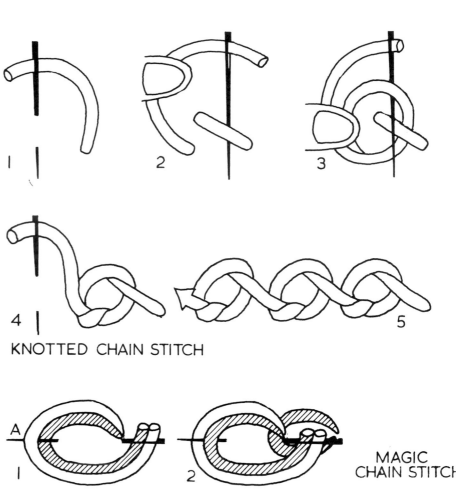

KNOTTED CHAIN STITCH

A

1

2

3

Pull the thread not
caught by needle to
the reverse

**MAGIC
CHAIN STITCH**

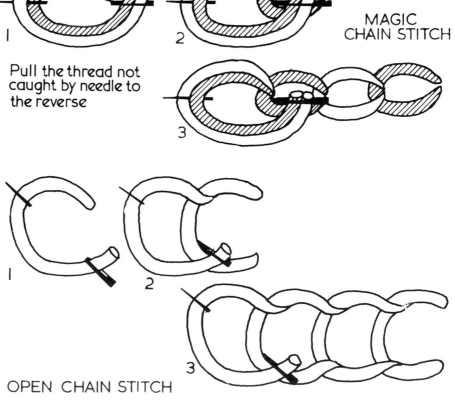

1

2

3

OPEN CHAIN STITCH

58

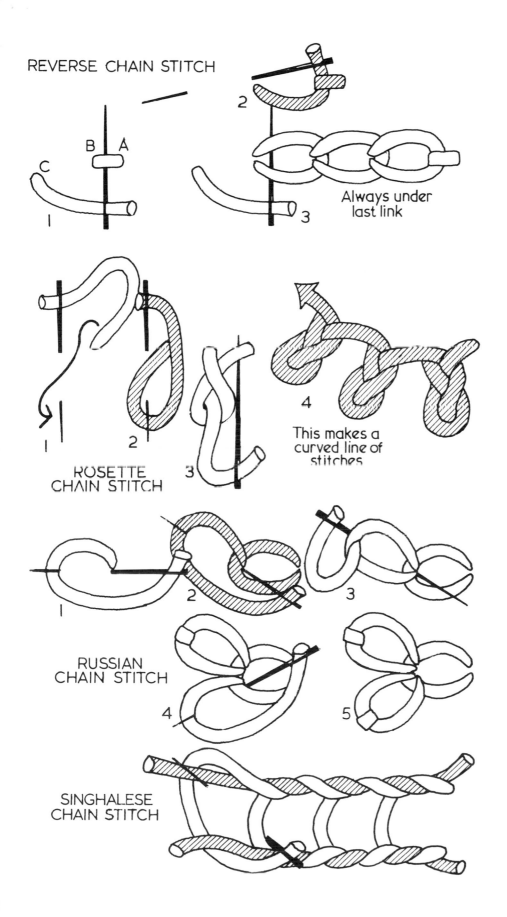

REVERSE CHAIN STITCH

B A

C

1

2

3

Always under
last link

ROSETTE
CHAIN STITCH

1

2

3

4

This makes a
curved line of
stitches

RUSSIAN
CHAIN STITCH

1

2

3

4

5

SINGHALESE
CHAIN STITCH

59

When a line of chain stitching is complete, it can be threaded, whipped or otherwise embellished

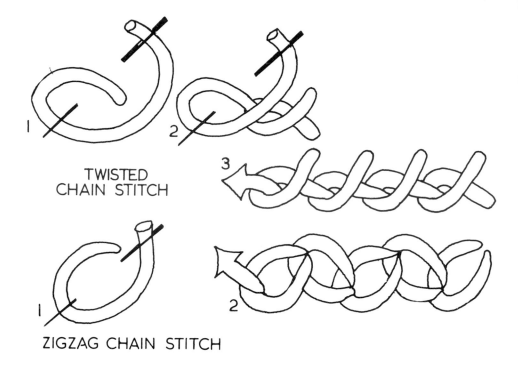

TWISTED CHAIN STITCH

ZIGZAG CHAIN STITCH

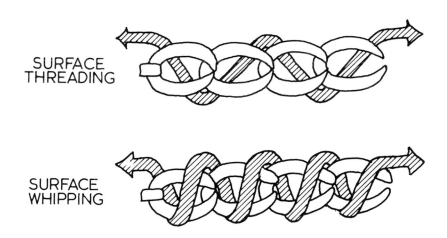

SURFACE THREADING

SURFACE WHIPPING

Tambouring

The name tambouring derives from a drum-shaped frame that is not now in general use. Similar in proportions to the musical tambour drum, it was held in the lap and the embroiderer thus had both hands free. Two hoops of circular wood, one fitting within the other, mounted on a curved wooden base, had the fabric stretched tightly between them. In later models, the circular base was discarded in favour of a vertical-legged frame, sometimes with a reel underneath the fabric so that a roll of continuous free-winding thread was always available.

Today tambouring is often done on a fanny or floor frame. A special hook is used, shaped as a crochet hook but with a removable notched needle at one end. In previous times, the main handle was usually ivory, bone or wood and if it was hollow spare needles could be stored within. Now plain pencil-shaped tambour handles are employed and a notched needle of the required size is fitted in and secured with a small screw. Since the embroiderer is unable to see what is going on beneath the ground fabric, it is a good idea always to insert the notch of the needle in alignment with the holding screw, which remains above the ground fabric and therefore gives an indication of the notch in the needle below. Another guide to placing the unseen needle beneath the fabric can be provided by a special tambour thimble with a notch in the top.

A length of thread, ideally one-stranded, is held in one hand beneath the ground fabric. The tambour hook is held upright, above the surface, in the other hand, and it is pushed a short way through the fabric. Helped by the hand beneath the surface, the hook loops the thread and brings it back up through the fabric. After a short distance, another such entry is made *through the previous loop*, now a stitch above the surface, and each subsequent stitch continues to be worked through the previous link.

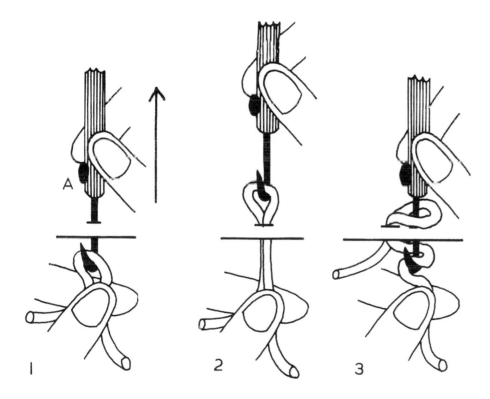

Method of working tamboured chain stitch: **1** One hand holds the thread beneath the ground fabric and the other hand inserts the tambour hook through the fabric and catches the thread in a loop. **2** When the tambour hook is pulled up through the fabric, the loop is brought up too. **3** After a short distance, the hook is taken through the first stitch and down again through the ground fabric. To enable the embroiderer to feel the unseen thread below the fabric more easily, it is always a good idea to align the notch of the hook with the screw (A) holding it into the tambour holder

61

9. Conservation

This chapter is essentially practical and it covers display and storage of embroidery as well as its basic conservation, cleaning and restoration.

Conservation should ideally be left to the professional, and to find such an expert a local museum should be contacted. If it does not have its own textile conservation department, the museum should be able to put the inquirer in touch with a conservator.

Although in the past embroideries were sometimes repaired, textile conservation as a profession is relatively new. Fortunately, with the increasing awareness of the value of textiles and of preservation generally, there has been a proliferation of such specialist organizations as the Textile Conservation Centre in England and the Canadian Conservation Institute. In the United States, there are many professional embroidery conservationists in cities across the country.

Caution, common sense, patience and dexterity are the qualities needed in an amateur who attempts to undertake conservation. He should know when *not* to attempt something, and remember the guideline that prevention is better than cure.

Display and storage

Eighteenth-century religious figure, thought to represent the Christ Child, which has undergone conservation at the Textile Conservation Centre at Hampton Court. After cleaning, couching repairs were worked on the gold-embroidered silk robe (height of figure 38cm [15in])

Flat embroideries on display should always be supported evenly. Large wall-hangings can be hung with touch and close fastening, matching pairs of hooked tape that when sealed together maintain a strong and even hold. Velcro, for instance, is sold in widths of 15, 20 and 30mm (approx $\frac{1}{2}$, 1 and $1\frac{1}{2}$in) but 10mm and 50mm (approx $\frac{1}{4}$in and 2in) are also available. One strip of tape is attached horizontally across the top of the back of an item and the other is fixed to a wooden dowel or direct to a wall. Smaller embroideries can be displayed with such aids as plastic V-shaped rods sometimes used for hanging posters. Lengths of self-clamping rod are placed along the top and bottom of an item to maintain even support.

Alternatively, embroideries can be mounted and framed as paintings (see chapter 6). Although items retain more textural effect when not put behind glass, delicate fabrics and threads do benefit from protective glazing.

Costume and other embroideries that require three-dimensional display should, as with flat wall-hangings and pictures, always be shielded from damp, moths, direct sunlight and extreme temperatures. The same conditions apply also to storage of any embroideries not on display.

Collectors sometimes store items in strong cardboard boxes with tight-fitting lids. It is a good idea to spray against moths before putting any embroideries away, and since some cardboard contains acid harmful to textiles, stored items should always be protected by sheets of white acid-free tissue or perma paper, the latter generally only available from museum suppliers.

Ideally embroideries should be stored flat. Larger pieces can be rolled round map holders or other cardboard tubes, protected by white tissue paper. Any folds should be loosely made around a wad of tissue paper and the folded article should be taken out from time to time and put away with folds in different places. Embroidered costumes hung from dress hangers, sometimes covered with bits of cotton cloth or tissue paper, should always be protected from the metal hook, and items stored by hanging or any other method should never be put in a polythene bag unless it is pierced to allow the item inside to breathe.

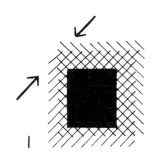

Dry Cleaning

Some owners trust a good dry-cleaner with their embroideries but until confidence is established, it is advisable to test the service with an item that is not valuable. Do-it-yourself spray and other commercial cleaners, some especially intended for needlepoints, have not all yet been extensively tested.

Surface dirt can be removed from upholstery and other embroidered items by a variety of methods. Magnesium carbonate, a white pharmaceutical powder, can be thinly sprinkled on the surface and after a short while carefully removed with a soft brush. Alternatively a vacuum-cleaner nozzle covered with a piece of fine nylon net can be worked in continuous circular movements over the entire surface of the item.

Washing

Washing of any embroidery should be undertaken with great caution, if at all. Articles with metal thread should never be immersed in water and anything to be washed must be carefully tested for running or bleeding with the cottonwool method. Most embroideries can simply be washed by immersion and gentle up-and-down agitation but delicate items can be protected by placing them between layers of nylon gossamer or ordinary dress net.

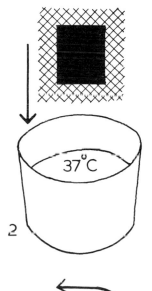

Before starting to wash an item, it is imperative to make sure that everything—other than the dirty embroidery—is immaculately clean. A plastic wash-bowl or large stainless steel sink should be half-filled with deionized, rain or soft tap water at blood temperature, 37°C (98°F): hotter water should only ever be used when necessary on cottons and linens. Several drops of a mild washing agent should

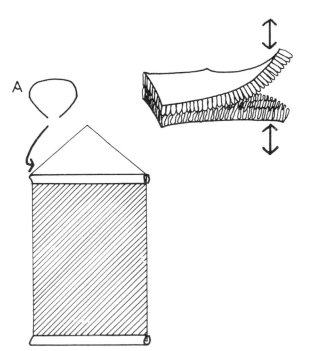

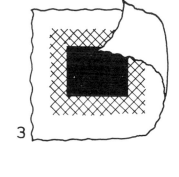

(*Left*) Touch and close fasteners consist of two strips, each with nylon tufts, which stick together. One half of the fastening tape is sewn horizontally along the top of a wall-hanging and the other is nailed to a board set on the wall. Another method of hanging embroideries is by attaching a plastic V-shaped clamp (seen in cross-section at A) along the top and bottom of an item

(*Right*) Method of washing embroidery: **1** An item can be sandwiched between two pieces of gossamer net or nylon dress net held with long tacking stitches. **2** It is then dipped in a container of hand-warm water with natural soap. When all the dirt has come out the item is rinsed in cold water. **3** The embroidery is wrapped in a large dry, clean towel and excess water is gently squeezed out. **4** The item is laid out, horizontally, on another towel to dry

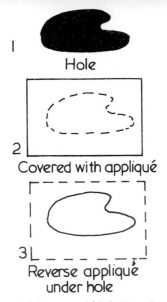

1
Hole

2
Covered with appliqué

3
Reverse appliqué
under hole

A hole in a ground fabric (1) can be disguised by overlaid appliqué (2) or reverse appliqué (3)

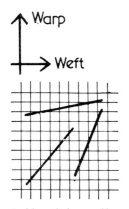

Warp
Weft

Long tacking stitches used in reinforcement need not be parallel to the warp or weft of the ground fabric

Similarly, an accidental snip through canvas (1) can be disguised by placing a small piece of similar canvas (2) behind the hole and, from the front, working stitches through the two layers all around the hole, the heavy dots here defining where stitches are worked through two layers of canvas (3)

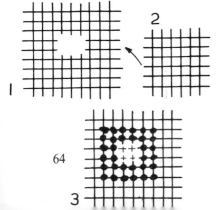

1

2

3

be put in the water, or pure soap flakes or dishwashing liquid can be used, the latter probably having additives that make it unsuitable for old, valuable or delicate items. Particularly small articles can be put into water and washing agent in a small screw-top glass or plastic container and gently shaken up and down.

Items being washed in a bowl or sink should be carefully immersed and, when the dirt is seen to have come out, washed in several rinses of cold water until that water remains absolutely clear. The article is then carefully transferred to an absorbent towel which is wrapped round it and carefully squeezed—not wrung hard—to get rid of excess water. It is next laid on another towel or on a large sheet of blotting paper and carefully fingered or held with stainless pins to its correct shape. The embroidery is then left flat on the towel or paper, out of direct sunlight or extreme heat, until it is completely dry.

Simple stains can sometimes be removed by sandwiching the item between two sheets of blotting paper and gently ironing it. Alternatively, grease can be removed by covering the stain with dry talc and leaving it for a few hours. Other stains require more complicated action, although it should be remembered that it is better to leave a stubborn mark alone rather than risk damaging the fabric.

Acetic acid (5 per cent) or white vinegar are useful stain removers for dealing with dried adhesives, beer, coffee, tea or wine stains. Methylated spirit (colourless) or industrial alcohol can be used to remove ballpoint or fibre-tipped pen marks and lipstick stains require a dry-cleaning fluid. In each instance the stained part should be placed over a clean white cloth. The mark is lightly dabbed with a ball of cotton wool soaked in the recommended fluid. As it absorbs the stain, the ball of cotton wool should be replaced by a clean ball and when no more stain is absorbed, carefully rinse the area of ground fabric previously stained, using another wad of cotton wool moistened in clean water.

Sometimes stains result during the process of embroidery. There is no need to panic if the embroiderer pricks his finger and blood gets on to the item. The stain should immediately be sucked or put under a cold tap.

Although such other methods of removing stains as allowing chewing gum to freeze and then carefully picking it off are elementary, others can be dangerous and scientifically unsound, and the amateur conservator should at all times practise caution.

Mending

One of the most useful materials in reparation is nylon gossamer fabric, a matted material with strong one-way support. It can be used as a sandwich for washing embroideries or for backing or other purposes, and can be sewn, painted or glued.

The strength and durability of a repair are most important when mending embroideries and invisible stitching is therefore less important than the practicality of that stitching.

Embroidery that has suffered moth or similar damage may have holes in the ground fabric. These can be disguised by motifs applied in onlay or reverse appliqué methods, or the whole item can be supported by a length of net placed behind it and held in place with strong tacking stitches. If darning is worked as reparation, stitches should always be executed parallel to the warp or weft of the ground, but other stitches, ideally executed in thread as close as possible to the colour of the ground fabric or the original embroidery thereon, need not be worked parallel to the ground-fabric threads. Wherever possible, repair stitches should be worked through the holes of existing or other original stitches.

During the third quarter of the
seventeenth century biblical
pictures were popular with
English needleworkers. This
version of the Judgement of
Solomon (I Kings 3) shows the
king, in the guise of Charles I
with a Charles II wig and
wearing an ermine-trimmed
cloak. The executioner to the
king's left holds up the living
baby whom he is about to cut in
half to share between two
women who claim maternity.
The other—dead—baby lies in
front of the throne (linen canvas
embroidered mainly in silk tent
stitch with satin stitch and
bullion knots and some raised
work. Small pieces of mica are
sewn as spangles for the castle
windows. 40 × 49cm [15¾ ×
19¼in])

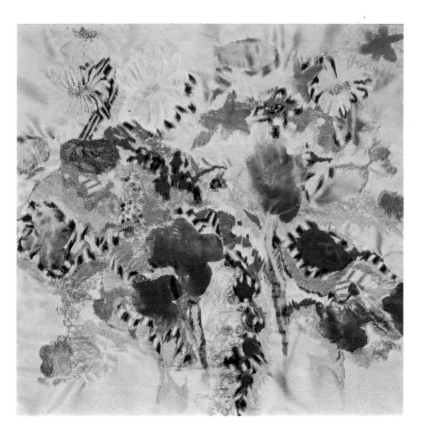

10. Couched work and filling stitches

Couched work is the technique by which threads are held in place by others. Threads are laid on the ground fabric and retained there by couching stitches worked in other threads at regular intervals. The couching threads pierce the ground fabric.

In technical terms couching implies a single thread thus laid and couched to the ground fabric. Although laidwork, in which many threads are laid and couched, is usually a filling technique, not all filling stitches need be couched. This chapter covers couching and laidwork techniques, including underside couching, or point couché rentré, and or nué, also known as shaded couching or Burgundian lazar, and surface filling stitches. Other specialized filling techniques are associated with drawn-thread work (chapter 16), metal-thread work (chapter 24) needlepoint (chapter 26) and pulled-thread work (chapter 30).

Couching and laidwork are employed both for decorative and practical purposes. Since the laid threads are kept above the surface of the ground fabric none is wasted by being hidden on the reverse and, also, metal threads not always easily sewn through a fabric can be laid and couched with another, thinner and more manageable, thread.

Surface filling stitches are used to infill a motif or other area of ground fabric and the many variants fall into two groups. Semé embroidery has single spot stitches or small devices either in geometric formation or scattered at random within a determined area. Ground-covering stitches cover the entire surface of that area.

One of the earliest examples of couched work is a fragment from an Altaian Scythian saddle cover from Pazyryk. In western Europe the Bayeux 'tapestry', worked c1070, provides an early example of the technique of underside couching. Although it was employed elsewhere, the best items decorated with underside couching came from England, and Opus Anglicanum, or English work, in which both underside and superficial couching and laidwork were ubiquitous, remained supreme from the middle of the thirteenth to the end of the fourteenth centuries.

The demise of Opus Anglicanum coincided with the beginnings in Europe of or nué, in which gold threads laid closely parallel to each other are couched with coloured silks in such a way that the couching stitches build up a coloured pattern. Worked to a large extent in Burgundy during the fifteenth century, the technique was especially popular until the seventeenth century.

Many forms of couched work continue to be worked today, especially in eastern Asia.

Materials

Canvas is not generally used as a ground for couched work but it is extensively employed for needlepoint filling stitches. A beginner might like to try some of the couched work techniques here set out, using all six strands of stranded cotton laid on an evenweave linen fabric and couched with one strand of differently coloured stranded cotton threaded through a chenille or crewel needle. Although single lines of couching can be worked on hand-held fabric, a frame is recommended for executing laidwork and other filling forms.

In couching one thread is held to the ground by another

(*Opposite, above*) Machine-embroidered cushion cover designed and worked by Caroline Jubb (yellow satin partly painted and decorated with applied cotton and velvet fabric and machine stitching, detail of cover 91 × 75cm [32 × 29¼in] overall)

(*Below*) Crewel embroidery designed and worked by Audrey Francini (linen twill embroidered in wool and some silk in a variety of techniques including chain and open chain, fly, herringbone, long-and-short and stem stitches, Romanian couching, spider's web and other fillings and French knots. 20.2 × 14cm [8 × 5½in])

67

(*Left*) Underside couching is especially associated with Opus Anglicanum, English Work, primarily executed from the middle of the thirteenth until the end of the fourteenth centuries. This is the back view of the Clare Chasuble, and as two of the coats of arms embroidered on a matching stole and maniple are those of Cornwall and Clare it was probably worked sometime before the divorce of Edmund Plantagenet, Earl of Cornwall, and his wife, Margaret Clare, in 1294. The main motifs here show the Crucifixion, the Virgin and Child, St Peter and St Paul and the Stoning of St Stephen (blue satin with cotton weft embroidered with coloured silks in split stitch, laid and couched work and silver-gilt underside couching, 115 × 66cm [45¼ × 26in])

(*Right*) Oriental couching is often especially intricate. This Japanese panel is worked in black and white silks and gilt thread and as well as couching, long-and-short stitch is employed (76 × 66.2cm [30 × 26¼in])

Methods of working

When laying either one or more threads on a ground fabric, it is necessary to push the ends through to the reverse: either take them through with a special thick couching needle, or plunge them, placing the end of a laid thread through a loop of another thinner thread worked from the reverse of the fabric. When that loop is pulled sharply back through the fabric it takes the end of the laid thread with it.

Couching and laidwork

Some forms of couched work are executed as single lines. Each laid thread is worked separately and the angle and frequency of couching stitches determine the pattern.

As well as the basic couching stitch, also known as convent or kløster stitch, forms of couched work, executed either in single lines as couching or in blocks of

1 Couching cross-section, the surface of the fabric represented by the dotted line. 2 Underside couching, again in cross-section, has the laid thread pulled through the surface. 3 In or nué, couching stitches form a design over laid threads

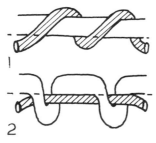

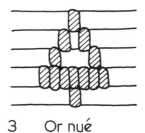

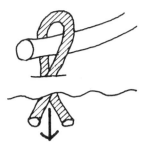 

Plunging the end of a laid thread
through the ground

BOKHARA
COUCHING

BURDEN
COUCHING

COLCHA
COUCHING

NEW ENGLAND
COUCHING

ROMAN
COUCHING

ROMANIAN
COUCHING

DOUBLE ROMANIAN STITCH

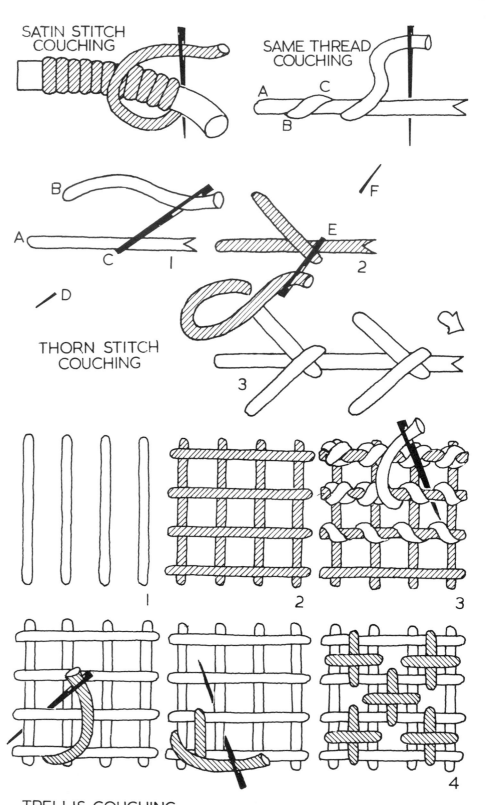

SATIN STITCH
COUCHING

SAME THREAD
COUCHING

THORN STITCH
COUCHING

TRELLIS COUCHING
Over a foundation of laid threads (1, 2) patterns can be
executed (3, 4)

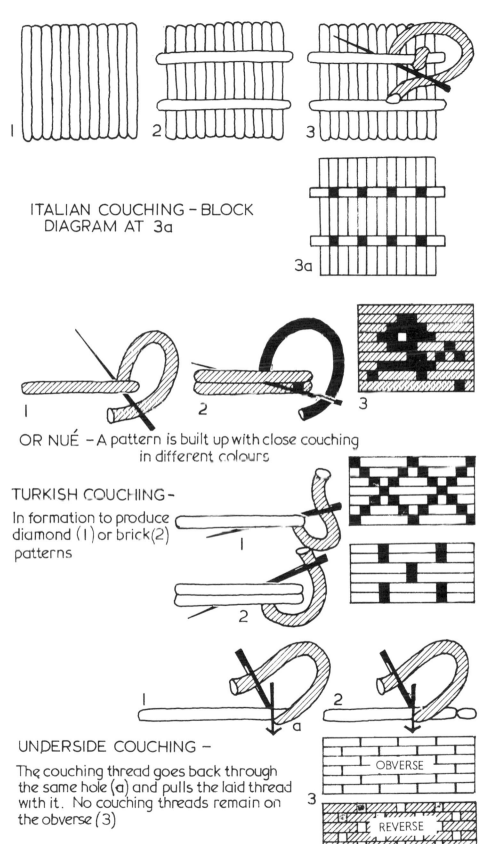

More dense laidwork forms include Italian couching—worked over two layers of laid thread, with block diagram of finished result at 3a; Or nué—a pattern is built up with close couching in different colours; Turkish couching—laid threads, usually metal, are couched in formations to give diamond or brick patterns; underside couching—the couched thread (1) goes back through the same hole (a) and pulls the laid thread with it. No couching threads remain on the obverse of the fabric.

ITALIAN COUCHING – BLOCK DIAGRAM AT 3a

OR NUÉ – A pattern is built up with close couching in different colours

TURKISH COUCHING –

In formation to produce diamond (1) or brick (2) patterns

UNDERSIDE COUCHING –

The couching thread goes back through the same hole (a) and pulls the laid thread with it. No couching threads remain on the obverse (3)

OBVERSE

REVERSE

Spot filling stitches, shown in block form to the right of the illustration

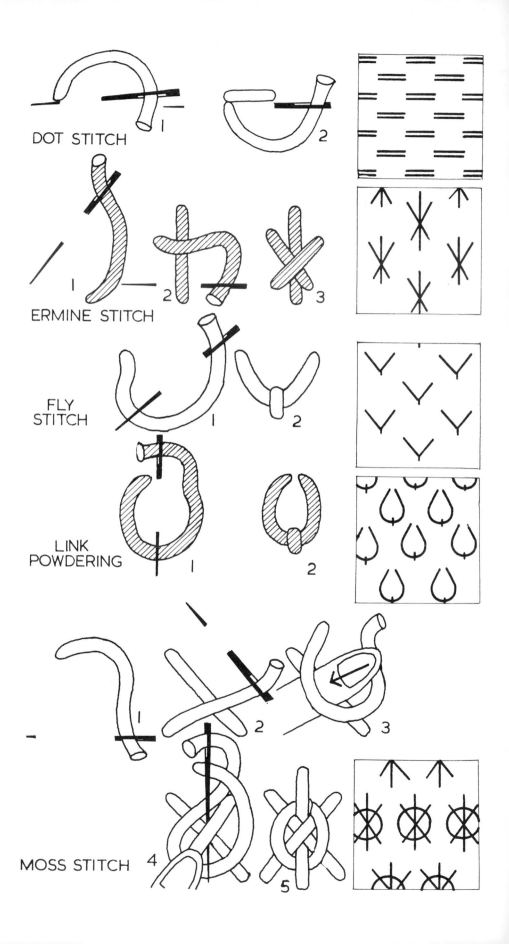

DOT STITCH

ERMINE STITCH

FLY STITCH

LINK POWDERING

MOSS STITCH

laidwork, include Bokhara, Burden and colcha stitches, New England or Deerfield stitch, also known as self-couching, Roman stitch and Romanian stitch, also known as antique, figure or oriental couching and with a related double Romanian stitch form. There are also satin stitch, same thread, thorn and trellis couching techniques and some of the more dense variants include Italian or Algerian couching, or nué, Turkish and underside couching.

Filling stitches

Spot filling techniques include dot or simple knot stitch, ermine stitch, fly stitch, also known as open loop and Y stitch, link powdering or detached daisy stitch, moss and sheaf stitches, spider's web and tête-de-boeuf fillings.

Ground-covering fillings include basket and brick and cross filling stitches, buttonhole filling stitch with closed, open and knotted versions, Ceylon and cloud or Mexican filling stitch and diamond, honeycomb filling and net passing stitches. Laced fillings include herringbone and laced-star filling stitches, the latter with Persian laced variation.

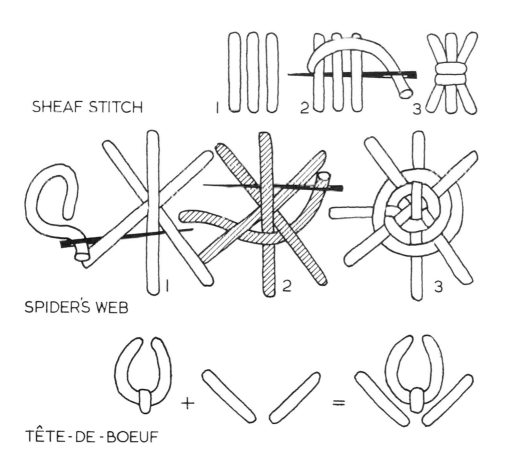

SHEAF STITCH

SPIDER'S WEB

TÊTE-DE-BOEUF

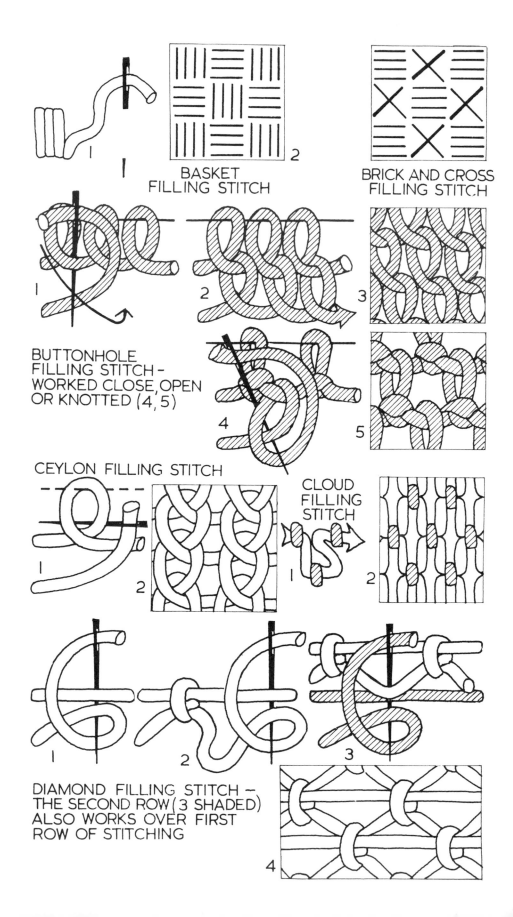

BASKET
FILLING STITCH

BRICK AND CROSS
FILLING STITCH

BUTTONHOLE
FILLING STITCH –
WORKED CLOSE, OPEN
OR KNOTTED (4, 5)

CEYLON FILLING STITCH

CLOUD
FILLING
STITCH

DIAMOND FILLING STITCH –
THE SECOND ROW (3 SHADED)
ALSO WORKS OVER FIRST
ROW OF STITCHING

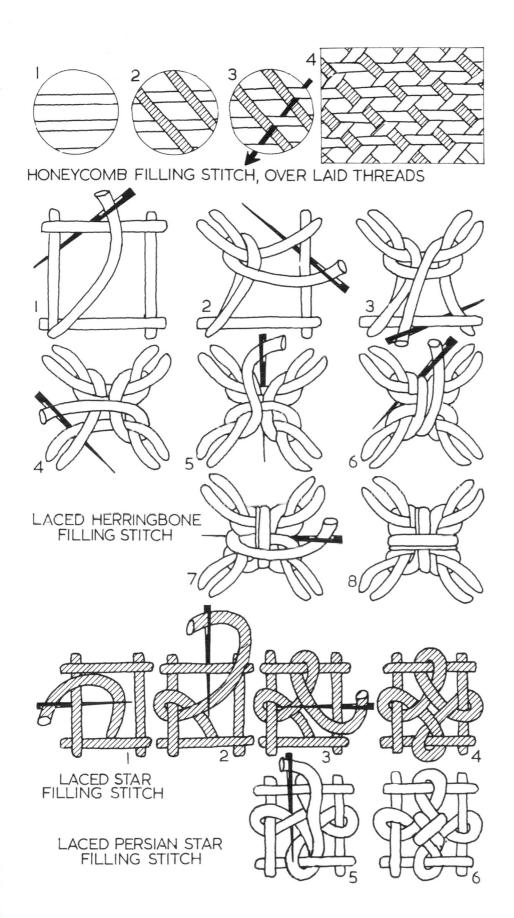

HONEYCOMB FILLING STITCH, OVER LAID THREADS

LACED HERRINGBONE
FILLING STITCH

LACED STAR
FILLING STITCH

LACED PERSIAN STAR
FILLING STITCH

11. Crewel embroidery

Crewel wool, also known as cruel, is a two-ply lightly twisted worsted yarn which is used in a variety of techniques, including needlepoint. 'Crewel embroidery', alternatively called 'crewel work' and, less accurately, 'Jacobean embroidery', implies crewel wools embroidered in crewel, stem and other stitches on linen in non-geometric, free-flowing and usually floral patterns.

Some of the earliest surviving fragments of embroideries worked in crewel wool, either on linen or woollen ground fabrics, were executed in Egypt and around the north-east of the Mediterranean from the fourth century.

One of the first known crewel embroideries worked in western Europe, possibly in south-east England, is the Bayeux 'tapestry', a panel which recounts the story of the conquest of England by William, Duke of Normandy, in 1066. Although the exact historical details are still unknown, it is possible that it was worked to commemorate the consecration of Odo, Bishop of Bayeux, in 1077. With a mean height of 0.5m and overall length of 70.35m (20in × 230ft), the Bayeux 'tapestry', executed in stem stitch as well as chain and split stitches and underside couching in plied wool thread on a linen ground, is one of the largest and most famous embroideries of all time.

Crewel embroidery as a specific form began to gain popularity in England in the late sixteenth century. There are records in such journals as the Hardwick Hall Inventory of 1601 which confirm that Lady Shrewsbury's bed chamber contained a 'Cloth of Checker work of Cruell about the bed'. Silk, employed in blackwork and other needlework forms, was expensive as it was imported, usually from the eastern Mediterranean. Wool, on the other hand, was available locally and offered a better defence against winter cold when used to decorate clothing and such household furnishings as wall-hangings, coverlets and cushions.

Many of the items surviving from this time were probably worked by ladies for their own use. Patterns were copied from herbals and other books and also direct from nature, in designs with delightful motifs of carnations, daffodils, cornflowers, pansies and other flowers, herbs and fruits, including the potato plant recently brought from the Americas by Sir Walter Raleigh.

With the Incorporation of the East India Company by Elizabeth I in 1600, and

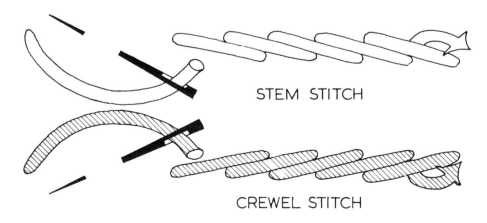

STEM STITCH

CREWEL STITCH

with the expansion of eastern trade generally, an oriental element was introduced into crewel embroidery design. Tree of life patterns, possibly copied by Indian draughtsmen from western European mille-fleurs tapestries were, in turn, imitated by English embroiderers. Seventeenth-century crewel work therefore often has a tree with gently curving branches and large leaves rising from rolling terrain or a specific mound known as terra firma. Around it frolic squirrels, rabbits and other animals and, especially after the Restoration of 1660, oak leaves and apples, royalist motifs, were often included in crewel designs.

Crewel embroidery began to lose popularity in England at the beginning of the eighteenth century, partly because needlepoint worked on a canvas ground was found to be more lasting. Many surviving early crewel pieces have, at some time or other during their lifetime, had the reserves of the main embroidery carefully cut away, and the embroidered sections applied, with hemming, to new and stronger ground fabrics.

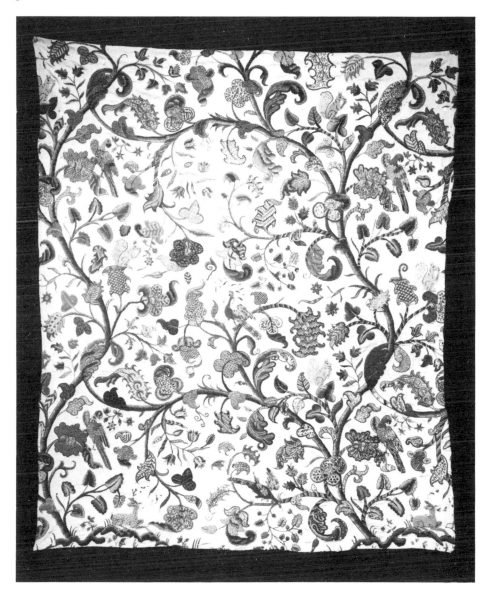

Seventeenth-century English curtain embroidered with crewel techniques (linen and cotton twill worked with long-and-short, stem and other stitches, 208 × 165cm [81¼ × 65in])

Pieces of crewel work are thought to have been brought to America by early settlers and others. Such ground fabrics as home-produced fustian and dimity, blends of cotton and linen, were probably employed during the late seventeenth century although no examples now survive.

In the eighteenth century American crewel began to develop its own characteristics. In order to make the embroidery thread cover more ground, American embroiderers worked both stitches and designs sparingly. Filling stitches, for instance, were often worked with the minimum of thread appearing on the wrong side of the ground fabric. Native fruits and flowers were included in designs, which were lighter overall with more of the ground unworked than in contemporary British examples.

American crewel, used especially for bed-hangings and coverlets and for such costume items as 'husifs', housewives' pockets, suffered a setback at the time of the Revolution. It recovered somewhat at the end of the nineteenth century when needlework schools and groups were established, particularly in New England, in an effort to repair the artistic damage done by Berlin woolwork.

One such organization was founded in Deerfield, Massachusetts, by Ellen Miller and Margaret Whiting. From 1896 to 1926, 'Deerfield blue-on-white work' was embroidered to these ladies' designs by outworkers. Although Deerfield embroidery used linen threads and fabric, many of the floral motifs were taken from eighteenth-century crewel embroideries.

In England, after Berlin woolwork and other embroidery fashions had become increasingly garish, there was a temporary return to 'art needlework' in the third quarter of the nineteenth century. William Morris, Walter Crane and Lewis Day were among the designers who produced patterns for crewel designs, mainly floral, with soft natural colours reminiscent of the vegetable dyes of former times.

Materials

Although any material which will not pucker may be used, crewel embroidery is best worked with crewel wools on a natural ground of unbleached linen twill or crash. Sharp crewel needles should be used, although blunt tapestry needles can be useful for interlacings and laidwork. Although some stitches can be worked with the fabric hand-held, a frame is recommended.

Stitches and designs for crewel embroidery

Crewel embroidery stitches are diagrammed elsewhere in this book (and they can be found via the index). As well as the main crewel and stem stitches, which are often synonymous and can be called outline, or stalk, stitches, many other straight stitches are employed, especially brick, long-and-short and split stitches. A variety of knots and couching and filling stitches, including brick-and-cross and buttonhole, are also used.

Crewelpoint

As explained in chapter 26, crewel can be adapted to canvas work, either in co-ordination with tent and other standard needlepoint stitches or by itself.

12. Cross stitches

Cross-stitch embroidery is a counted-thread technique using any of the many variants of stitches formed by at least two straight stitches, usually diagonal and crossing each other.

Basic cross stitching has two diagonal stitches of equal length bisecting each other at right angles. Ideally the uppermost stitch should slope up to the right. When more than one cross is worked all the uppermost stitches should lie in the same direction.

Cross stitch is one of the most versatile of all embroidery forms. It can be worked

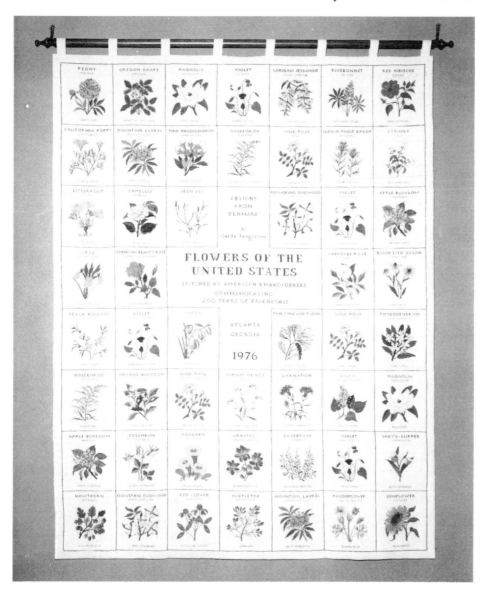

Cross-stitch wall-hanging designed by Gerda Bengtsson of the Danish Handcraft Guild in Copenhagen and executed, under the sponsorship of Felker Art-Needlework of Decatur, Georgia, by fifty-one men and women in the Atlanta area (linen, with thread count of 34 per 2.5cm (1in), embroidered in Danish flower thread and stranded cotton, 147.3 × 111.7cm [58 × 44in])

on most ground fabrics, including canvas. Intricate floral cross-stitch designs on fine linen ground fabrics are sometimes known as Danish embroidery because of the proliferation of patterns from Scandinavia. At the other extreme, peasant motifs are worked in cross stitch, sometimes in monochrome, on regional costumes in eastern Europe and many other parts of the world.

The origins of cross-stitch embroidery are unknown, although it was in use in the Near East by about the eighth century. In South America, some surviving pre-Colombian textiles dating from about the twelfth century include cross-stitch decoration.

Long-armed or long-legged cross stitch, with two diagonal stitches of unequal length bisecting each other at right angles, was popular with central European embroiderers in the Middle Ages, and the technique was also used by Icelandic embroiderers from about the sixteenth century.

Ordinary cross stitch was not especially popular in the British Isles until Tudor times when it was taken up by ladies, some of them highly skilled needlewomen of the calibre of Mary, Queen of Scots, and Bess of Hardwick. Working with silks and wools on linen canvas, they decorated such items as cushion covers, wall-hangings and small panels which were then applied to sumptuous velvet or silk fabrics.

In America, rather later, cross stitch was also to become popular with famous ladies, including Martha Washington (1731–1802) who in 1766 began work on twelve cushion covers, each 47.6×39.4cm ($18\frac{3}{4} \times 15\frac{1}{2}$in), decorated in yellow and golden silk floss and wool on canvas imported from England.

On both sides of the Atlantic, cross stitch was also supreme in sampler embroidery, worked on linen or cotton ground fabrics. Girls of all ages have used cross stitch in lettering and for numerical, pictorial and other motifs on their 'test pieces' (see chapter 32).

Materials

Since cross stitch is a counted-thread technique it is advisable to work on canvas or an evenweave fabric with the same number of warp and weft threads to a specified square. Alternatively, a block-weave canvas with a number of warp and weft threads interwoven to form a block can be used. Cross stitches worked on a matted ground such as felt can be symmetrically aligned by the needlepoint technique of temporarily laying waste or single-weave canvas over the ground and working stitches over both materials (see chapter 26).

Most embroidery threads, including wools, are suitable for cross-stitch work, and plied yarn can be used with one or more strands at a time. Beginners might like to work with pearl cotton on a linen ground fabric. To avoid splitting that fabric a tapestry needle should be used and it is a good idea to work on a frame.

Stitch forms

As well as basic cross stitch, versions illustrated include chained cross stitch, crossed-corners cross stitch or rice stitch, diagonal stitch, double cross stitch, also known as Leviathan or Smyrna cross stitches, and Italian or arrowhead cross stitch. The list continues with long-armed or long-legged cross stitch, alternatively called plaited Slav stitch, and marking and Montenegrin cross stitches. It proceeds with reversed cross stitch and two-sided or reversible cross stitch, also known as brave-bred stitch. Half a cross stitch is diagrammed in chapter 26.

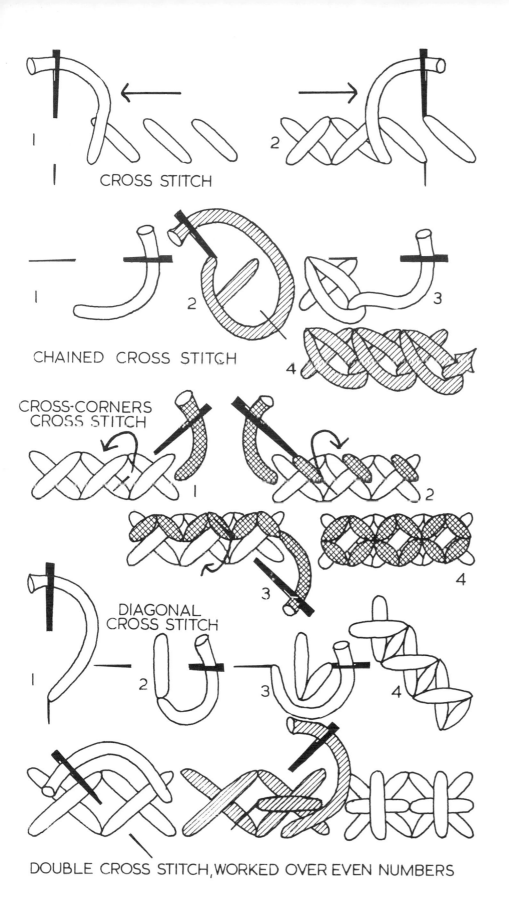

CROSS STITCH

CHAINED CROSS STITCH

CROSS-CORNERS
CROSS STITCH

DIAGONAL
CROSS STITCH

DOUBLE CROSS STITCH, WORKED OVER EVEN NUMBERS

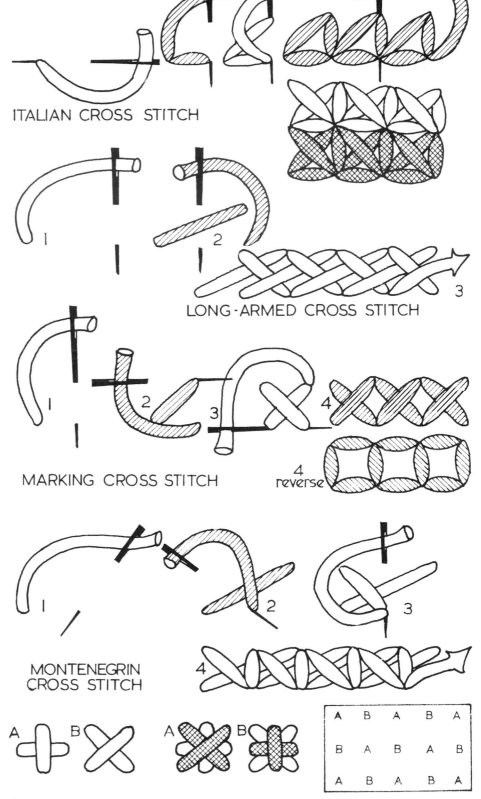

ITALIAN CROSS STITCH

LONG-ARMED CROSS STITCH

1 2 3

MARKING CROSS STITCH

4

4 reverse

MONTENEGRIN CROSS STITCH

1 2 3

4

(*Opposite, above*) Cushion cover with a simple cross-stitch design of ancient Middle Eastern motifs. Each quadrant of the design has stylized motifs of (from the centre) a palm tree, a cypress tree, a 'true' tree and a 'false' tree, all separated by flowers in pots. Instructions for making this cushion are given at the end of chapter 12 (Scotscraig linen and cotton mixture embroidered with Anchor Pearl Cotton No 5, 40.6cm [16in] square overall)

(*Below*) Bargello pocketbook made by 'Elizabeth Lord of Lyme who married Jared Eliot, 2 April 1760' (linen canvas embroidered with wool flame stitch, 8 × 17cm [3⅛ × 6¾in] when closed)

A   B   A   B

A	B	A	B	A
B	A	B	A	B
A	B	A	B	A

*REVERSED CROSS STITCH WORKED ALTERNATELY

82

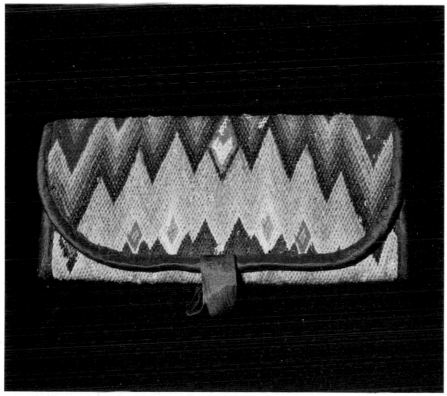

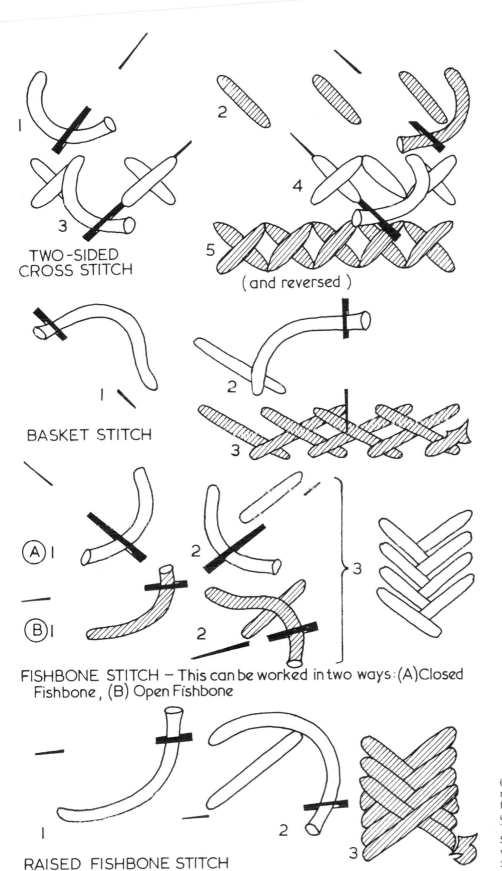

TWO-SIDED
CROSS STITCH

(and reversed)

BASKET STITCH

FISHBONE STITCH – This can be worked in two ways: (A)Closed
Fishbone, (B) Open Fishbone

RAISED FISHBONE STITCH

(*Opposite*) One of the famous
needlepoint panels, worked in the
first few years of the seventeenth
century and still to be seen at
Traquair House, near Peebles,
Scotland (linen canvas embroidered
with wool and silk tent stitch, 75 ×
58cm [$29\frac{1}{2} \times 22\frac{7}{8}$in])

85

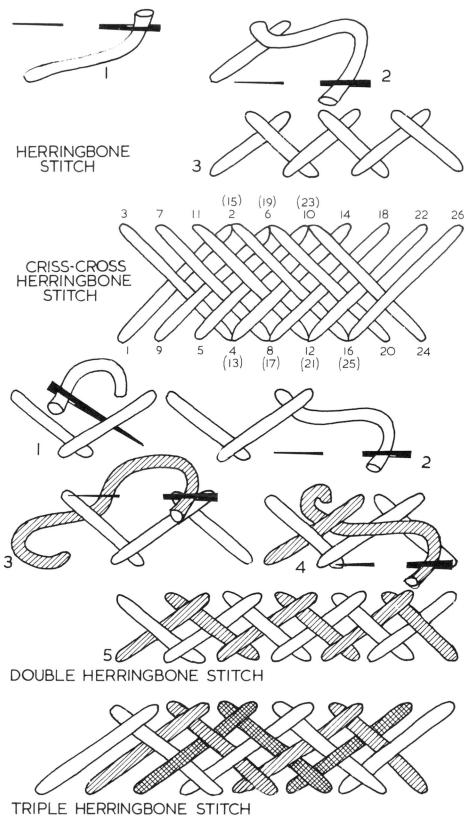

HERRINGBONE
STITCH

CRISS-CROSS
HERRINGBONE
STITCH

DOUBLE HERRINGBONE STITCH

TRIPLE HERRINGBONE STITCH

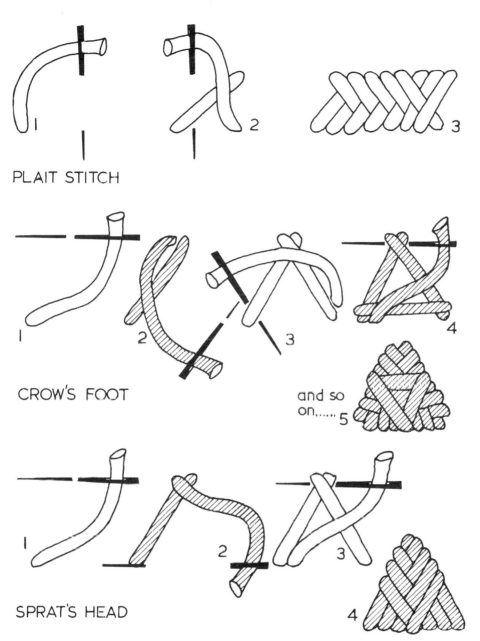

PLAIT STITCH

CROW'S FOOT

and so on...... 5

SPRAT'S HEAD

Other forms related to the cross-stitch family shown here include basket stitch and fishbone stitch, with closed, open and raised variations. Herringbone stitch, also known as mossoul, Russian cross or Russia stitch, has criss-cross, double and triple versions which can be laced, threaded or tied. Plait stitch, also known as Spanish stitch, is included, as are such formations as crow's foot and sprat's head.

Cross-stitch design (see colour illustration on p 83)

A cushion cover with motifs taken from typical Middle Eastern designs can be made in the following way:

Materials

2 pieces of fabric 40 × 45cm (15¾ × 17¾in)—the sample was made from Scotscraig, a sixty-five per cent linen and thirty-five per cent cotton mixture; many embroiderers find that an evenweave fabric is more suitable to use for counted-thread embroidery
2 balls pearl cotton No 5 in colour one—the sample used Anchor pearl yellow No 0290
1 ball pearl cotton No 5 in colour two—the sample was made with Anchor pearl green No 0255
tapestry needle No 18
35cm (13¾in) Velcro 1.5cm (approx ½in) wide
1 cushion pad 35 × 37cm (13¾ × 14½in)
(also, if required, two pieces of cotton or other lining the same size as the main fabric)

Instructions

1 The edges of the main fabric are bound with machine or hand sewing.
2 One piece of fabric is marked vertically and horizontally into quarters, indicated by small running stitches.

This diagram shows one quarter of the finished Middle Eastern cross-stitch cushion cover design. The main motifs, from the left, are a palm tree, a cypress tree, a 'true' tree and a 'false' tree, with small flower pots in between

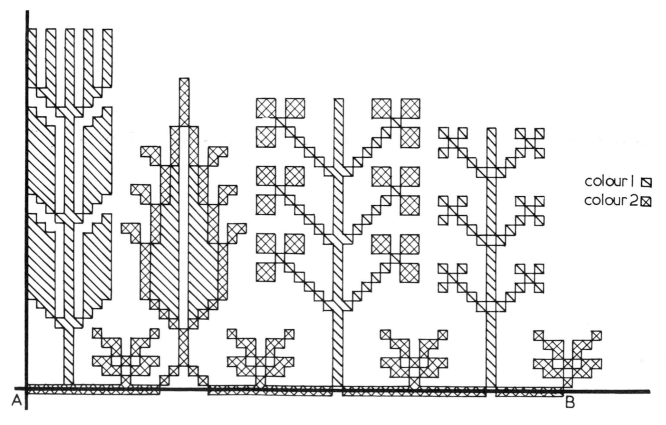

colour 1 ◨
colour 2 ⊠

3 With one longer edge of the fabric uppermost, the design is started at the centre (A on the diagram) and a base line worked to B. Colour two thread is used, worked in cross stitches over two threads. The charted design pivots horizontally on this base line and to centre the finished embroidery the base line is worked one thread up and one thread down from the marked line of running stitches.

4 When the first line AB has been worked, the fabric and charted design are turned through 180° and the other half of the base line of cross stitches is worked from left to right.

5 The rest of the embroidery is completed, the charted design being worked four times in all, once in each quadrant of the ground fabric.

6 When all the cross stitches are worked the running stitches are removed and the item is pressed carefully from the wrong side. If required, both pieces of fabric can be attached to lining.

7 Wrong sides out, both pieces of fabric are machined together around three edges, one shorter side being left open.

8 Velcro is attached to the open edges.

9 The cushion cover is turned right side out and corner tassels worked (as diagrammed in chapter 3).

10 The cushion pad is placed inside the cover and the item is sealed by the Velcro fastening.

13. Cutwork

In cutwork, areas of ground fabric which have been bordered with buttonhole stitch are carefully cut away. The resulting holes may be partly infilled with stitches sometimes so intricately formed as to be the true 'needlepoint' or needle-lace. The ground fabric and stitches are usually white, and the main forms of cutwork are broderie anglaise or eyelet embroidery, Renaissance embroidery, with cut reserves, reticella or Italian cutwork, with even more of the ground fabric cut away, and Richelieu embroidery, similar to Renaissance but with picots embellishing holding buttonhole bars.

The last three forms of cutwork reached a zenith in Italy in the sixteenth century. Although Renaissance and Richelieu cutwork remained as embroideries, reticella, a particularly highly skilled art worked chiefly in Venice, became more a needle-lace than an embroidery. Reticella was executed on fabric from which most of the threads had been cut or carefully withdrawn to form squares and these were then buttonholed around and infilling worked with long stitches taken from one side to the other of a hole and then bound together with buttonholing. The amount of remaining ground fabric diminished so much that eventually stitches were formed with no ground fabric at all, the design worked above a marked parchment pattern.

Detail of an early twentieth-century English baby's robe decorated with broderie anglaise (white cotton fabric and thread embroidered with buttonhole, satin and stem stitches, skirt 91.5cm [36in] long)

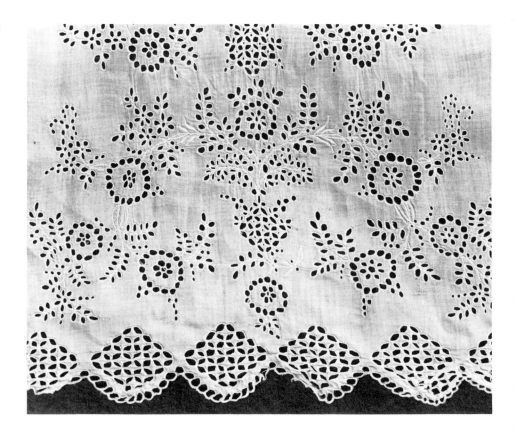

Renaissance cutwork. After the rabbit and earth outlines were worked with close buttonhole stitching, buttonhole bars were formed above the fabric. The reserves were then cut away from the wrong side of the fabric, leaving the bars untouched (Glenshee linen embroidered with half a hank of blue coton à broder No 18, 11.7 × 12cm [4⅝ × 4¾in])

Eighteenth-century Italian cloth illustrating fine reticella cutwork (linen cambric decorated with buttonhole, overcast and padded satin stitches, French knots and eyelets, 46 × 45cm [18 × 17¾in])

When small broderie anglaise holes are made, small running stitches are first worked just outside the circumference of any area to be cut away. The area is pierced with a stiletto and the raw edges bound with overcasting worked over the running stitches. If the hole is over 6mm (¼in) in diameter, radial cuts are made with scissors almost as far as the circumference. Each segment is turned back and overcasting is worked over the running stitches and through the area turned back. Excess can later be carefully cut away from the rear

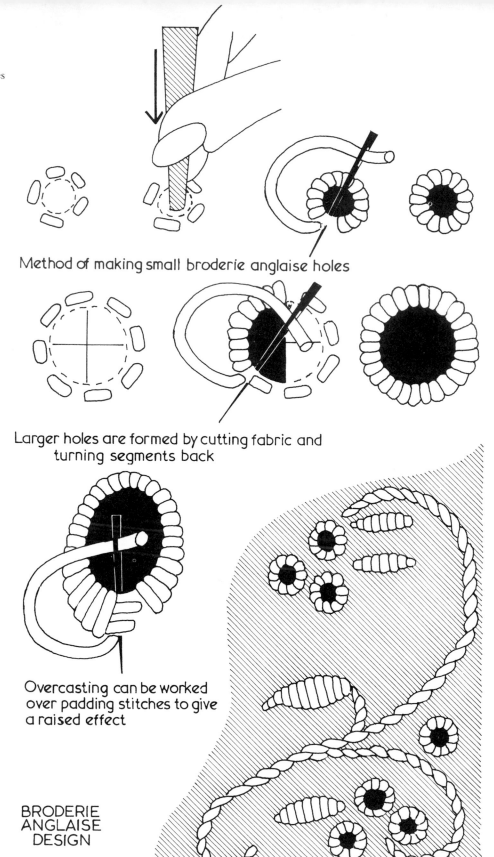

Method of making small broderie anglaise holes

Larger holes are formed by cutting fabric and turning segments back

Overcasting can be worked over padding stitches to give a raised effect

BRODERIE
ANGLAISE
DESIGN

Since the first mention of cutwork in England in 1577 it and whitework have been closely connected, especially for lingerie and baby clothing and for table-cloths. One particular form of English work is broderie anglaise, which evolved in the middle of the nineteenth century from Ayrshire work (see chapter 36), a whitework especially practised in the northern part of the British Isles.

Materials for cutwork

A good quality linen or cotton ground fabric is recommended, sewn with pearl cotton, soft cotton, coton à broder or linen thread. To avoid knotting the thread during working only a short length should be used, threaded through a sharp

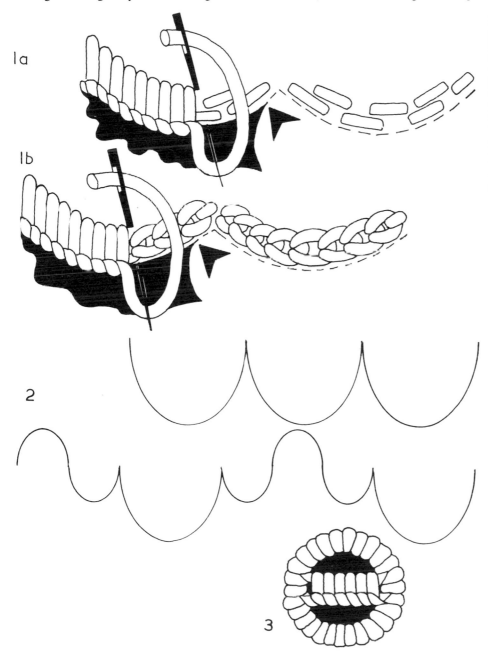

1 Broderie anglaise items often have scalloped edges bound with buttonhole bars. These can be formed over either straight (a) or chain (b) stitches to achieve a padded effect. The fabric should be cut along the required edge only a short way (arrowed) before the buttonhole stitch is worked. 2 A wide variety of different scallops can be worked. 3 Buttonhole bars are sometimes worked across broderie anglaise holes, a technique known as Pisa stitching

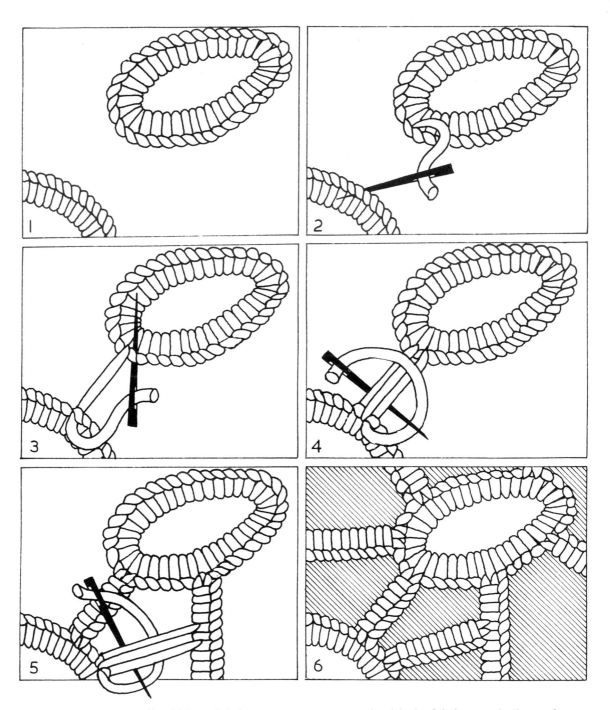

needle. Although it is not necessary to work with the fabric stretched on a frame, having that fabric held taut does maintain embroidery tension.

Broderie anglaise

Traditionally worked with a white soft cotton on fine linen cambric, flowing designs, usually floral, are formed from round or oval cut holes bound with overcasting. Surrounding surface embroidery is worked with satin and stem stitches and the edges of an item are often scalloped with buttonhole stitch.

Running stitches are worked just outside the required edge of a small hole and a pointed stiletto pierces the fabric. The raw edges of the cut hole are then bound with overcasting worked over the running stitches. Any holes larger than 6mm ($\frac{1}{4}$in) in diameter should be cut with scissors. Radial cuts are made nearly to, but not quite reaching, the required edge. One section at a time of fabric is then folded back and overcasting worked over the running stitches and through the turned back fabric, any excess of which can afterwards be trimmed from the rear. If required, a raised effect can be achieved by overcasting over padding stitches.

As well as scalloped edges worked with buttonhole stitch, sometimes padded with chain or straight stitches in the manner illustrated, buttonhole stitches can also be worked as bars across broderie anglaise holes. When bars are thus worked, broderie anglaise can be known as Pisa stitching.

Renaissance embroidery

The main motifs are first outlined in close buttonhole stitch, with the knot of each stitch at the side next to the area of fabric which will subsequently be cut away. It is a good idea temporarily to support the entire area of ground fabric being decorated by tacking it to a piece of paper.

(*Opposite*) Renaissance cutwork: main motifs must first be outlined in close buttonhole stitch (1). Tack the fabric to a temporary card backing before working buttonhole bars from motif to motif above the fabric (2–4). Branched bars can be formed from a finished bar to the outline of a motif (5). When all the bars are finished the backing paper is removed and the reserves cut away from the rear, leaving the buttonhole bars intact (6)

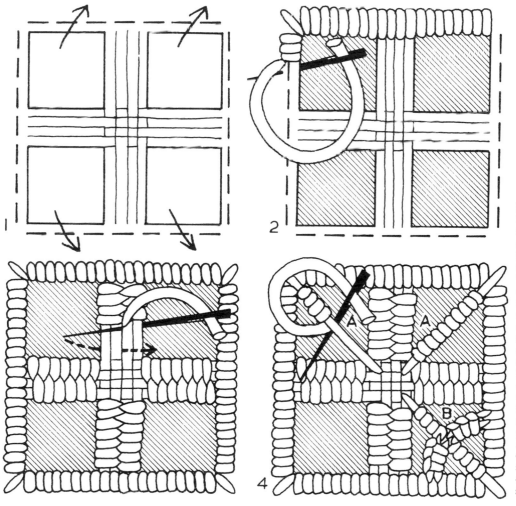

Reticella cutwork is characterized by square motifs. Small running stitches are worked two threads outside a required area and the interior is carefully cut to the motif outline and withdrawn (if 'panes' are required, even numbers of warp and weft threads can be left uncut, as in diagram 1). Buttonhole stitch or overcasting is then worked around the entire area (at the ends of warp and weft threads still left intact, overcasting becomes satin stitch, as in diagram 2). Then remaining warp and weft threads are bound together with overcasting or needleweaving (3). Using the same technique diagrammed in Renaissance cutwork, extra bars can be formed from straight stitches and decorated with overcasting (4A) or buttonhole stitch (4B)

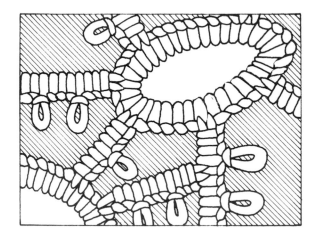

Richelieu cutwork is Renaissance cutwork with added picots

Buttonhole bars are then worked in the reserves of the fabric, with long straight stitches taken back and forth and attached to worked buttonhole motif edgings only at either end of each stitch. Three such stitches worked through the same buttonhole stitches form a bar foundation which is then bound with close buttonhole stitches *making sure that these do not pierce the ground fabric beneath the bar foundation*. Using the same principle of working three long straight stitches between two supports, branched bars can be formed with the bar foundation worked from a bar already completed to the original buttonholing bordering a main motif.

When all the bars are finished, the temporary paper backing is removed and, making sure that the buttonhole bars are not severed, the areas of reserves are carefully cut away, from the reverse, with a pair of sharp scissors.

Reticella cutwork

What is generally known today as Italian cutwork consists of squares cut away and then bordered and infilled.

Running stitches are worked two threads outside a required motif and the area of that motif is then cut away, although if vertical or horizontal bars are required in the finished pattern, even numbers (say 2, 4, 6 or 8) warp and weft threads can be left uncut and not withdrawn. Cut edges are then bound, either with overcasting or buttonhole stitch, and the whole item can be temporarily backed with strong paper before remaining threads are bound with needleweaving and extra bars formed, as in Renaissance cutwork, with long straight stitches.

Surface embroidery around a cut area of reticella work is generally executed with bullion knots or satin stitch.

Richelieu work

This form of cutwork follows the same format as Renaissance cutwork except that the buttonhole bars are further embellished at intervals with picots.

Finishing techniques for cutwork

Apart from broderie anglaise, all other forms of cutwork can subsequently be mitred and hemmed with drawn-thread techniques or hemming. Renaissance and Richelieu work often have an outer edge which is not turned over as a hem but bound with close buttonhole stitch, with added picots in the Richelieu version.

14. Darning

In general sewing terms, darning usually implies parallel lines of long running stitches along the warp and weft of a ground fabric worked to repair or to strengthen it. Darning is a form of embroidery if its stitches are worked in another colour thread or worked solely for ornamental purposes. Pattern darning, with stitches of predetermined length, can be worked aligned with either warp or weft. A speciality of embroiderers in many parts of the world, pattern darning can form diapered, or lozenge-shaped patterns. Other forms of darning covered in this chapter include damask and huckaback techniques and filet darning or lacis.

The more usual form of parallel lines of vertical and horizontal stitches became especially prevalent in English needlework in the eighteenth century and some girls worked darning samplers. Decorated with a thread of either the same or a contrasting colour, these sometimes had large crosses, one in each corner, and different darning patterns could be combined with cutwork and other techniques. In America, darning stitches were also used to decorate bed rugs, especially at the end of the eighteenth century.

Later, William Morris and his contemporaries designed embroideries that were subsequently worked in darning, and 'darned work' was a popular component of the art-needlework movement at the end of the nineteenth century in both England and the United States.

Materials

It is preferable to begin ornamental darning on an evenweave ground in order to facilitate counting threads to form stitches of a required length. Advanced embroiderers sometimes prefer to work on satin or another ground with less well defined threads. Stranded and soft cotton, tapisserie and Persian wools can all be used for pattern darning and, except on canvas, a crewel or chenille needle is generally used. Pattern darning need not be worked on a frame.

Methods of working

When working ornamental darning stitches, it is essential that regularity of stitch length and alignment are maintained in order to build up a required design. Various forms of darning can be executed as diagrammed.

Owl worked in different vertical darning patterns and outlined with back stitch (linen with thread count of 26 per 2.5cm (1in) embroidered with three strands of dark brown stranded cotton, motif 13.5 × 6.5cm [5¼ × 2¼in])

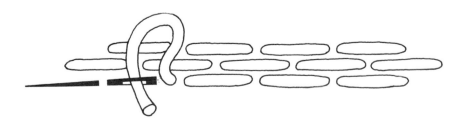

Darning consists of parallel lines of long running stitches forming a required pattern

97

Darning sampler worked by Gerarda Gerritsen in 1763 (cotton embroidered with silk **pattern darning**, Algerian eye, chain and cross stitches, 37cm [14¼in] square)

Filet darning

A net ground with large square meshes is held securely in a square or rectangular frame and the interstices of the net can be infilled, either with needleweaving or with a filet interlacing sometimes known as toile stitch.

Huckaback darning

Originally worked on huckaback towelling with 'floating threads', occasional loops of weft threads, this can be transposed to any fabric and only tiny lengths of ground are taken up by the needle at each stitch.

Surface darning

This is a laidwork form and is covered in chapter 10.

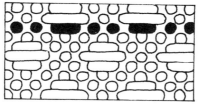

DARNING PATTERNS
(ONE LINE SHADED)

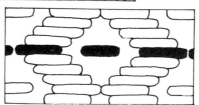

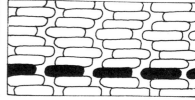

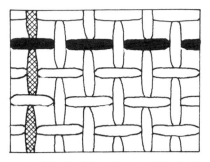

BASKETWEAVE DARNING

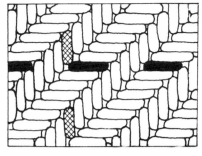

DAMASK DARNING

(FASTENING
KNOT)

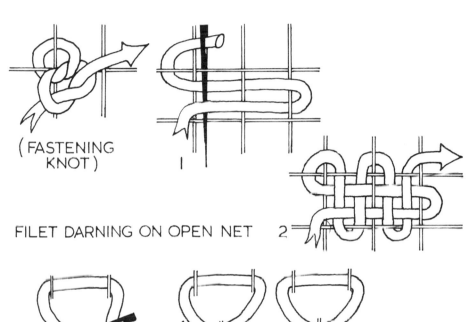

FILET DARNING ON OPEN NET

2

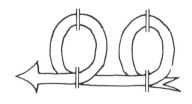

HUCKABACK DARNING

3

SURFACE DARNING, A
LAIDWORK FORM

The needle weaves in and
out of laid threads

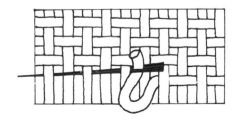

15. Designing

This brief guide to designing for needlework includes sources of design today and methods of enlarging, reducing and transferring those designs to the ground fabric.

Some embroideries are designed for others to execute. For many centuries artists and draughtsmen produced cartoons which were either painted direct on to a fabric stretched on a frame, or transposed by 'pouncing'—dusting pulverized charcoal or another fine powder over a parchment or paper pattern needle-pricked to indicate the design; the powder falls through the holes to the ground fabric beneath.

Designs from Richard Shorleyker's *A Scholehouse for the Needle*, published in 1632

Some themes have long been popular with embroiderers. This tree of life motif was possibly worked in India for a European market in the eighteenth century (satin embroidered with silks, 259 × 170cm [102 × 67in])

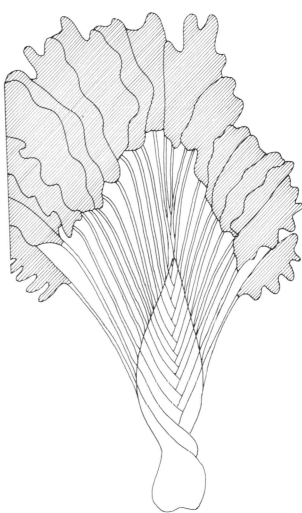

The earliest dated book of patterns for embroidery was produced in Germany in 1523. The best known of the books that were later published in England are *The Needle's Excellency* by James Boler (tenth edition 1634) and *A Scholehouse for the Needle* by Richard Shorleyker (1632). Outline and some block designs were printed in heavy black ink from carefully cut wood blocks and many different embroiderers often worked the same motif. Lions, carnations, roses and, later, the tree of life, have long remained popular themes and can still be seen as recurring motifs in different needleworks.

By the eighteenth century women's magazines began to appear with needlework designs. Such publications became more readily available and by about 1820 they were supplemented by a regular supply of Berlin woolwork designs (see chapter 26).

(*Above, left*) Designs can be taken from everyday or unusual sights. This *Hyphaene thebaica*, or doum palm, was photographed in Zaire

(*Right*) A line drawing taken from the doum palm could be worked in appliqué, blackwork or many other techniques

Sources of design today

Many kits for embroidery are available, some excellently designed for the novice embroiderer, others requiring more advanced stitch techniques. Fabric can be stencilled or printed with the required pattern, one repeat of a recurring design can be already worked, or plain fabric can be accompanied by a printed paper pattern. Although kits are commercially produced it is nonetheless possible to add an individual touch by, for instance, working an extra border in colours and stitches complementary to the main picture.

Commercial transfers can be obtained with designs that are ironed on to fabric. And, as in the past, books, magazines and pamphlets are available with ideas specifically for embroidery. Books based on flowers, architecture or a myriad of other subjects can also offer ideas for original embroideries.

One of the most important things to remember is that it is not necessary to be a

Curtains and other furnishings can be copied by embroiderers to decorate cushions and other co-ordinating items (1).
Using shapes cut from different 'shades' of newsprint, various collages can be formed to give an indication of how an embroidered design might look (2)

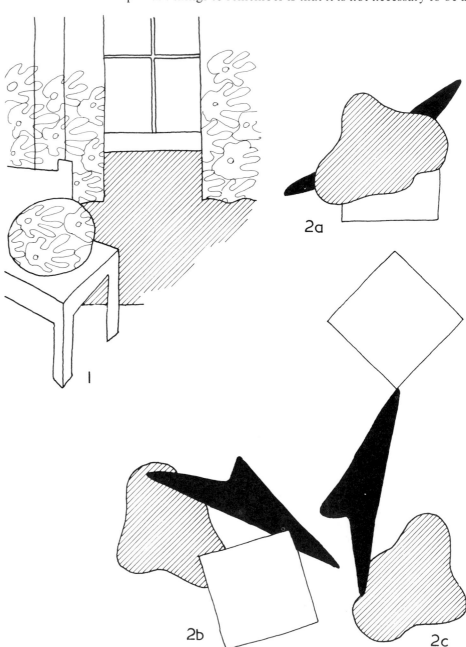

Tile design taken from J. Bourgoin's *Arabic Geometric Pattern and Design* (Dover 1973)

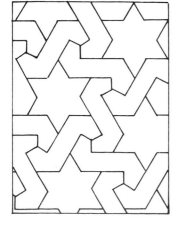

skilled artist in order to be able to design needlework. Everyday life and holidays and other special events contain many elements suitable for transposition in traditional as well as experimental forms of needlework. Wrought-iron gates and tessellated floors can suggest blackwork motifs. Printed signs could offer ideas for the balance of embroidered lettering on a banner.

Other ideas can be gleaned from sunsets, from crowds of people or from scenes on television. Pictures of flowers in gardeners' seed catalogues can be transposed in fine cross stitches. A repeat of a printed pattern from wallpaper or curtains can be copied as an embroidered cushion to accentuate the overall design of a room. Family crests can be worked in crewel or needlepoint. Appliqué and patchwork designs can be inspired by stained-glass windows or by greetings cards.

Some people like to visualize a design by drawing it on paper. Others experiment, as in blackwork, with collages of newsprint and other paper, moving pieces around to produce different effects. There is no hard and fast rule and an embroiderer should interpret ideas as he thinks best. Without starting on complex designs, the beginner can without difficulty create original patterns which are not irrevocable and can if necessary be altered as embroidery progresses. Even if the embroiderer is still not satisfied when the work is done, at least he or she has taken the plunge into *creative* design.

Siting, enlarging and reducing

The alignment of a design on fabric is important. Unless an asymmetrical balance is deliberately intended, a motif should be centred by finding the mid-point as

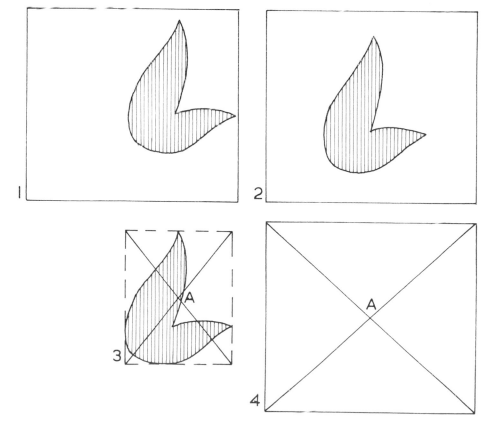

Sometimes designs are deliberately set off-centre (1) but centrally placed motifs might be preferred (2). To find the central point of a motif, it should be enclosed in a rectangle or square and diagonals drawn as illustrated (3). The central point (A) is then set on to the marked central point of the fabric (4A)

A simple border design (1) can be taken through a corner of 90° by (2) placing a mirror at an angle of 45°. The resulting corner pattern depends on where the mirror is placed (3)

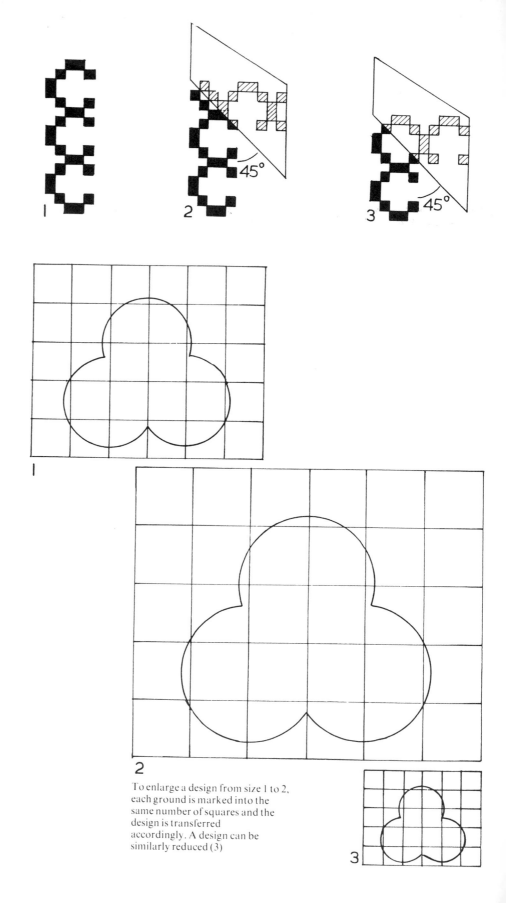

1

2

3

45°

45°

1

2

To enlarge a design from size 1 to 2, each ground is marked into the same number of squares and the design is transferred accordingly. A design can be similarly reduced (3)

3

shown and aligning it to the centre of a mitred ground. Border patterns can be turned through an angle of 90° with the aid of a mirror.

One method of enlarging or reducing a design is shown; alternatively a design can be enlarged by projecting it on to a light table and tracing around the outline.

Transferring designs to fabric

An embroiderer soon develops a preferred method of transposing designs; some of the ways are as follows:

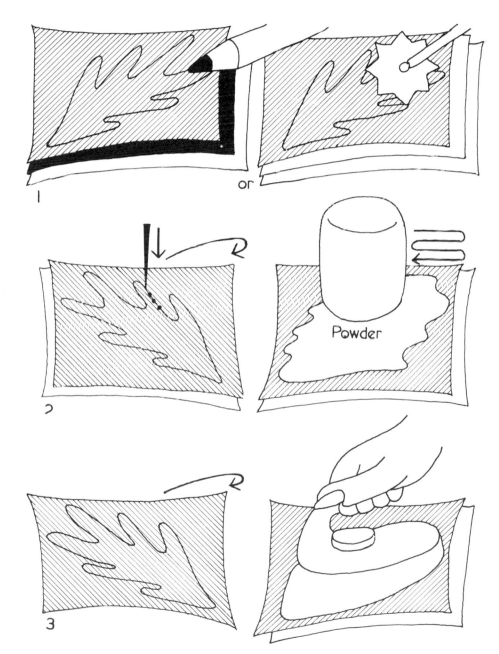

Methods of transferring designs to fabric: **1** Using dressmakers' carbon paper, trace the outline with a pencil or dressmakers' wheel. **2** Pouncing, with powdered charcoal or cuttlefish rubbed through marked holes is still employed. **3** Commercially-bought transfers can be ironed on to the fabric

Dressmaker's carbon is placed, operative side down, on the front of the ground fabric. A paper pattern is then placed on top and the outline traced with a French embroidery roulette or dressmaker's wheel, or forcefully marked with a hard pencil, so that the pattern is passed through the carbon to the fabric.

Pouncing, today sometimes called perforation, can still be employed. The paper pattern is laid upside down on thick felt or a towel and the design carefully pricked out with a stiletto or needle. The perforated pattern is then placed right side up over the ground fabric and a pounce of powdered charcoal or cuttlefish is carefully rubbed over it so that some flecks pass through the perforation. After

Methods of transferring designs to fabric: **1** Loose-weave canvas can be laid on another ground and counted thread stitches worked through both layers, after which individual warp and weft threads of canvas are carefully removed. **2** Tracing paper or vanishing muslin can be laid on the fabric and the embroidery worked through both layers; the tracing paper is then carefully pulled away or the vanishing muslin ironed off

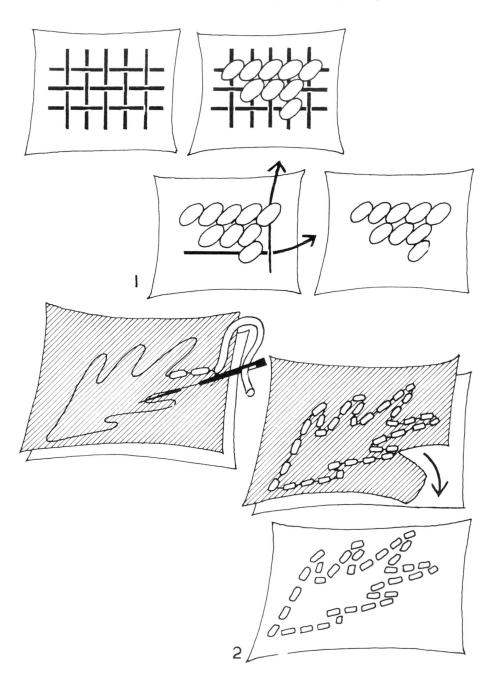

the perforated paper has been removed the design can be 'sealed' on to the fabric with a light spray of methylated spirits.

A transfer pencil can be used to mark a design, in reverse, on tracing paper. This is laid, design side down, on the fabric, and the design is transferred as instructions indicate, possibly with a warm iron.

A counted-thread design can be transferred by simply counting blocks of a paper pattern and stitching over the corresponding number of threads of fabric.

Tracing paper or vanishing muslin marked with a design outline can be laid on top of the ground fabric as in lettering (see chapter 22). Running or tacking stitches are worked through both layers and then the paper or muslin is carefully torn off, using the end of a needle to prise away any parts that may be caught by embroidery.

The first three methods described above indicate where on the fabric a design should be. These marks can be made more visible before embroidery commences. Running or darning stitches can be worked along the lines of the marks, or they can be highlighted by a marker. It is important that marking stitches worked with needle and thread are temporary and can easily be removed after embroidery is finished, and that any fibre-tip pens used should be thoroughly tested for colour fastness on each piece of fabric employed (sizing on some canvases, for example, can affect a marker that might otherwise be colour fast). Lead pencils should be avoided as they smudge, and ink or ball-point pens should never be used.

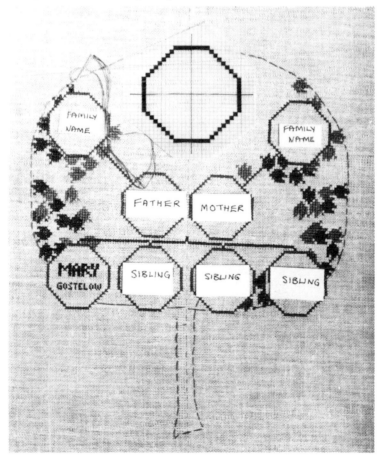

This design for a family tree sampler has endless permutations. The basic fruit motif can be worked as many times as required and arranged to accommodate family numbers. Here two strands of Anchor stranded cotton are being used for cross stitch executed over two threads and family names are formed in sewing cotton over one thread. The ground fabric is Needlewoman ivory linen with 30 threads per 2.5cm (1in) and the size of the whole tree will be 25 × 20.3cm [9$\frac{7}{8}$ × 8in]

16. Drawn-thread work

For drawn-thread work, warp and/or weft ground threads are cut and *withdrawn* one by one before the fabric is embellished with embroidery. It is sometimes called drawn work, but this term in fact includes both drawn-thread work and pulled-thread work (see chapter 29). Russian drawn-thread work, included at the end of this chapter, has threads withdrawn from the reserves, or background, of a main design.

Usually worked on linen, all drawn-thread techniques have in the past been particularly associated with Scandinavia, the Baltic Republics and other northern regions.

Materials

A strong evenweave fabric such as Glenshee linen or Danish Aida should be used, and after threads have been withdrawn in the manner explained below embroidery

Butterflies, their wings formed from different drawn-thread patterns, worked with stranded cotton on linen with thread count 10 per cm (26 per in), motif 14 × 15cm (5½ × 5⅞in)

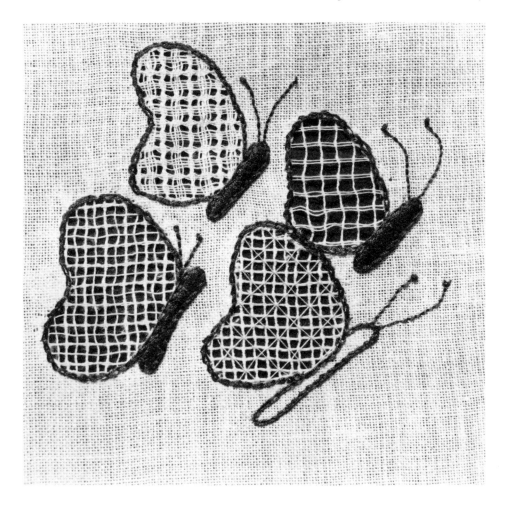

is generally worked in pearl or stranded cotton or coton à broder with a tapestry needle. Small items are usually hand-held, although if a large area of trellis is to be infilled it is a good idea to use a frame.

Methods of working

Each thread of ground fabric to be withdrawn is removed separately. If an entire thread is to be withdrawn, the point of a needle is inserted under the thread near the edge of the fabric and used to ease up the thread. When the resulting loop is long enough to be hand-held it is pulled until the whole thread is removed. If a small section of a thread is to be removed, the thread is cut at each end of that section and the thread between carefully removed in the same manner.

Several neighbouring threads are usually withdrawn to produce a trellis for subsequent embroidery. When a trellis is to pass through a corner, individual threads are cut a short distance before that corner and, after the surplus lengths have been withdrawn, the remaining threads are secured by being woven back into the fabric, or by holding temporarily with small tacking stitches until a permanent embroidery cover is worked, or by being cut close to the edge of the corner and secured with buttonhole stitch or overcasting.

If drawn-thread work is being executed around the edge of a cloth, threads are

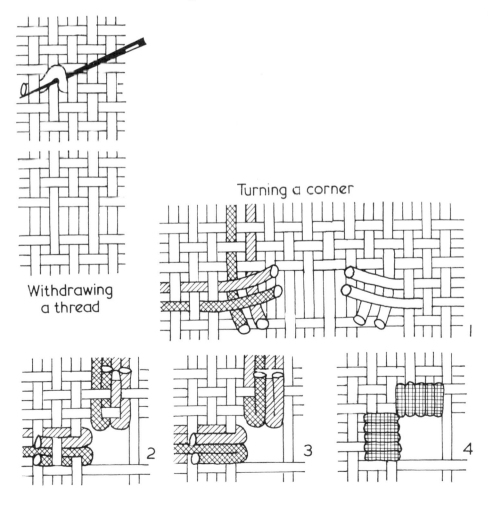

Withdrawing a thread

Turning a corner

When a thread is withdrawn, the point of a needle is carefully inserted under the thread, towards the edge of the fabric, and the thread pulled out. When turning a corner, threads at the outer edges of the required corner are carefully cut two or three threads inside that corner, and internal lengths of thread withdrawn (1). Exposed ends are then secured by being woven back into the fabric (2), by being folded back and temporarily held by tacking stitches which are covered by subsequent stitching (3), or by being cut close to the edge of the hole and held with buttonhole stitch or overcasting (4)

Needleweaving can be worked on a 'fence' of an even number of threads exposed after others have been withdrawn (1–3). Working on a larger 'fence' produces a wider band of needleweaving (4). This technique can also be combined with overcasting

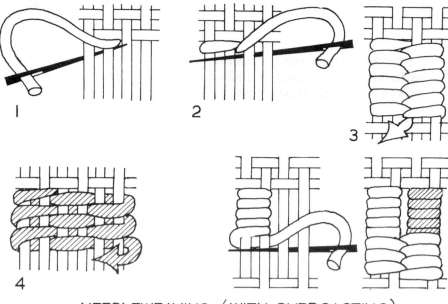

NEEDLEWEAVING (WITH OVERCASTING)

DARNING STITCHES

After threads have been withdrawn, many other techniques can be worked, including darning stitch patterns.
Russian drawn-thread work implies a motif outlined in heavy chain stitch, threads withdrawn from the reserves and the remaining trellis bound with overcasting or Russian drawn ground

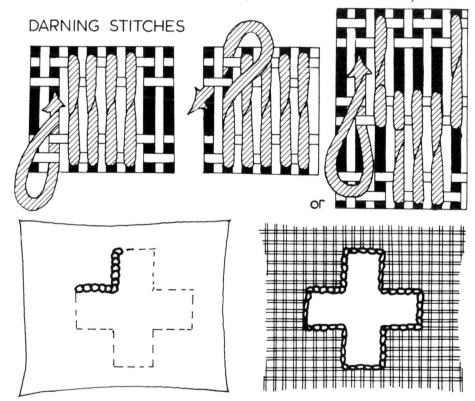

or

RUSSIAN DRAWN-THREAD WORK

withdrawn before a hemming technique is worked. Withdrawing threads weakens the overall tension of the ground fabric, so unless interlaced, ladder or zigzag hem-stitches are to be used, not too many threads should be withdrawn for each border band.

Needleweaving is an important constituent of drawn-thread work. Other tech-niques include darning stitch worked in a variety of formations, buttonhole and overcast bars and such pulled-thread stitches as reversed faggot stitch, known as

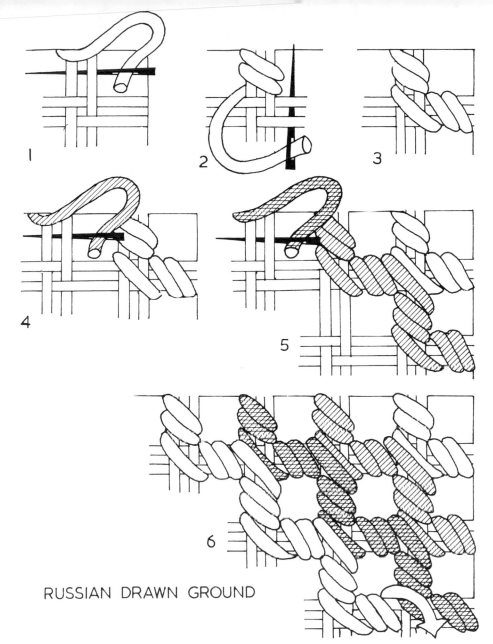

1

2

3

4

5

6

RUSSIAN DRAWN GROUND

ground stitch when worked on a trellis left after threads have been withdrawn, and diamond and diagonal stitches. When basic drawn-thread and pulled-thread forms have been mastered they can be combined with cutwork techniques.

Russian drawn-thread work

In this technique, as in Assisi work, the reserves are decorated while the main motifs are left unworked. Especially popular in Archangel and other northern areas of the Soviet Union, Russian drawn-thread work, usually executed in white on white linen, is still employed for bed and table linen decoration.

A design is first outlined in heavy chain stitch. Threads in the reserves are then carefully withdrawn, usually two threads alternately being withdrawn and left. The end of each thread to be withdrawn is carefully cut as close as possible to the chain stitch before it is removed. When all the reserves are thus formed into trellis formation, they are usually bound with Russian drawn ground, also known as overcast filling stitch, although needleweaving may be preferred.

17. Equipment

As well as fabrics and threads (see following chapter), an embroiderer needs several items of equipment.

First and foremost are steel needles in a variety of shapes. Sizes are expressed numerically: the *higher* the number the *finer* the needle and the smaller the eye. The main forms of needles used for embroidery are:

Crewel needles, general-purpose, sharp-pointed needles used in any technique such as appliqué and cutwork in which the ground fabric is pierced. Sizes 9 (fine) to 3 (thick) are most popular.

Chenille needles are of the same thickness or gauge and size as tapestry needles but have sharp points.

Tapestry needles have blunt points. They are employed in any technique in which the thread passes between adjacent threads rather than piercing them. The most

The higher the number of an embroidery needle, the finer the needle, including the eye through which the thread has to pass. The needles shown here are:

1 *Crewel*, sizes 9 (fine) and 3 (thick)
2 *Chenille*, size 24 (fine) and 18 (thick)
3 *Tapestry*, size 24 (fine) and 18 (thick)
4 *Couching*

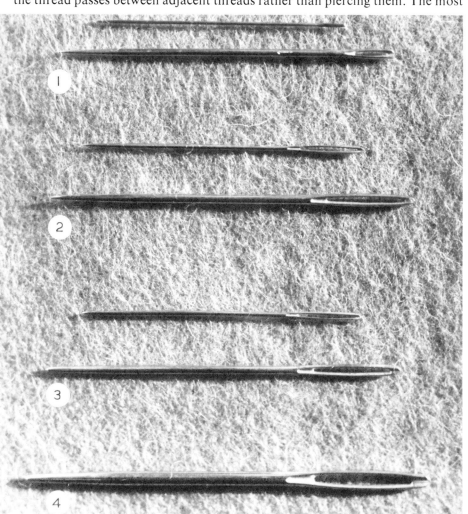

frequently-used sizes are from 24 (fine) to 18 (thick).
Couching needles also known as heavy embroidery or short pile rug needles, are especially thick with blunt points. They are of one size and they are used primarily for plunging the ends of heavy thread laid and subsequently couched, in Italian quilting and for working heavyweight cross stitch used for floor coverings.

Small needles are easily lost. In the past they were sometimes kept in needlecases made of ivory, tortoiseshell or wood. One of the simplest methods of keeping needles handy today is to use a small magnet, but a small needlebook with 'leaves' of felt or another soft substance might be preferred. Needles should be kept dry to prevent rust, but if some rust does form it can be removed by pushing the needle into a small cushion, traditionally the shape and size of a strawberry, filled with emery powder.

All equipment brought into contact with embroidery should be spotlessly clean and any pins used for temporarily holding motifs should always be stainless.

At least two pairs of scissors are recommended. One pair of tailor's, dressmaker's or general-purpose scissors is needed for cutting fabric, and a smaller pair, with short sharp blades, is used for careful cutting, as in cutwork. A seam-ripper is also useful, for even the most experienced embroiderer has occasionally to undo stitches.

Some useful items of equipment include an expanding metal rule, ideally marked both in centimetres and inches, dressmakers' and embroiderers' lightweight scissors, a seam-ripper, a magnetic block to hold needles and pins, and a wire-looped needle threader

Other small items of equipment include a tape measure or metal rule, and a needle-threader with fine wire loop which, when holding thread, passes easily through a needle's eye (or a calyx-eyed or open-ended needle might be preferred). Some embroiderers wear at least one thimble, and pencils and eraser, graph and plain paper and adhesive are also useful. Sometimes embroiderers find magnifiers valuable, either hand-held, free-standing or suspended round the neck, ideally with their own illumination.

Blocking, mounting and finishing and such processes as designing, and techniques including needlepoint, require special items of equipment which are covered elsewhere in this book.

Many forms of embroidery are best worked on a frame or hoop and numerous wooden and plastic types are available. They can be hand-held or clamped to a table or convenient ledge. Some have their own floor-standing supports and yet another type, with a shorter 'stalk', is known as a table, lap or fanny frame as the embroiderer can either have it on the table in front of him or on table and chair beneath, sitting astride the frame or with part of its foot under his leg.

Round and oval frames consist of two rings, the outer one adjustable with a

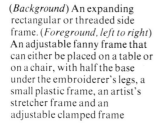

(*Background*) An expanding rectangular or threaded side frame. (*Foreground, left to right*) An adjustable fanny frame that can either be placed on a table or on a chair, with half the base under the embroiderer's legs, a small plastic frame, an artist's stretcher frame and an adjustable clamped frame

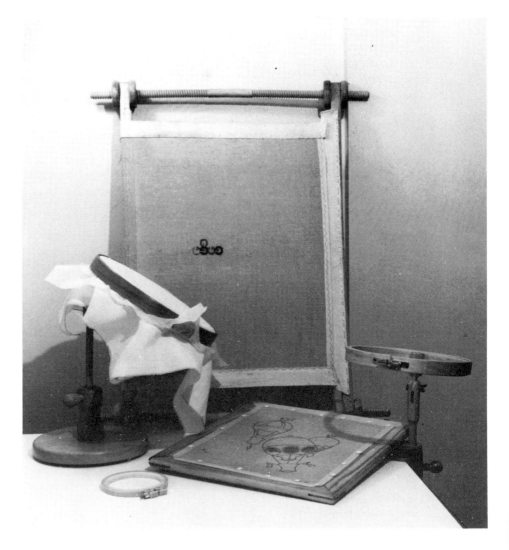

screw. A piece of fabric is placed over the inner ring, the outer ring is then put on top and the screw tightened. In order to prevent the fabric from slackening while work is in progress, and also to prevent the fabric being marked, the inner ring can be bound with tape or cotton strips and when the ground fabric is placed in position a piece of tissue paper can be put on top before the outer ring is screwed on. A large area of ground fabric can be worked on a small round or oval frame as the rings can easily be removed to another section of fabric.

On a square or rectangular frame the entire ground fabric is usually held at once, the warp and weft threads carefully aligned with the frame. The most economical

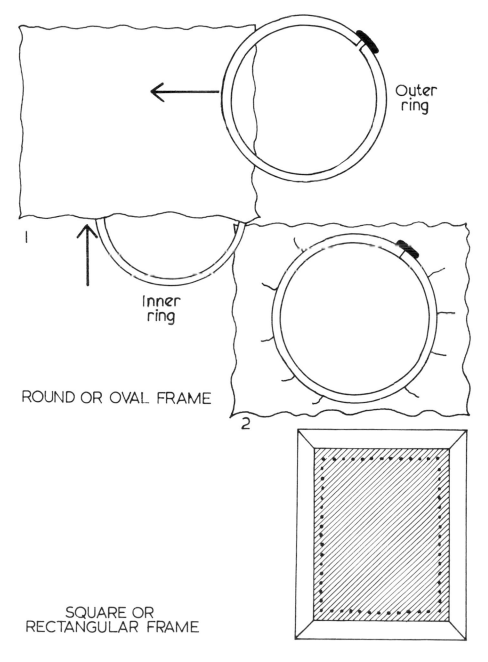

Outer ring

Inner ring

ROUND OR OVAL FRAME

SQUARE OR
RECTANGULAR FRAME

1 When fabric is held on a round or oval frame, the inner ring of the frame is placed beneath the fabric and the outer ring above it. 2 The screw of the outer ring is then tightened, sandwiching the fabric between the two rings. The easiest method of forming a square or rectangular frame is to use two pairs of artists' stretching mounts, with ends cut at 45°. The fabric (here shaded) is then placed with warp and weft threads in alignment with the frame and secured with drawing pins

One advantage of a circular or oval frame is that only one small area of ground fabric need be held taut at once, and when that section of embroidery has been worked the frame can easily be moved to another area

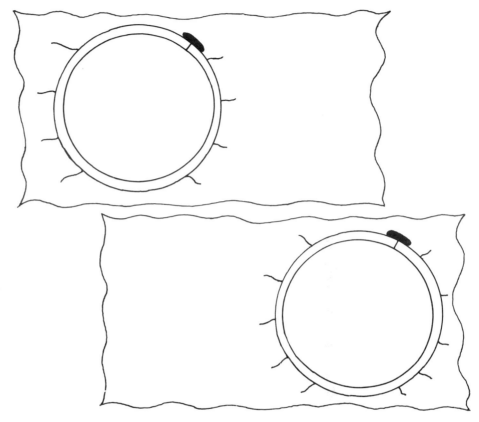

form is obtained by buying two pairs of artists' framing, lengths of wood with ends cut at 45° and with connecting tongues. One pair of 20cm (approx 8in) and one pair of 18cm (approx 7in) lengths give a resulting frame 20 × 18cm (approx 8 × 7in) and a piece of fabric, the edges protected against fraying, can be held in place with tacks or pins. More complicated frames, available from needlework stores, have rollers and screws, and sometimes the fabric being embroidered has to be laced into position as indicated by the maker's instructions.

An embroiderer soon finds which type of frame is most convenient. Fanny frames are becoming increasingly popular as the embroiderer has both hands free, although some people prefer to work on a square or rectangular frame which will not distort or mark the fabric.

18. Fabrics and threads

Apart from paper or matted felt, woven fabrics are used for embroidery grounds. When choosing a fabric it is important to remember that many hours of work may be spent embroidering it; it is false economy to buy inferior material.

Much embroidery is worked on canvas, originally a strong material made from hemp, used primarily for sail-making. Now the term has widened to include wool, cotton, acrylic, hemp, linen, jute, metal or plastic 'material' with a lattice-like mesh.

Measurement of canvas indicates the thread count, the number of single or close-pairs of warp or weft threads to a given length, usually 2.5cm or 1in, or 5cm, nearly 2in.

A beginner will find a selection of canvases available, usually beige, yellow or white and mostly cotton or polyester or a mixture:

Single-weave canvas, known variously as mono or congress canvas, has single warp and weft threads interwoven.
Double or Penelope canvas has pairs of warp and weft threads interwoven.
Interlock or lockthread canvas has two fine warp threads locked around a single weft thread, and the resulting 'lattice' does not distort during embroidery.

Most canvases are initially kept rigid with a thick layer of size applied after weaving, but the canvas softens with handling. Some embroiderers, however, prefer to work canvas techniques on a limp fabric such as scrim, now a fine openweave cotton, linen or mixture. Other embroiderers prefer the wide mesh of rug canvas,

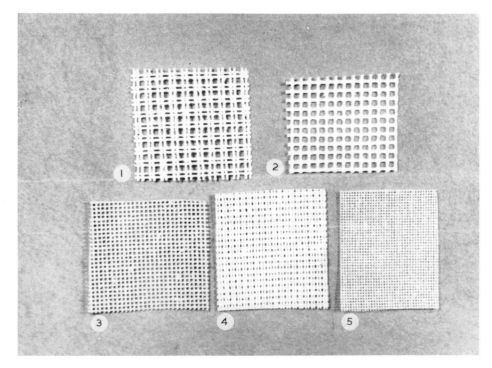

Some popular canvases include:
1 Double or Penelope canvas, 10 pairs of threads per 5cm (2in);
2 Interlock or lock thread canvas, 14 threads per 5cm (2in); **3** Single or mono canvas, 28 threads per 5cm (2in); **4** Double canvas, 20 pairs of threads per 5cm (2in);
5 Single canvas, 48 threads per 5cm (2in)

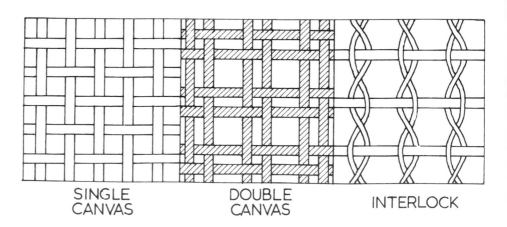

SINGLE CANVAS DOUBLE CANVAS INTERLOCK

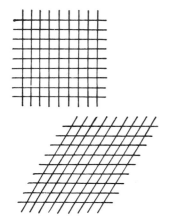

Unless worked on a frame, any canvas that is not interlock tends to distort during stitching

either double or single weave (raffia canvas). Rug canvases are especially useful for working floor coverings and other heavy items.

In the past, especially in the nineteenth century, a wider variety of canvases was available, including:

Berlin silk canvas, particularly used for Berlin woolwork with reserves unworked
German canvas, a limp cotton canvas with each tenth thread coloured, usually blue or yellow, to aid counting
Moskowa canvas with gold, silver, black, blue and other coloured threads interwoven
Mummy canvas, a close, irregular mesh which was generally used for chair furnishings
Railroad or net canvas, a stiff black or white linen and cotton canvas with low thread count
Thread canvas, another heavy-duty canvas
Winchester canvas, a single-weave canvas with irregularity in thread sizes, called after the needlepoint project in Winchester Cathedral organized in the 1930s by Louisa Pesel.

Fabrics without an obvious mesh are also measured according to their thread count, usually to 2.5cm (1in). Some cotton, linen, wool, silk and man-made fabrics are 'evenweaves', with a thread count of the same number of regularly spaced warp as weft threads and some can also be termed 'stuffs', a word originally implying lightweight wool cloth with no nap brought to England by sixteenth-century Flemish weavers but now taken to mean any fabric without nap.

As well as the selection of materials illustrated, embroiderers sometimes work on velvet or other grounds with cut pile. Muslin, originally cotton from India and Persia and especially popular for tambour work in the late eighteenth and nineteenth centuries, is still employed by many western embroiderers. Monk's cloth, also known as abbot's, belfry or druid's cloth, a heavy cotton basketweave fabric, is particularly used in America. Many other fabrics, including sumptuous cloths of gold and silver, silk partly woven with the appropriate metal, are not now generally available.

One of the most common weaves is plain or tabby, with regular one-over and one-under formation. Twill weave implies exposed weft threads passing over more than one warp and satin weave is similar except that weft threads pass over an irregular number of warp threads so that the warp is almost entirely hidden. Gauze

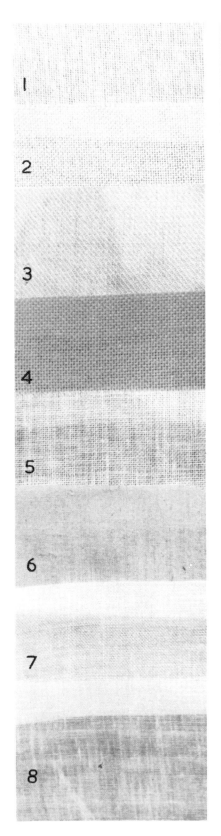

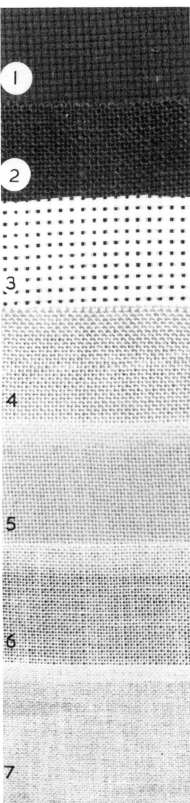

Some popular fabrics include (*left side*) **1** Glenshee crash, 50 per cent linen, 50 per cent cotton, used for appliqué grounds and household furnishings; **2** Glenshee mercerized cotton D, the finest weave cotton (26 threads per 2.5cm), used for counted thread techniques; **3** Needlewoman linen twill, a hard-wearing fabric primarily used for crewel embroidery; **4** Hardanger Danish 425, cotton, 24 pairs of threads per 2.5cm (1in) used for Hardanger and other counted thread techniques; **5** Danish linen 1416, 34 threads per 2.5cm (1in), the finest linen evenweave used for intricate cross stitch; **6** Unbleached calico used for smocking and other techniques; **7** Medium weight linen TF 8/8 used for cross stitch work; **8** Fine weight linen cambric, a handkerchief linen and shirt material suitable also for church embroideries and whitework (*right side*) **1** Danish Aida 419, cotton woven with 9 blocks of threads per 2.5cm (1in), used for cross stich work; **2** Hessian, used for many purposes; **3** Binca cotton with 6 blocks of threads per 2.5cm (1in), often used by beginners; **4** Glenshee mercerized cotton A, the coarsest weave cotton, with 16 threads per 2.5cm (1in); **5** Needlewoman evenweave worsted, 18 threads per 2.5cm (1in), a soft wool ground fabric; **6** Needlewoman evenweave linen 595, 21 threads per 2.5cm (1in); **7** Glenshee evenweave linen, available 18, 26 or 28 threads per 2.5cm (1in)

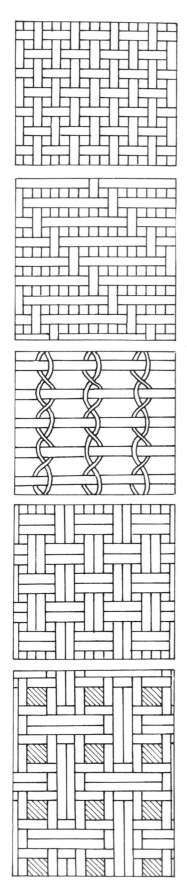

has fine warp threads twisted together before penetration by a thicker weft. Hardanger is woven in pairs and Aida in blocks.

Embroidery thread or yarn is generally made from silk, wool, cotton, flax or man-made fibre (metal threads are covered in chapter 24). The thread is composed of fine filaments, each known as ply or filé, either put singly or twisted together in S or Z formation for strength (1, 2, 3 or 4-ply and so on) to form a strand, which lies by itself or is laid with other strands in groups. Individual strands of stranded cotton and other yarns can easily be separated.

Keeping differently coloured threads tidy can be aided by a wooden or plastic palette with holes. Hanks of one colour thread are passed through a hole and lightly knotted. Metal clothes' hangers, plastic rings and plastic holders taken from sets of beer or soft drink cans make inexpensive and portable lightweight palettes. The horizontal bars of old-fashioned folding clothes driers (or clothes horses) can be used as storage lines for many different threads.

Types of weave include (*top to bottom*) plain or tabby, regular twill, gauze, Hardanger and Aida, the last shown with spaces between blocks of threads shaded for extra clarification

Stranded thread consists of two filaments tightly twisted in S formation forming a 2-ply strand. Six of these are then loosely twisted in Z formation

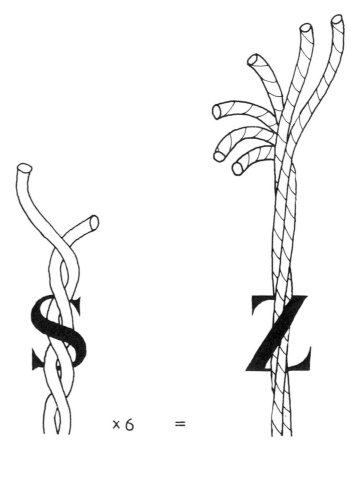

x 6   =

A selection of popular threads: (*left, top to bottom*) Gütermann silk twist, 100 per cent pure silk, 10m (11yd) spool; Anchor machine embroidery cotton No 30, 10g reel; Anchor machine embroidery cotton No 50, 10g reel; (*centre, top to bottom*) Anchor coton à broder, a single fine shiny thread, highly twisted, in 40m (44yd) white and 30m (33yd) colours and black skeins;

Anchor stranded cotton, the most versatile thread, stranded, loosely-twisted and shiny, in 8m (9yd) skeins. One or more strands can be separated from a length of thread; Anchor soft embroidery, a matt, fairly thick and loosely-twisted thread, 9m (10yd) skein; Appleton tapestry wool, moth resistant, 5.5m (6yd) skein; Appleton crewel wool, moth resistant, soft 2-ply, 32m

(35yd) skein; Anchor tapisserie wool, moth resistant and fast colours, thicker 4-ply wool, 13.7m (15yd) skein; Persian yarn, 3 strands of 2-ply wool, available in Britain by 5m (approx 6yd) skeins, in America by weight; (*right, top to bottom*) Gütermann fine silk, 50m (55yd) spool; Anchor pearl cotton No 5, a twisted shiny thread, 10g reel; Anchor pearl cotton No 8, a finer thread, also 10g reel

19. Hardanger

Hardanger is a counted-thread embroidery worked on linen or cotton of the same name, characteristically woven in pairs of two warp and weft threads. A geometric design is embroidered in cotton or linen in kløster blocks, groups of parallel satin, here known as kløster, stitches surrounding square areas of fabric which are then carefully cut away and sometimes partly infilled with bars.

This form of embroidery originated around the Hardanger Fjord in western Norway before the end of the eighteenth century. Women in this area spun their own flax and wove their own fabric which they then made into household and clothing items, often beautifully embroidered with blocks of Hardanger work.

Hardanger enjoyed particular popularity in America at the beginning of the twentieth century and it is practised today in many parts of the world.

Close-up of a typical Hardanger design

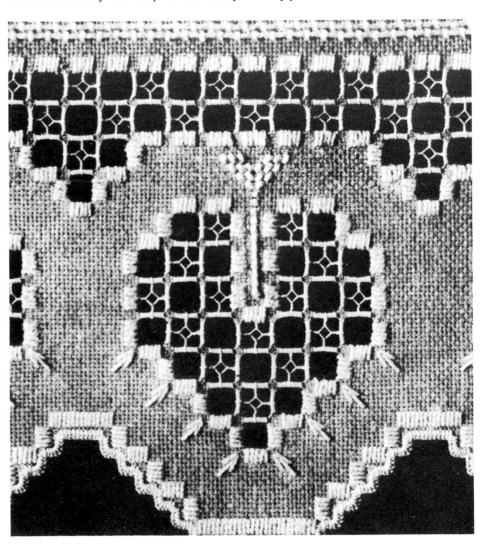

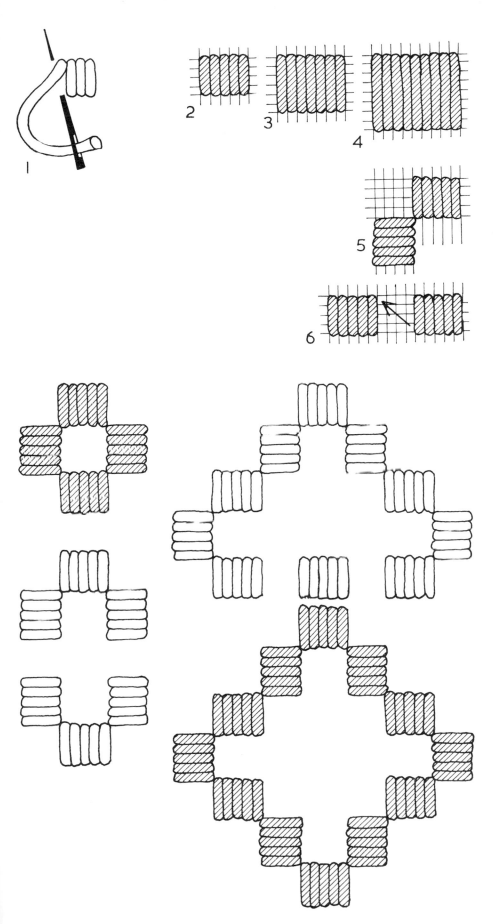

The first stages of working Hardanger involve the forming of kløster or satin stitch blocks. In this diagram, with each pair of threads represented by one square, the working of close satin stitch is shown (1), as are typical blocks of five stitches over four pairs of threads (2) and alternatives, seven stitches formed over six threads (3) and nine stitches over eight threads (4)

A second block may be worked at right angles to the first, with two corner stitches executed through the same hole (5). If preferred, a gap of the same number of threads as the length of each stitch may be left and a second block worked on the same plane as the first (6)

Kløster blocks are generally worked to produce square, triangular, rectangular or diamond-shaped motifs

Reserves outside motifs worked with kløster blocks can be decorated with close parallel satin stitch, possibly worked in triangular or eight-pointed star formations

The area within each kløster motif is then cut away as indicated by arrows (1) and threads withdrawn (2). It is important to make sure that no cuts are made that would produce raw edges

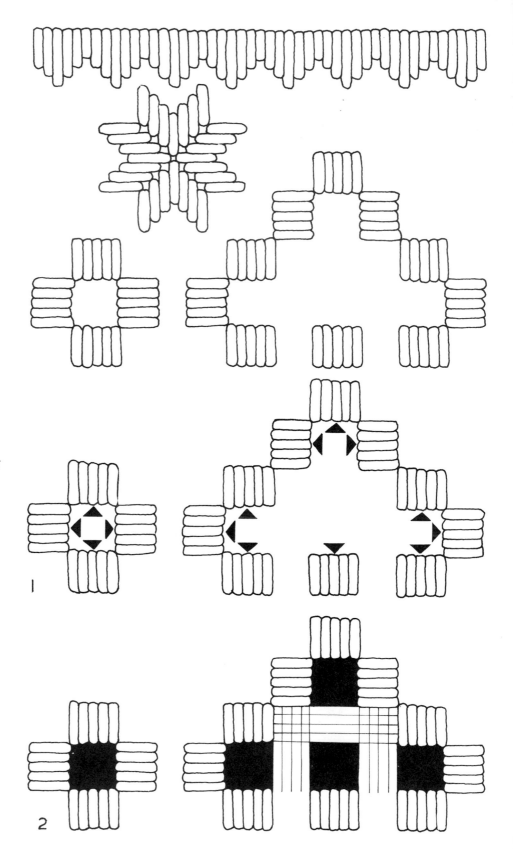

1

2

124

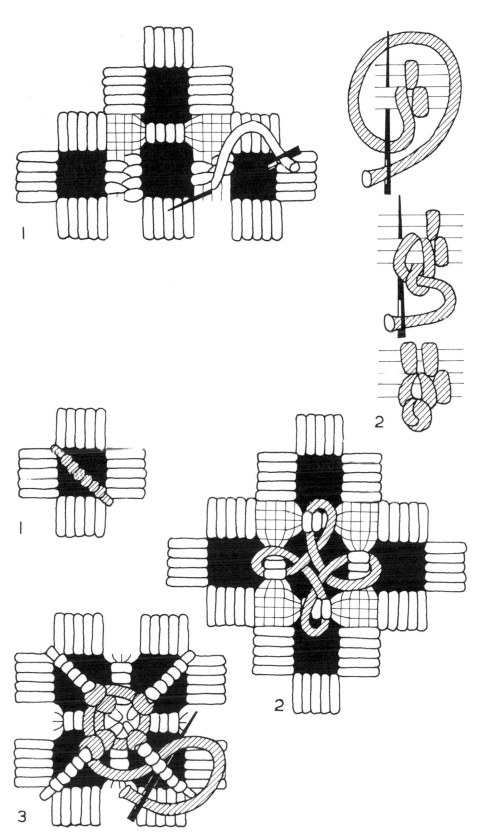

Remaining warp and weft threads
within a motif can be overcast or
bound with needleweaving (1).
For further decoration, picot
loops can be combined with
needleweaving (2)

2

As in cutwork, extra bars can be
formed (1) and lace star filling
stitch (2) or laced spider's web
(3) can be worked

1

2

3

Materials

Hardanger cotton fabric, with 18 or 24 pairs of threads per 2.5cm (1in), is available in traditional white or in colours. It is a strong fabric and does not fray easily. Suggested threads, ideally in white or a pale shade, are pearl cotton No 5 for kløster blocks and surface stitchery and pearl cotton No 8 for subsequent bars and filling stitches. Fabric is usually hand-held during embroidery.

Methods of working

Kløster blocks are worked to produce squares, triangles, rectangles, diamonds or other geometric motifs. Each block is formed from an odd number of satin stitches, each worked over an even number of threads. Blocks of five stitches, for example, should be worked over four threads, or blocks of seven stitches over six threads. At the end of each block, either another block is started at right angles, the first stitch of the second block worked into the same hole as the last stitch of the first block, or a gap is left, over the same number of threads as the length of each satin stitch, before starting another block on the same line.

Satin-stitch devices in the reserves around the outside of kløster block motifs are then worked, often in triangles or eight-pointed stars.

The area within each kløster motif is next carefully cut away and threads withdrawn (no cuts should be made that would produce a raw edge). The resulting trellis can afterwards be decorated with needleweaving or overcasting, and extra bars can be formed from long straight stitches. Picots can be worked on the bars, and laced-star filling stitch or spider's web formed around the bars.

Hardanger cloth made from 20cm (8in) of Danish 425 white Hardanger, 120cm (47in) wide, embroidered with one ball each of Anchor pearl cotton shade 0387, No 5 for the kløster blocks, and No 8 for the overcasting (finished dimensions 14 × 44cm [5½ × 17¼in])

Finishing

Cloths decorated with Hardanger can be finished with single or interlaced hem stitch. Alternatively an edging of close buttonhole stitch worked in scallop or pointed formation, or, as in the illustration, close parallel satin stitches in diamond shapes can be employed.

20. Hedebo

Like Hardanger, Hedebo is a cutwork but today the holes are circular and oval and bordered with Hedebo stitch.

Hedebo takes its name from the *heden* (heath lands) south of Copenhagen, where in about 1760 women began to embroider on linen they had woven themselves from locally grown flax. They adapted floral designs from carved and painted patterns on furniture in their homes. Motifs were outlined with chain stitch, and infilled with geometric bands of drawn-thread trellises bound with needleweaving or overcasting, and the reserves were sometimes decorated with surface stitchery.

By about 1840 square cuts similar to reticella were formed, giving towels and pillowcases, marriage nightgowns and shirts a lighter appearance than that of earlier examples.

Hedebo panel designed and worked by Dorrit Gutterson (evenweave linen embroidered with pearl cotton, 31.1cm [12¼in] square)

127

'The air balloons', designed and worked by Posy McMillen (canvas embroidered with pearl and stranded cottons and metal thread in various techniques including Hedebo, overall dimensions 25 × 19cm [9¾ × 7½in])

A third form of Hedebo evolved some ten years later. Circles were cut, bordered with embroidery and infilled, and surrounding surface embroidery was less in evidence. As a result of commercial pressure, often from dealers exporting needlework throughout Europe, indigenous motifs were sometimes forgotten and replaced by international floral sprays required by the market. Hedebo embroidery as it is now was popular with local heathland embroiderers only from about 1850 to 1870, although it is now extensively worked elsewhere in the world, especially in America where it is sometimes done on canvas.

Materials

Traditionally, single evenweave natural linen is decorated with two-stranded linen thread slightly darker than the fabric. A pointed needle should be used and the fabric must be supported on a frame.

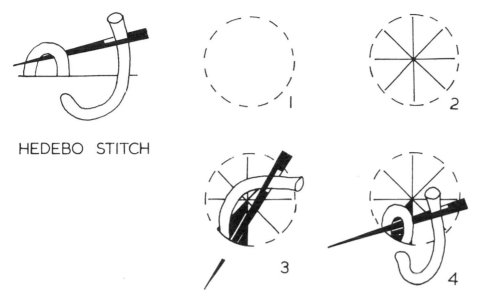

HEDEBO STITCH

The steps taken when starting to bind a hole with Hedebo stitch

Methods of working

Hedebo stitch, also known as Hedebo buttonhole stitch, is different from ordinary buttonhole stitch in that the needle passes through the loop of thread from back to front (see diagram).

When the required design has been marked on the ground fabric, small running stitches are worked around the outline of an area that is to be removed. Radial cuts are then made within that area, close to but not through the running stitches. One segment of the resulting 'wheel' is turned back and Hedebo stitch worked through the ground fabric and the turned-back segment. When all the segments of the wheel have been worked, untidy ends of turned-back fabric can be cut away from the reverse.

A finished hole can be infilled with buttonhole bars bound with Hedebo stitch. Circular infilling rings can be made with a Hedebo 'ring', a short stepped rod, or around a pencil. Thread is wrapped several times round the required width of the gauge and secured. The thread ring is slipped off the gauge and worked with Hedebo stitch all around its circumference. It is then held in place in a finished hole of ground fabric by a retaining web or network of straight stitch dividers which are themselves bound with Hedebo stitch. Incomplete rings can, as an alternative, be made with Hedebo bars formed from long straight stitches that are not pulled tight, resulting in loose tension and a curved appearance to the finished bar.

Other infilling, sometimes so dense and intricate that the effect is of lace, can be formed with Hedebo stitch worked in rows in pyramid fashion, the top of the pyramid held in place with a retaining straight Hedebo bar.

The same method of working, and infilling, cut devices can be applied to any curvilinear motif such as leaves. When all the cutwork is finished, surface embroidery is worked with eyelets and satin stitches. Stems of floral sprays are traditionally worked with neat parallel satin stitches at right angles across the flow of a stem.

In addition to straight dividers, formed as buttonhole bars but bound with Hedebo stitch, circular dividers can be formed with the aid of a stepped gauge or pencil. Thread is wrapped around the gauge several times (1, 2). The ring is taken off and bound with Hedebo stitch (3) before being placed in a cut hole in the main ground fabric and held in place with straight dividers

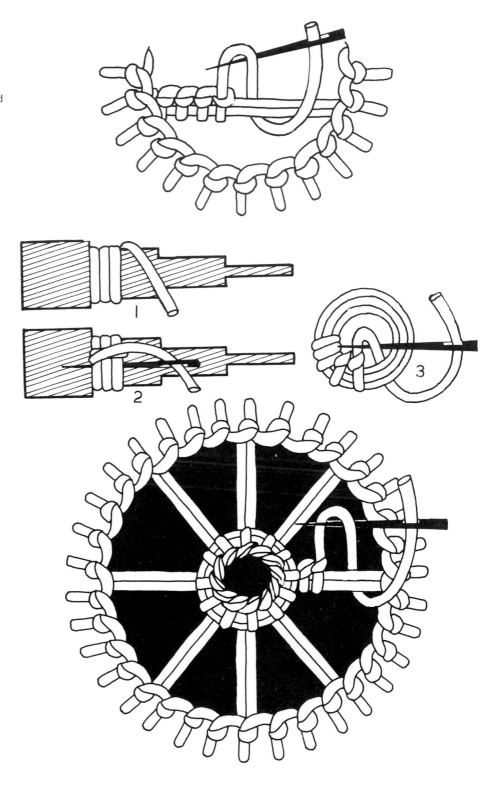

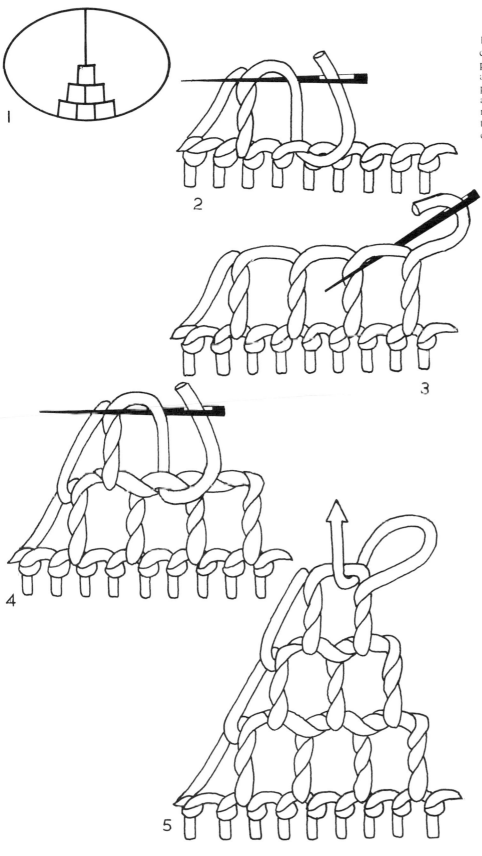

Pyramids can be built up from the circumference of a hole to produce a blocked design such as (1). The method of working a pyramid is shown in stages (2–5) and it is held in place by a long retaining stitch carried across to the other side of the hole or to a convenient internal bar

Complicated geometric block
shapes can be worked in
Hedebo. A flower design, with
stems worked in small parallel
satin stitches, could have a
different pattern within each of
the cut holes of flowers and
leaves

21. Knots and loop stitches

Knots, which add raised texture to an item, are formed by thread loops placed around the needle before it enters the fabric. Individual or groups of knots can be made in this way, or knots can be worked in conjunction with other stitches.

As their name implies, loop stitches are worked by taking the thread around the needle, which does not necessarily immediately enter the ground fabric.

Knotting

In the seventeenth and eighteenth centuries laid and couched knotting was practised widely in the British Isles. The embroiderer first made knots, formed around a small shuttle, at about 6mm ($\frac{1}{4}$in) regular intervals along a length of linen, silk or wool thread. This knotted thread was then laid on ground fabric and couched, between each knot, with another thread. Sometimes the knotted threads were laid so close together that no ground fabric was visible.

Used principally for whitework coverlets and polychrome chair coverings, knotting was a ladies' pastime and is not now much worked.

Section of a Chinese sleeve band mainly worked in Pekin knots with an outer surround of laid and couched cord (satin embroidered with silks, motif 9cm [3$\frac{1}{2}$in] square)

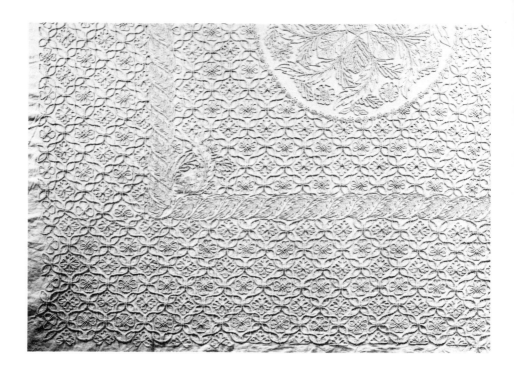

Corner of a knotted and couched cord coverlet worked by Mary Delany (1700–88) and presented to her godson, Thomas Sandford, on his birth in 1765 (overall dimensions 254 × 241cm [100 × 95in])

Methods of working

A thumb placed over a loop of thread may facilitate the working of many knots and loop stitches and an embroiderer quickly develops the easiest way of forming each stitch. Thumb holds are not indicated in the illustrations.

Among the many forms of knots popular with embroiderers today are Basque knot and bullion knot, which has many other names, including caterpillar, coil or grub knots, Porto Rico rose, post stitch and roll, round or worm stitch. A double bullion knot can alternatively only be called trilby stitch.

The list of knots illustrated continues with coral knot, also known as beaded or coral stitch, German knot, knotted outline stitch or snail's trail. The double coral knot is alternatively termed Danish, Old English, Palestrina, Smyrna or tied coral knot.

A four-legged knot has no other common name but the popular French knot can be called French dot or knotted, twisted or wound knot. The Gordian knot is known sometimes as braid stitch and the Italian knot is also called long-legged knot. Knot stitch as such may be known as Antwerp edging or knotted blanket stitch and the Pekin knot, a Chinese speciality, is not surprisingly variously called Chinese knot or forbidden knot.

Seeding and dot stitch, covered in chapters 5 and 10 respectively, can also be called simple knot stitch. Many knotted stitches can be adapted for use in needlepoint.

One of the largest groups of loop stitches is the buttonhole or blanket stitch family which includes basic buttonhole stitch and an alternating variation also known as quill stitch. Buttonhole bars are illustrated, as are closed and crossed buttonhole stitches. A knotted buttonhole stitch, somewhat different from the knot stitch mentioned above, is here followed by German knotted buttonhole stitch and padded or raised buttonhole stitch. Spaced buttonhole stitch can be called grouped

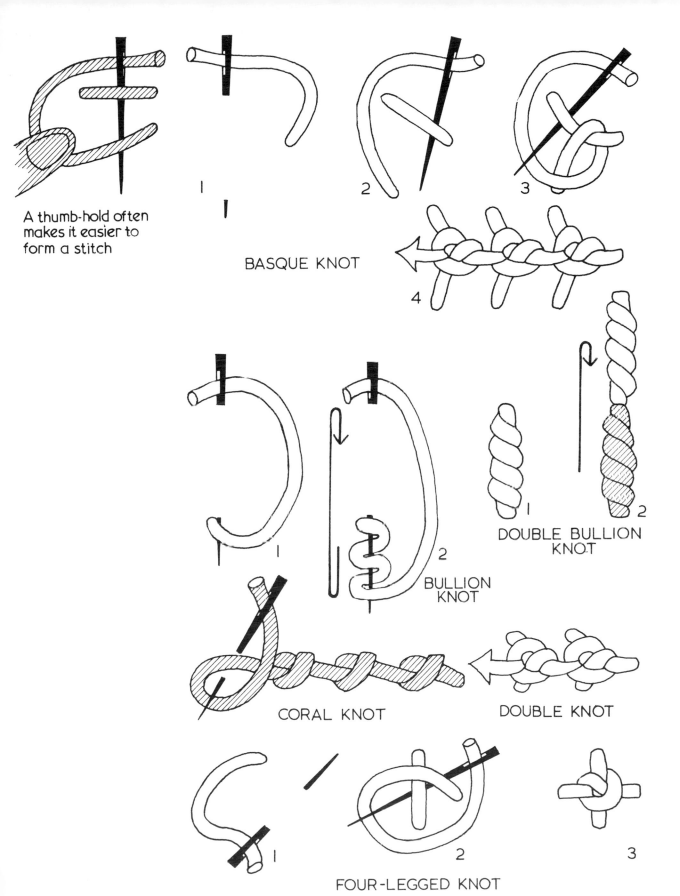

A thumb-hold often makes it easier to form a stitch

1   2   3

BASQUE KNOT

4

1

BULLION KNOT

2

DOUBLE BULLION KNOT

1   2

CORAL KNOT

DOUBLE KNOT

1   2   3

FOUR-LEGGED KNOT

135

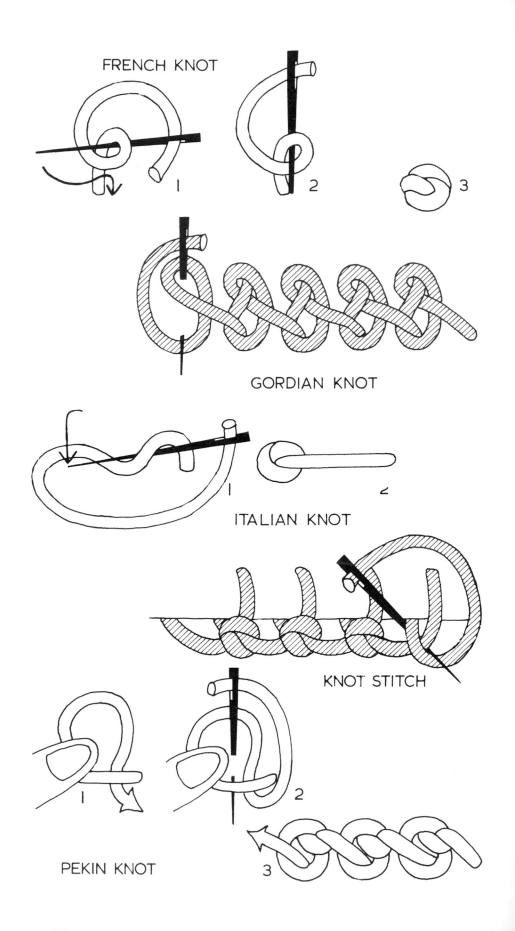

FRENCH KNOT

1 2 3

GORDIAN KNOT

ITALIAN KNOT

1 2

KNOT STITCH

PEKIN KNOT

1 2 3

136

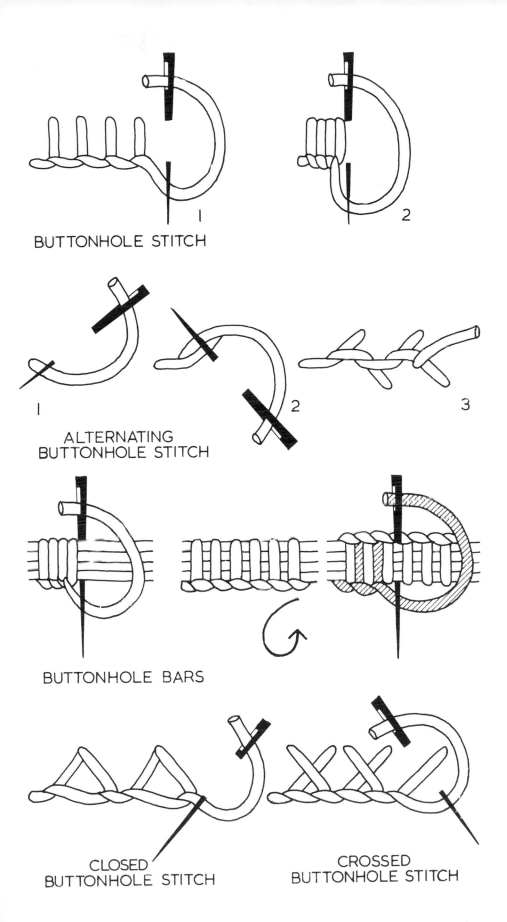

BUTTONHOLE STITCH

1

2

ALTERNATING
BUTTONHOLE STITCH

1

2

3

BUTTONHOLE BARS

CLOSED
BUTTONHOLE STITCH

CROSSED
BUTTONHOLE STITCH

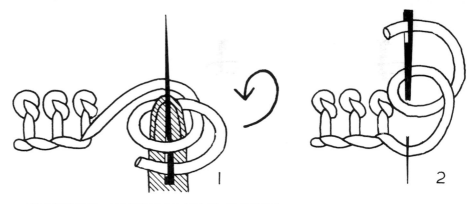

KNOTTED BUTTONHOLE STITCH

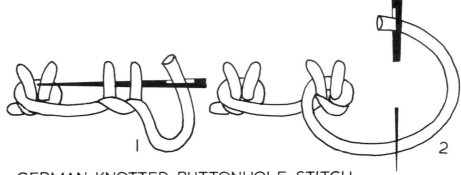

GERMAN KNOTTED BUTTONHOLE STITCH

PADDED
BUTTONHOLE STITCH

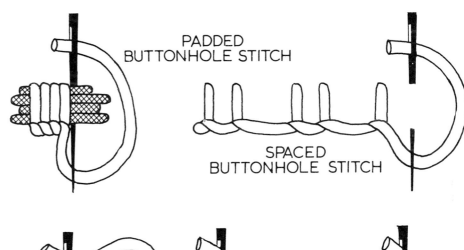

SPACED
BUTTONHOLE STITCH

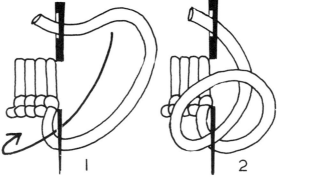
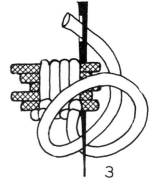

TAILOR'S BUTTONHOLE STITCH — PADDED

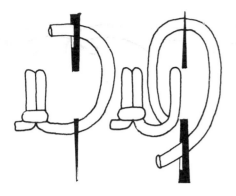

UP-AND-DOWN
BUTTONHOLE STITCH

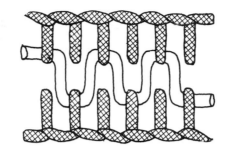

THREADED
BUTTONHOLE STITCH

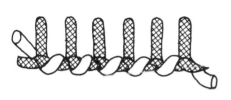

WHIPPED
BUTTONHOLE STITCH

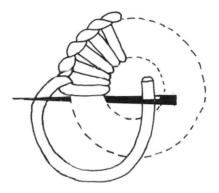

BUTTONHOLE WHEEL

buttonhole stitch and the list continues with tailor's buttonhole stitch and tailor's padded buttonhole stitch. The marvellously named up-and-down buttonhole stitch completes the variants illustrated.

A basic buttonhole stitch can be threaded, whipped or worked in a wheel formation. It will be noted, too, that Hedebo stitch (see chapter 20) can also be called Hedebo buttonhole stitch.

Other loop stitches include Basque stitch and Cretan stitch, also known as fish stitch or long-armed or stacked feather stitch, with closed and open Cretan variations. Diamond stitch is a useful filling stitch.

The feather-stitch family is also called by briar or single coral names. A basic feather stitch has chained and closed variations, the latter also known as double chain stitch. The illustrations continue with double feather stitch, sometimes called double coral stitch, and slanted or single feather stitch, alternatively known as slanted buttonhole stitch. Spanish knotted feather stitch has no other usual names, nor has straight feather stitch.

Fly stitch is variously called open loop or Y stitch; ladder stitch has no alternative common names. Pearl stitch, rope stitch, Sorbello, Türkmen, Vandyke, wave and wheatear stitches complete the looped-stitch diagrams.

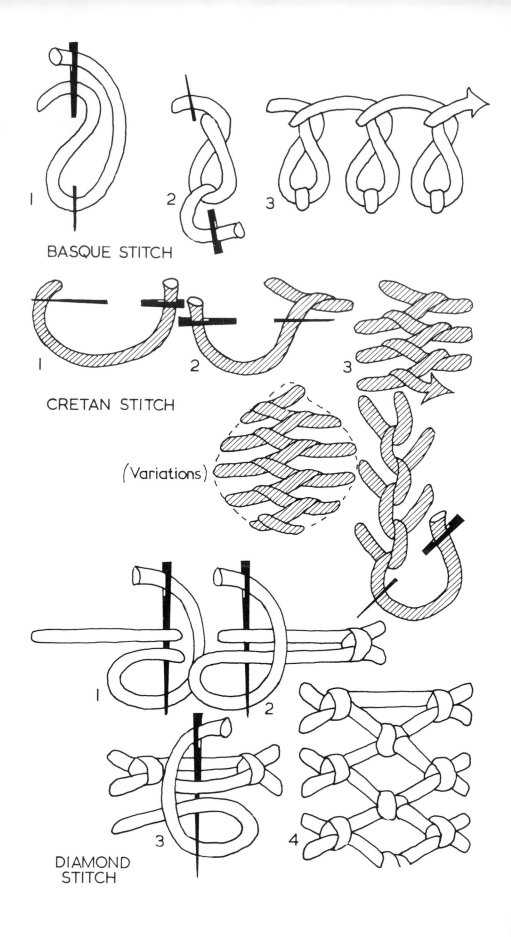

BASQUE STITCH

CRETAN STITCH

(Variations)

DIAMOND
STITCH

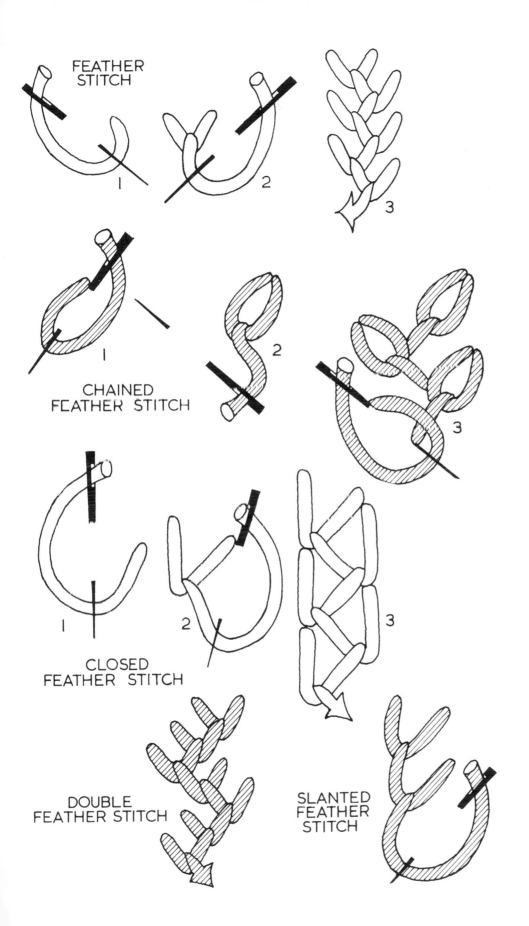

FEATHER
STITCH

1

2

3

CHAINED
FEATHER STITCH

1

2

3

CLOSED
FEATHER STITCH

1

2

3

DOUBLE
FEATHER STITCH

SLANTED
FEATHER
STITCH

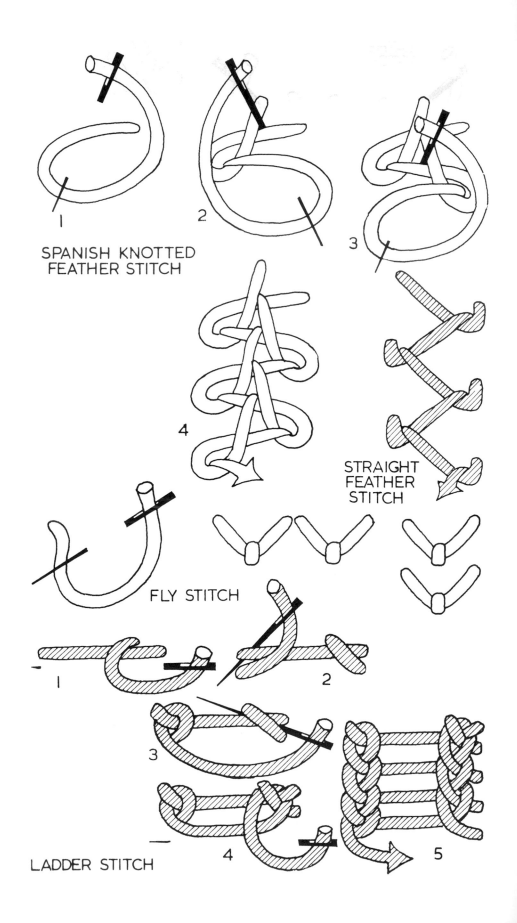

SPANISH KNOTTED
FEATHER STITCH

1

2

3

4

STRAIGHT
FEATHER
STITCH

FLY STITCH

1

2

3

LADDER STITCH

4

5

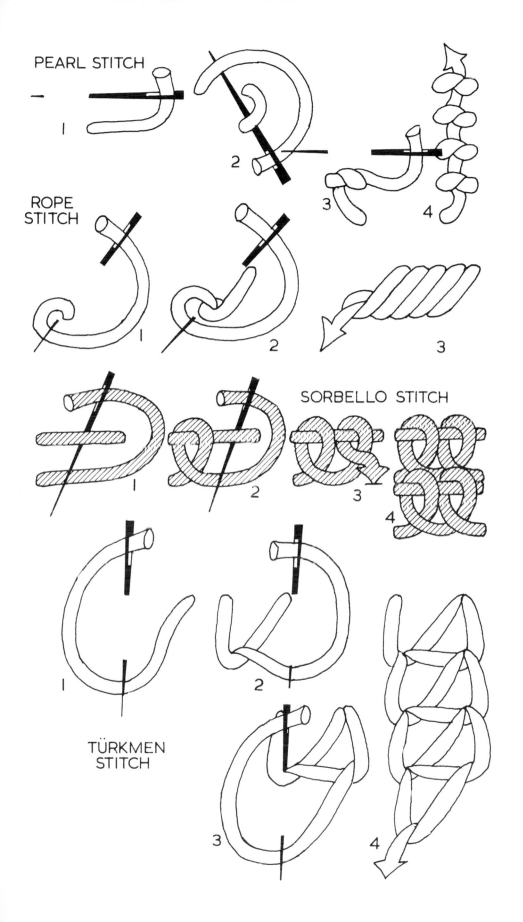

PEARL STITCH

1   2   3   4

ROPE
STITCH

1   2   3

SORBELLO STITCH

1   2   3   4

1   2

TÜRKMEN
STITCH

3   4

143

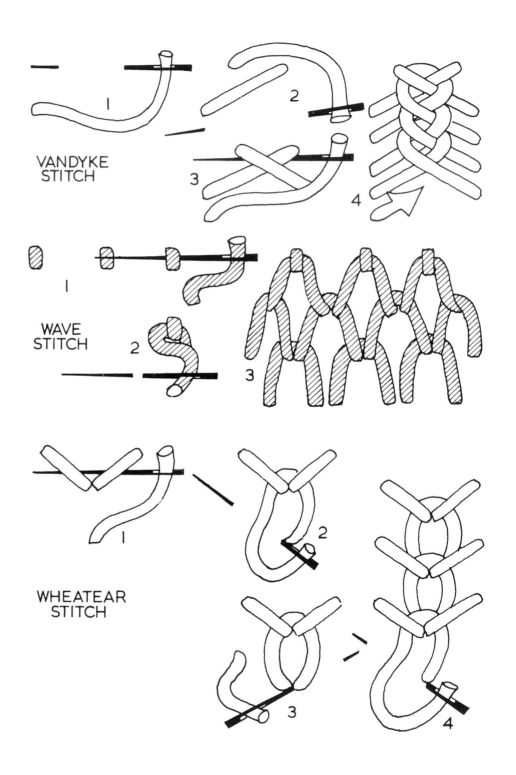

VANDYKE
STITCH

WAVE
STITCH

WHEATEAR
STITCH

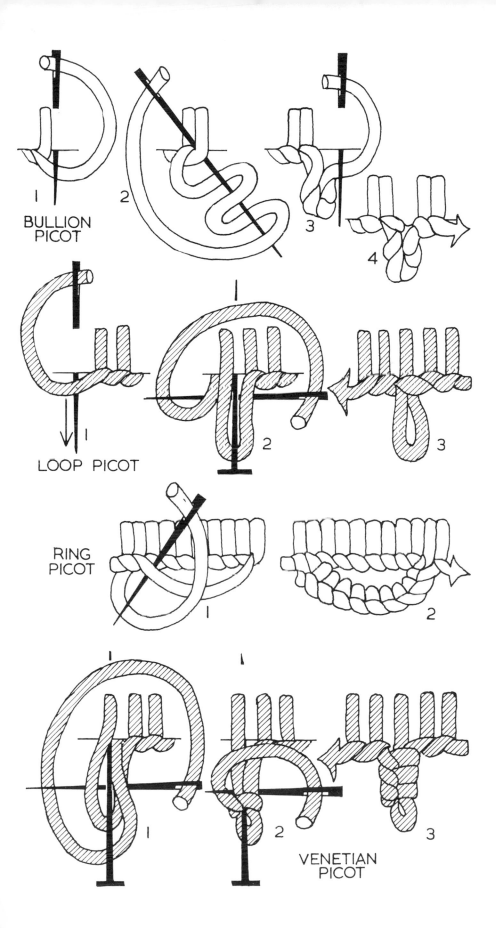

BULLION
PICOT

1 2 3 4

LOOP PICOT

1 2 3

RING
PICOT

1 2

VENETIAN
PICOT

1 2 3

145

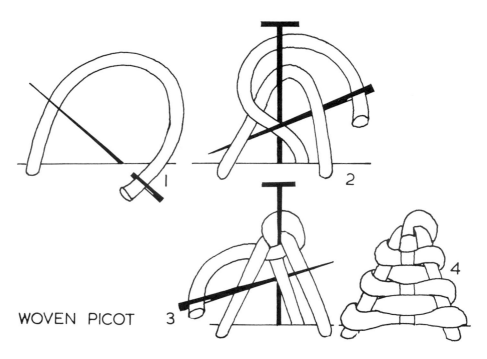

WOVEN PICOT

Picots

Usually forming an edge to an item or a needlework bar, picots are small loops of thread, sometimes twisted and bound with stitches. (For a short time in the second quarter of the twentieth century picot-edging referred to bias-cut skirts hemmed with machine stitching which was then cut to produce tiny lengths of thread.)

When working one of the picot forms illustrated, the embroiderer will discover whether it is easier to work from left to right or vice versa. Some versions are best worked around a T-pin or a second needle, removed when the loop is finished.

Among the most popular picots are bullion picot and loop picot, also called pinned picot. Ring picot is alternatively known as buttonhole ring picot, and Venetian as buttonhole picot. The last picot shown here is a woven picot.

22. Lettering

Embroidering letters and numbers is one of the accomplishments of the many embroiderers who like to sign and date their work, say as 'M.W. 1776'.

The art of calligraphic embroidery can be traced at least to the tenth century. One of the earliest examples is a silk fragment, 2.5 × 20cm (1 × 7⅞in), embroidered in silk chain stitch with an inscription which gives the name of a vizier and calligrapher who served at the Abbasid court from 928 to 930. Contemporary examples from Western Europe include the stole and maniple of St Cuthbert, now at Durham Cathedral, which says 'AELFFLAED FIERI PRECEPIT—PIO EPISCOPO FRIDESTANDO' ('Ethelfleda ordered this work for the pious Bishop Frithestan', who is known to have held the see of Winchester from 909 to 931).

Hebrew inscription on a sixteenth-century cloth, with texts from Genesis and the Psalms and signed 'Karla daughter of Alomo iben Pschat' (white linen embroidered mainly in red silk cross and long-armed cross stitches, 49.5 × 44cm [19½ × 17¼in])

Lettering was mainly used on religious and other ceremonial embroideries, although that eminent needlewoman Bess of Hardwick (1520–1608) had many of her pieces inscribed ES (Elizabeth Shrewsbury), and sometimes also with Latin names of flowers and fruits.

In 1598 Jane Bostocke signed and dated a sampler but, in the main, lettering came into everyday use for secular needlework in the seventeenth century. For nearly two hundred years it was extensively employed on samplers and other items in many parts of the world.

Especially during the nineteenth century many special pattern books were published, with Gothic, Old English and other scripts. Monograms were then often worked, on handkerchiefs and household linens, and decorated with satin or padded satin stitches or double-running stitch, in lettering alternatively called writing stitch.

Although Ann Macbeth (1875–1948) and other designers experimented with lettering, its use declined during the general demise of needlework at the beginning of the twentieth century.

Today embroiderers are making striking use of lettering in church work, using appliqué and other hand and machine techniques, and lettering in general is now associated with the skills of crewel embroidery, cross stitch, machine embroidery, needlepoint and samplers.

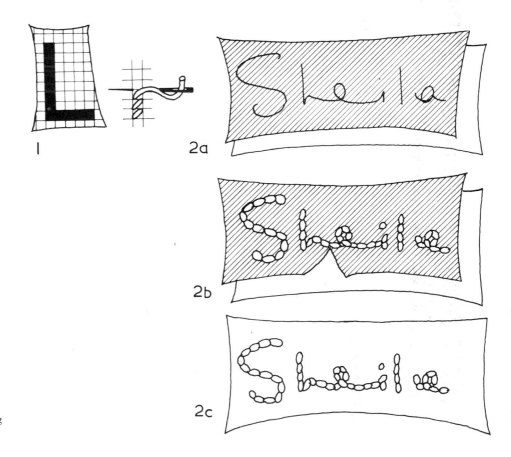

There are various methods of transferring designs from paper to fabric. Square charts can be copied on evenweave fabrics, with one stitch worked for each block of paper design (1). Alternatively, letters of an inscription can be written on tissue paper or vanishing muslin which is then laid on fabric (2a) and stitching is worked through both layers (2b) before the paper or muslin is carefully pulled or ironed away to reveal the lettering on the fabric beneath (2c)

148

Materials

Exact proportions of letters are easiest to achieve when worked on a canvas or even-weave material. Any kind of thread is suitable, and sometimes the fabric need not be held on a frame.

Methods of working

Transposing even lettering to canvas or evenweave fabric can easily be done by counting threads. Alternatively, tissue paper or vanishing muslin marked with the required script can be temporarily held over the fabric. Stitching is worked through both layers, after which the paper or vanishing muslin is carefully removed.

Lettering patterns are sometimes graphed as blocks, with each square of the chart indicating one or a certain number of stitches. These patterns are especially popular for cross stitch and tent and other needlepoint stitches. Other patterns, marked with lines, indicate outline stitches and the embroiderer counts the lines rather than blocks. These designs are more suitable for double-running or back stitches.

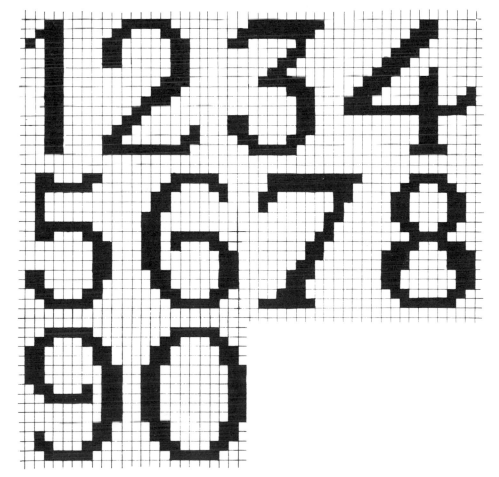

A block design, each square of the graph usually indicating one stitch

This alphabet design, especially suitable for back or double-running stitches, makes use of vertical, horizontal and diagonal lines. It is taken from *The embroiderer's alphabet* (Editions Th. de Dillmont)

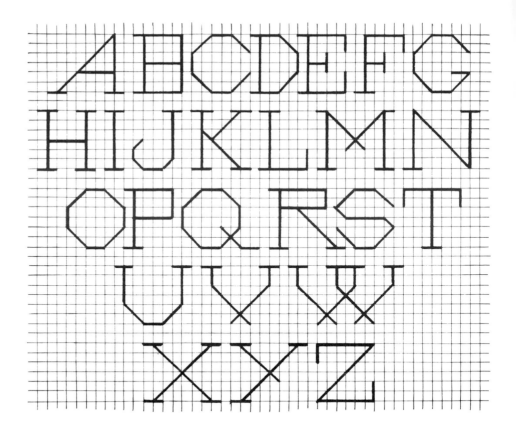

Different effects can be achieved by shading letters and by partial infilling. These letters are adapted from a nineteenth-century work *Lapidaire Monstre*, reprinted in Alexander Nesbitt's *Decorative alphabets and initials* (Dover, 1958)

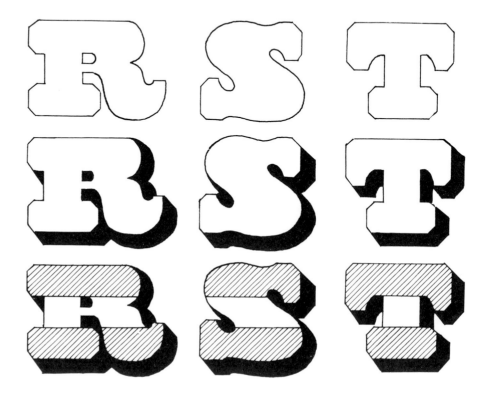

It is sometimes necessary to move letters closer together for balance (1). Letters can be worked at different angles to produce interesting patterns (2). In the past, many monograms, espicially in whitework, were executed in padded satin stitch (3). The monogram FG is here set out in three different ways (4)

An inscription should be carefully planned before any embroidery commences. Paper and pencils can be used to experiment with three-dimensional and filled letters, similar to those illustrated.

Sometimes letters have to be moved closer to their neighbours for overall balance. When the paper pattern is satisfactory, the central point of the design should be noted and stitching is worked on the fabric from that central point outwards, working both to left and right.

23. Machine embroidery

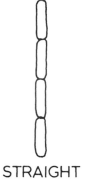

STRAIGHT

ZIGZAG

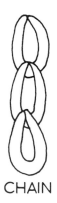

CHAIN

Machine stitching, worked with even tension, as it appears on the front of an item. In machined chain stitch, a hooked needle, working through the previous stitch, brings a loop of thread through from the reverse

This section deals with individual machine embroidery rather than with commercially produced work.

Embroidery on a domestic sewing machine is closely related to many other chapters in the book, especially those covering appliqué, blocking and mounting, designing, drawn-thread work, fabrics and threads, lettering, metal-thread work, net embroidery, padded and raised work, patchwork, quilting, shadow work and whitework.

The basic categories of machine embroidery include four worked on sewing machines operating with two reels of thread. Straight-line stitching is produced on a straight-stitch machine. Zigzag or satin stitches can be worked on a swing-needle machine, and these and built-in stitch patterns can also be formed with automatic machines.

'Creative machine embroidery', as it is generally known, is worked with any of the above three machines. The automatic-feed mechanism is covered and the foot taken off, so that the movement of fabric is controlled by the embroiderer.

Chain-stitch machine sewing is produced on a one-reel machine, and although this is extensively used by embroiderers, especially in Africa and the Middle East, to decorate table-cloths and clothing, it seldom enters the realm of creative machine embroidery in this particular context.

The two-reel sewing machine as it is today largely owes its form to American inventions made from 1845 to 1854, although an early machine had been established in London in 1790 by a cabinet-maker, Thomas Saint. Isaac Singer produced the first ordinary domestic sewing machine in New York in 1851 and a Winterthur gentleman called Rieter perfected a machine that executed a high-relief embroidery extensively used for whitework on muslin and net, or with more sombre colouring for decorating mourning apparel.

Other innovations were made in Europe. Isaac Groebli's 1865 design for a Schiffli machine enabled the embroiderer to work a large number of effects, including eyelets, and the chain-stitch machine was perfected by a Frenchman, M. Bonnaz, and subsequently manufactured by Ercole Cornely.

These inventions led to the growth of machine-embroidered items produced for commercial purposes and the subsequent demise of such hand needlework techniques as Ayrshire work (see chapter 36).

Creative machine embroidery as such evolved in the late 1920s and '30s and it is now popular in many parts of the world, often used by men to make spectacular wall-hangings, banners and individual fashion items.

Materials and equipment

It is obviously preferable to use an electric or treadle sewing machine as the embroiderer then has both hands free to control the flow of the fabric.

Although many different threads can be used on most materials other than canvas, a special machine embroidery thread is recommended. This comes in two thicknesses, 30 (thicker) and 50 (finer) and fifty shades are available, on 10g spools.

Machine embroidery should always be worked on a small circular frame with narrow ring surround.

Methods of working

The machine should be set up with the feed mechanism removed or covered, as indicated in the makers' instructions. If a thick thread is required to show on the right side of a finished item, it should be wound on the lower spool of the machine with a finer thread set above, the end threaded through the needle's eye.

Fabric is then stretched tightly on the frame, with the fabric *below* rather than above it, as illustrated, so that the fabric lies flat on the machine's base. If the thread on the lower spool is intended to decorate the right side of the finished item, then the fabric should face downwards on the machine's base, otherwise it can face upwards (see p 154).

The embroiderer holds each side of the frame with both hands. A small stitch is taken to pull the end of the underneath thread up through the fabric and, extremely slowly at first, a few stitches are executed. Because there is no feed mechanism, the direction and length of stitches is entirely dependent on the movement made by the embroiderer's hands.

Pulling the frame gently to one side will produce a stitch in the other direction

(*Below, left*) Men and some women in many parts of the Near East decorate table-cloths and other items with continuous lines of chain stitching, sometimes known as 'Damascus embroidery', worked on Cornely machines (detail of cotton table napkin 38cm [15in] square)

(*Right*) Machine-embroidered alphabet designed and worked by Pat Russell on a Bernina machine (felt 95 × 35cm [37½ × 13¾in])

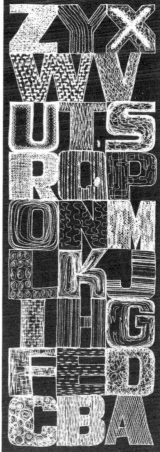

Before any embroidery is done, the foot is removed from the machine and a special clamp, usually supplied in the accompanying toolbox, is fitted over the feed mechanism

(Drawings in cross-section) If a thick thread is being used, it should be wound, by hand if necessary, on the underneath spool and a thinner thread passed through the needle's eye. Fabric on a frame lies on the machine's base under the needle. If a thick thread is being worked from the underneath spool, the frame must be set so that the right side of the fabric lies downwards (A) and embroidery is worked from the wrong side. It is also possible to work with the fabric right side up, as at (B)

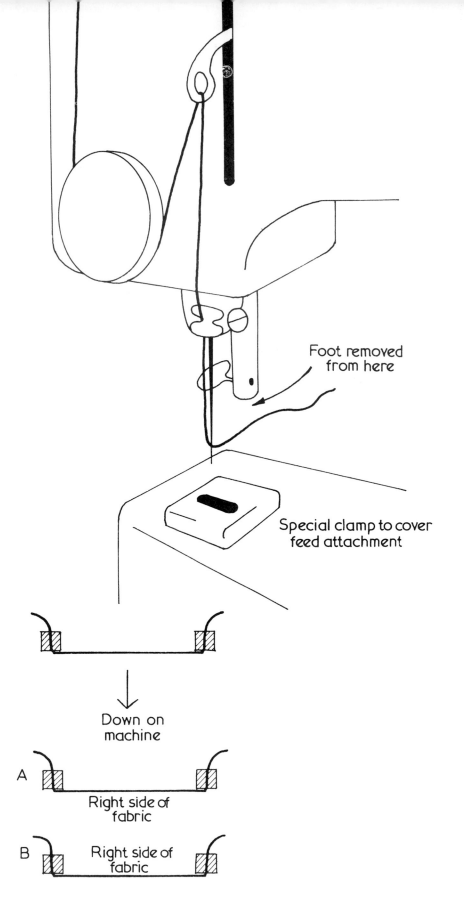

Foot removed from here

Special clamp to cover feed attachment

Down on machine

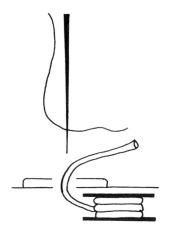

A Right side of fabric

B Right side of fabric

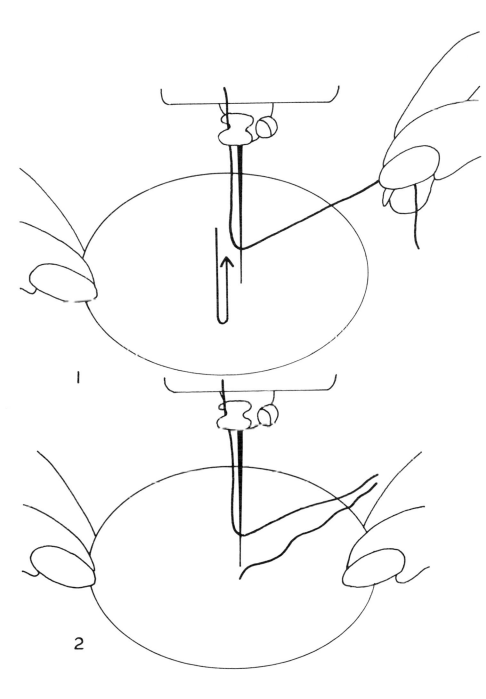

1 The frame is set beneath the needle and one stitch is taken to pull the thread from the underneath spool through the fabric. The frame is held in both hands and the embroiderer is ready to begin

1

2

Pulling the frame slowly to the *right* produces stitches moving in a *left* direction.

Tightening the tension of the thread in the upper spool results in 'whipping'.

After ground threads have been withdrawn remaining threads can be bound with close zigzag stitches to produce machine drawn thread work

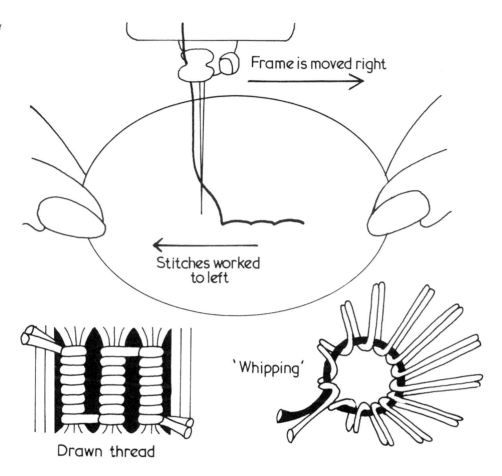

Frame is moved right

Stitches worked to left

Drawn thread

'Whipping'

of corresponding length. In other words creative machine embroidery 'writes in reverse'.

Once this process has been mastered the embroiderer can experiment with different threads and with altering the machine's tension. Holes can be made in the fabric, and subsequently bordered by stitching, and possibly partly infilled by taking the machine's needle from one side to the other, to produce machine-worked cutwork. Ground fabric with some threads withdrawn can have remaining threads bound with machine stitching to give an effect of machine drawn-thread work.

24. Metal-thread work

As its name suggests, metal-thread work makes use of threads or strips of gold, silver, silver-gilt or another metal, usually laid and couched with silk. Spangles or sequins, small flat discs of metal (see chapter 25), and silver or golden pieces of leather, are also applied in this way.

Most surviving examples of early western metal-thread work are church pieces. One of these is St Cuthbert's maniple, partly worked with brilliant pure gold only $\frac{1}{200}$ of an inch thick, with 128 laid gold threads and 16 couching silk threads per inch.

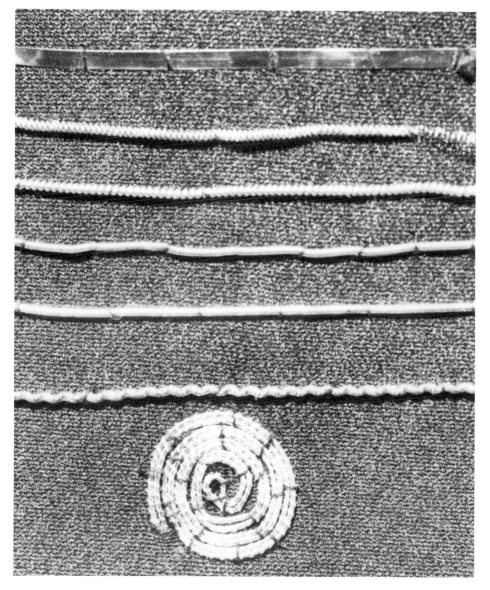

Some types of gold thread are (*from the top*) gold plate, bright check purl, rich gilt pearl purl, rich gilt rough purl, rich gilt smooth purl, medium rococo and substitute Jap gold

Metal-thread work was sometimes known as 'gold embroidery', even though from the eleventh century threads of a debased red gold mixed with copper, or of silver-gilt, made from thin films of gold on silver bases, were also employed. Because it was difficult to manage single metal threads they were sometimes wrapped in spirals round a central core of silk or linen. Threads were expensive, and for reasons of economy as well as the practical difficulty of taking heavy threads right through a ground fabric, they were usually couched, so that the maximum amount of the precious metal stayed above the surface of the fabric.

By the sixteenth century, metal thread was incorporated into blackwork and polychrome decoration on rich people's clothing. In more recent times metal threads have continued to be used for church vestments and furnishings and also for decorating ceremonial costumes and trappings and other elaborate clothing.

Metal-thread embroidery is also especially associated with the Far East. In China, for example, pairs of gold threads are traditionally laid together and couched with one brightly-coloured silk thread.

Today in many countries metal-thread embroidery is an art that beginners wish to master. The materials are still expensive and intricate work is required but even a novice can have fun experimenting with short lengths of different metal threads.

Materials

Standard metal threads used in the west today are gold, silver and lurex and other substitutes. Other parts of the world have evolved such distinctive materials as the tin thread used by some Lapps.

Some threads generally available have distinctive working instructions. Here are set out simply the material requirements and, at the end of the section, instructions for subsequent embroidery.

Although it is advisable to work on a firm strong ground fabric which will prevent the item puckering, metal-thread work can in fact be executed on most popular fabrics. If a light silk or organza ground is used it can be backed with muslin before any embroidery is started.

Some metal threads will tarnish if they come into contact with the embroiderer's hands, and expensive threads should be used sparingly and carefully and, where possible, handled with tweezers.

Among the most popular threads generally available today are:

Passing threads, taking their name from the fact that they 'pass over' the surface of the ground. They are fine but strong, smooth, coiled threads, spiralled around a silk or cotton core which can be seen when a short length of thread is 'uncoiled'. Wavy passing threads are less fine and slightly crinkly.

Tambour threads are finer core-wrapped threads used for surface stitchery and machine embroidery.

Plated threads are continuous lengths of flat and narrow shiny metal.

Purls or *bullions* are hollow spiral threads formed with no central core. They are pliable but, once uncoiled, it is difficult to form the spiral again. The four main forms of purl are:

1 check purl, also known as frieze purl, in which the wire is bent slightly at regular intervals to give a faceted appearance to the thread. Check purl can be mottled or bright.

2 pearl purl, also known as minikin or badge, bead or wire purl. This is a coarser thread, often used for ceremonial regalia, and the coil can be slightly pulled apart so that stitches can be formed between the coils. When two or more lines of pearl purl are laid closely parallel, the resulting effect looks like small knobs or pearls set together.

3 rough purl, a muted wire thread with soft polished finish.

4 smooth purl, which has an unusually bright and highly polished finish.

Japanese gold is made from thin strips of paper covered with real gold leaf and coiled around a bright orange, yellow or red silk core. This is no longer readily available and substitute Jap gold and silver threads are used instead. Available in various weights, the higher size number denotes the heavier thread.

Lurex and other man-made 'metals' can take the place of many of the threads mentioned above.

Cords and *braids* are available in a whole range, including gimp, soutache and rococo, and they are mainly used for ceremonial decoration.

Other materials required for metal-thread work include:

Couching threads: in the past Maltese silk, a tightly twisted strong thread also known as horsetail, was generally used. Couching threads now include stranded cottons and Gütermann silks, both of which can also be used for tacking, hemming and parts of embroidery that do not use metal threads. Only a short length of couching thread should be used at a time.

Beeswax: if the couching thread is drawn over a piece of beeswax, it can withstand possible friction from the metal thread without knotting and twisting.

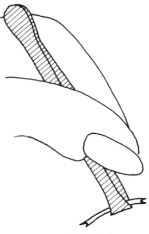

To prevent metal threads from tarnishing they should if possible be handled with tweezers

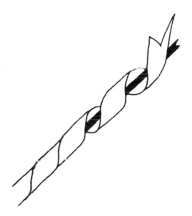

Jap and imitation Jap threads consist of metallic strips wrapped round a central silken or cotton thread which can be seen by untwisting the spiral

By unravelling a purl or bullion thread it will be seen that there is no central core

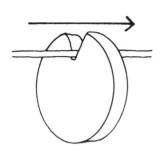

Before a length of couching thread is used it should be pulled over a block of beeswax to prevent it from knotting through friction caused by working with laid metal threads

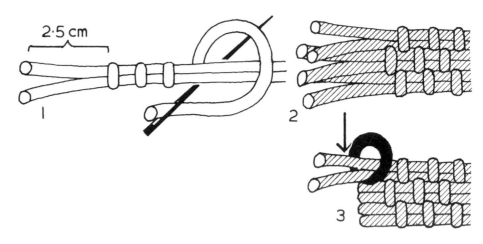

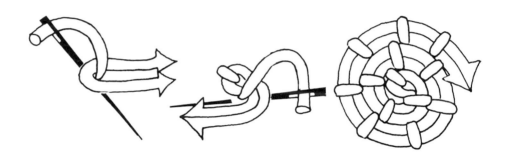

1 Usually two lengths of metal thread are laid and couched at a time, with couching stitches at right angles to the direction of the threads. At least 2.5cm (1in) extra thread should be left at the end of each length. 2 The raw ends are all left exposed until a block of embroidery is finished. 3 The surplus ends are then taken down through the fabric by plunging, using another thread—here black.
Circular motifs are formed with one continuous length of thread couched at the halfway point and the ends folded. Thereafter, as the spiral is worked outwards, couching stitches are worked over two thread widths.
Pointed motifs are initially formed with a pair of outer threads turned sharply at the apex of the design. Pairs of infilling threads are then worked as indicated, the raw ends left exposed until the whole motif is worked. These are then taken through to the reverse of the fabric

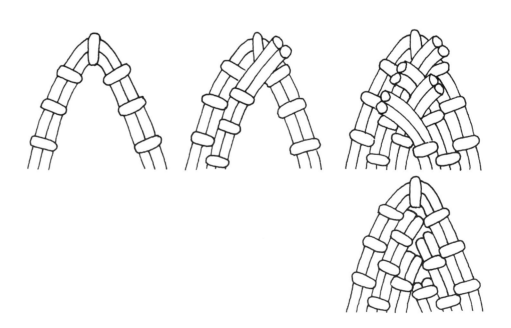

Transparent tape: because ends of many metal threads tend to unravel, it is a good idea to secure them with a short length of tape.

Needles: the couching thread is usually threaded on a crewel needle size 8–10. A couching needle is also required for passing metal threads through fabric, although a chenille size 8 can be employed instead.

Scissors: a small pair of florists' or other scissors is useful for cutting lengths of purls.

A stiletto is similarly useful for helping metal threads pass through required angles, for piercing the ground fabric prior to plunging the end of a heavy metal thread through it, and also for handling delicate metal threads. (This task was once assigned to a mellore, a tool with one pointed end for making holes and one spatula-shaped end for flattening threads.)

A cutting board or piece of card covered with felt or velvet is handy when cutting short lengths of purl.

Metal thread should always be worked on a frame.

Many metal-thread embroiderers like to work with two thimbles, one on each forefinger.

Storage of unused metal threads is facilitated by wrapping them in acid-free tissue paper or keeping them in an airtight tin to prevent tarnishing. Another tip to help retain the brightness of the metal is to tack a small piece of fabric on to worked areas of stitchery to prevent them coming into contact with the embroiderer's hands.

Methods of working

Although a few are worked direct on to the ground fabric, metal threads are mostly couched, sometimes over padding (see chapter 28). If metal threads are laid over

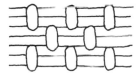 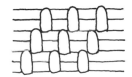 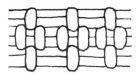

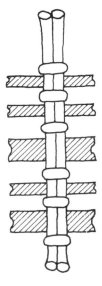

As in other laidwork, metal threads can be couched in brick, step and diamond formations.
Metal threads can be laid over strings sewn to the ground fabric, and are then couched in the normal way; the size of the string determines the depth of the resultant padding

161

cut-out shapes of parchment, vellum or cloth laid on the ground fabric the technique can be called guimped work.

The ground fabric should be stretched taut on a frame and the required couching thread passed over the top of the beeswax block.

Many embroiderers prefer the Chinese method of couching two threads at a time, a skill that speeds working and also results in a cleaner 'outside line'. Two lengths of thread, each not more than 190cm (72in), should be cut and threaded through one or two couching needles and laid progressively on the ground fabric. At least 2.5cm (1in) must be left unworked at each end of the threads and no plunging or taking the couching needles through the fabric is done until an entire block of embroidery is finished. Threads are couched with another needle threaded with the chosen couching thread, and this makes small stitches at right angles across the laid threads, each couching stitch being roughly 6mm ($\frac{1}{4}$in) from its neighbours.

As with other forms of couching, a variety of brick and other patterns can be built up by consecutive rows of couching and the rule of 'no plunging' again applies until an entire block of design is completed.

Purls are couched somewhat differently. Small lengths, usually no longer than 6 to 10mm ($\frac{1}{4}$ to $\frac{3}{8}$in), are carefully cut and couched to the ground with long stitches, giving an impression of bullion knots. It is advisable to cut purl on a felt- or velvet-covered board in order to prevent the metal jumping up when being cut. Each length should be cut with scissors exactly at right angles across the thread.

If possible without being touched by hand, one length of purl is then picked up by a fine crewel needle threaded with waxed silk. The needle enters the ground fabric to take a stitch and re-emerges to take up another length of purl.

The only exception to the method of working purls is pearl purl, which can be laid a long length at a time. This is stretched slightly so that the couching silk can slip between the coils and stitches are less visible.

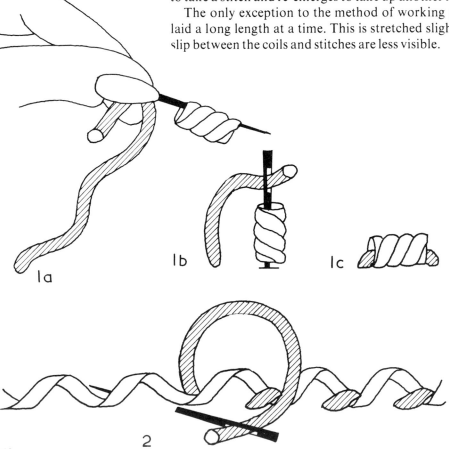

Pieces of purl or bullion no longer than 1.25cm ($\frac{1}{2}$in) are carefully cut on a cloth-covered board and picked up with a threaded needle (1a) before being sewn to the ground as a bullion knot (1b, c). Alternatively a longer length of purl can be slightly unravelled and couched between each coil (2)

25. Miscellanea

At various times in the past such unusual techniques as camera work, needle-worked surrounds to early photographs, have temporarily been in vogue. This chapter brings together some embroidery forms that are not covered elsewhere in the book. These are set out in alphabetical order.

Beadwork

Beads have been used by embroiderers for many centuries. Coloured or enamelled glass beads have had the widest application although wood, plastic and many other beads are available. Some famous types of beads, past and present, include:

OP beads, large cylindrical opaque glass beads imported from Germany in the middle of the nineteenth century.

Pipes or pypes, small glass tubes imported from Venice since the sixteenth century and especially used at that time for decorating dresses and doublets.

Pony or big beads, irregularly-shaped opaque china beads, generally blue, white, yellow or black, first brought from Venice to America in the early part of the nineteenth century and especially used by Plains Indians.

Pound beads, transparent glass beads in many different colours, sold by weight and imported in the early nineteenth century from Germany and Italy.

Rocailles, a family of transparent glass beads which includes round rocailles, also known as seed beads, round beads with round holes; square rocailles, or toscas, round beads with square holes, and charlottes, facetted beads.

A bead usually has one hole through which thread passes

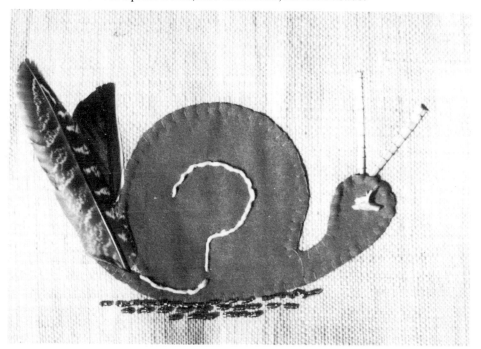

This raffia material is decorated with one piece of ultrasuede and with lengths of straw, feathers, beads, unravelled string and a small bone from a mackerel's head (motif dimensions 13.3 × 21cm [5¼ × 8¼in])

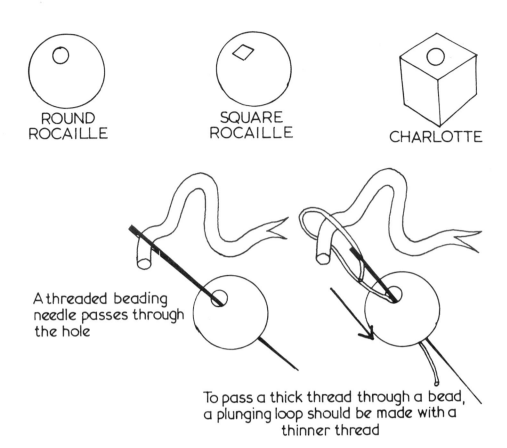

ROUND
ROCAILLE

SQUARE
ROCAILLE

CHARLOTTE

A threaded beading
needle passes through
the hole

To pass a thick thread through a bead,
a plunging loop should be made with a
thinner thread

Beads are generally threaded on coton à broder or another embroidery thread with the aid of a specially long and fine 'beading' needle, usually size 12. If it is difficult to pull the thread through a bead's hole, a loop of finer thread can be employed as shown in the diagram.

Beads are used for embroidery purposes in a number of ways. Individual beads can be attached to the ground fabric, a form of decoration especially popular with European and American needlewomen in the middle of the nineteenth century. After the needle emerges from the ground fabric, it penetrates one bead before being taken back into the material. Alternatively, more than one bead can be threaded on to the needle each time it emerges.

Another form of bead decoration is achieved by threading many beads on to one length of thread which is then laid on the ground fabric and couched with another thread which forms a couching stitch between each bead.

Tambour beading, sometimes called Lunéville work after a French town where the technique was popular in the latter part of the nineteenth century, is worked with a tambour hook (see chain stitch, chapter 8). A great number of beads are threaded on to embroidery thread. The outline of a required design is drawn on the reverse of the ground fabric and the embroiderer works with this, the wrong, side uppermost. The beaded thread is held beneath the frame and, as in ordinary tamboured chain stitch, each entry and exit of the vertically-held tambour hook brings up a loop of thread, each loop separated by one bead. The final effect, therefore, has the beads individually attached on the obverse of the item and the linked chains of stitching on the reverse.

From 1901 to 1927 the family of Sir Richard Paget (third from left), intrigued by a Stuart raised-work picture dated 1683, worked a group portrait in traditional style. Sir Richard designed the picture, set on a terrace at Cranmore Hall, and he himself formed all the faces and hands from wax which were subsequently cast in plaster and painted, and carved mannequins from teak. The ladies were required to make their own clothes and those of their husbands using fine needlepoint lace techniques, and all of the other stitching was worked by Sir Richard's mother.

(*Left to right*) Lord Gladstone, then Home Secretary and later first Governor General of South Africa, with his wife, Dorothy Paget; Sir Richard Paget, holding a stick formed from fused silica, a newly developed material on which he was working, and his wife, Lady Muriel Finch Hatton, daughter of the eleventh Earl of Winchelsea. The first Sir Richard Paget, here seated, had in fact died in 1908 but he is seen, as is Lord Gladstone, wearing Privy Council uniform. Lady Paget is followed by her children Hilda, later Mrs Archibald Balfour, and Geoffrey. Colonel

and Mrs Percy Bruce (Alethea Paget) are seen with Jarvis and Sheila, later Lady Crawshaw who was able, before the picture was completed, to work her own dress on knitting needles and, in front, Sylvia, later Lady Chancellor, and in the cradle, Pamela, to become Lady Glenconner
(overall size 52.1 × 61cm, [20½ × 24in])

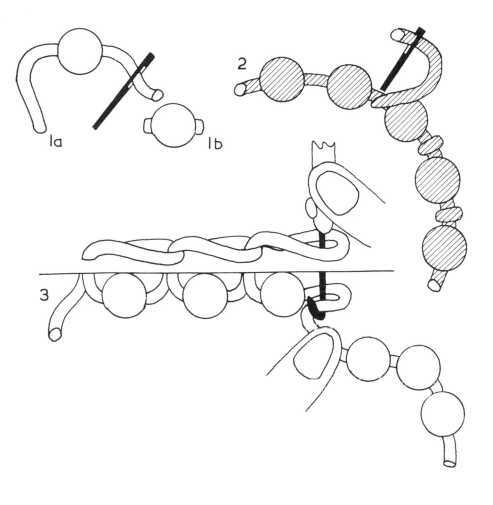

There are three main ways of attaching beads to fabric: **1** After a threaded needle emerges from the fabric it passes through one or more beads (a) before re-entering the fabric (b). **2** Many beads on one thread are laid on the ground fabric and the thread is couched with another thread between each bead. **3** A great number of beads are threaded on to a continuous thread held beneath the fabric. A tambour hook is used to pull up one loop of this thread between each bead. This produces a line of stitched beads below the surface and tambour chain stitching above the surface

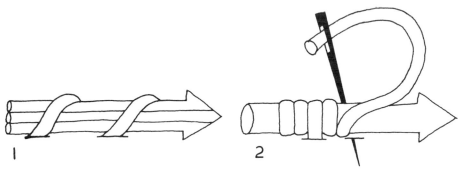

1 Bundles of hairs can be laid and couched. **2** Alternatively single hairs can be wrapped round quills or other 'fillers', with the hairs entering the ground fabric at every third coil

Hair embroidery

Human hair was used by western needlewomen at the end of the eighteenth and in the early nineteenth centuries to make printwork embroideries. Individual hairs threaded on fine needles were worked, usually in straight stitches, to form pictures often en grisaille and reminiscent of engravings. (It should be noted that printwork, also known as engraved or etched embroidery, does not necessarily imply hair embroidery. This form of decoration, popular throughout the nineteenth century,

Mirror work:
one method of attaching pieces of glass, mica or mylar to the ground fabric is with long straight stitches forming a circumferential net, and with subsequent lacing (shisha stitch)

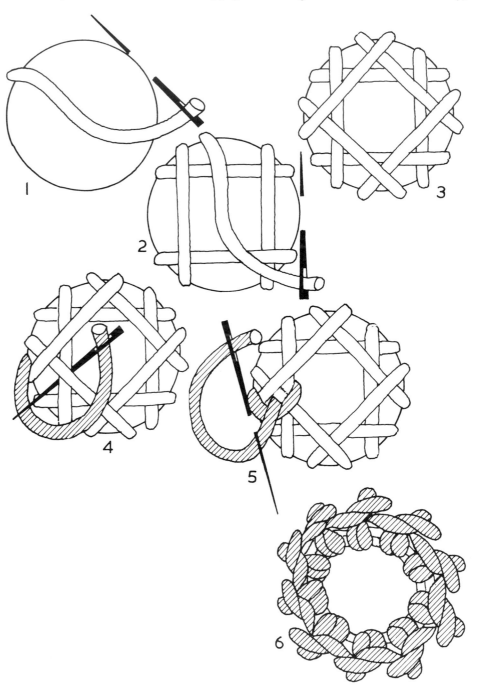

entailed the needleworked copying of engravings, usually with black and grey fine silk thread worked on cream taffeta or other silk ground fabrics.)

Horse and reindeer or moose hairs have also been used as embroidery thread, especially in North America and Siberia. Sometimes bundles of hairs are laid and couched, and in other instances individual hairs are tightly coiled around a quill filler and then couched with hair.

Mirror work

Also known as shishadur or shisha work, this technique uses small pieces of mirror glass, mica or mylar applied to fabric. Because there are no piercing holes the pieces are either held in place with circumferential interlacing or shisha stitch, or a 'looking-glass frame' of another fabric is itself applied, above the mirror, to the ground fabric.

Otolith embroidery

During the latter part of the nineteenth century some embroiderers used beetles' wings and fishbones as spangles. Small sections of the iridescent wings of rose-

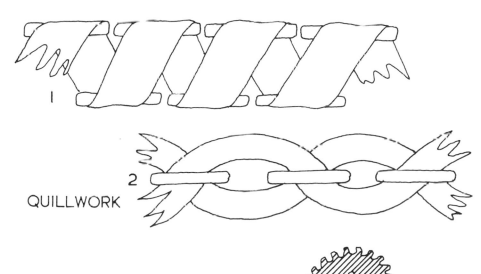

QUILLWORK

Quillwork: after quills have been made pliable they can be laid in pleats and couched with straight stitches (1) or two quills can be threaded through straight stitches (2). Ribbonwork consists of applying gathered ribbon, usually in floral designs

RIBBONWORK

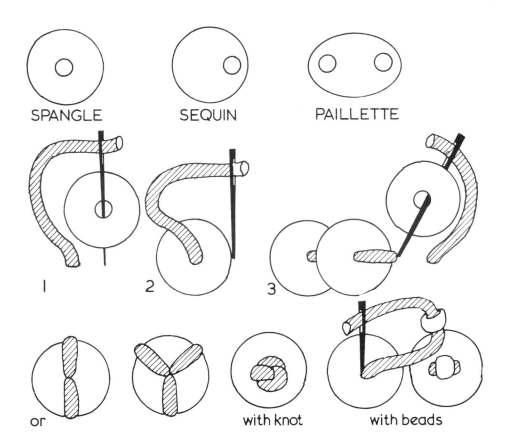

SPANGLE   SEQUIN   PAILLETTE

1   2   3

or   with knot   with beads

Some of the ways by which spangles, sequins and paillettes can be attached to the ground fabric include single long running stitches, two or three worked from each hole: or else French knots or retaining beads can be employed

(*Opposite*) Mid-nineteenth-century net panel worked in metal thread and straw techniques mainly in long-and-short and satin stitches and with applied paper flowers

beetles or small bones from heads of cod, haddock or other fish were sewn on to fabric. The bones were cleaned and boiled so that they became transparent and shiny and, when dried, they could easily be pierced by a needle.

Quillwork

Worked in the past by Indian women in many areas of North America, this peculiar couching technique used dyed quills from birds or porcupines usually laid on to hide or birch-bark; in the latter case the work can be called bark embroidery.

To make them pliable, quills were softened in water and flattened by hand or teeth. They were then couched with sinew, sometimes with the quills folded in pleated formation, or as linked chains as in the diagram on p 169.

Ribbon embroidery

Also known as silk ribbon embroidery, this was especially practised in the third quarter of the nineteenth century. Lengths of gathered ribbon were applied to fabric, often with floral designs as the crinkly edges of the ribbons looked like petals.

Seed embroidery

Seeds, usually from cucumbers, melons or Indian corn, are dried, dyed and sewn as beads or spangles to the ground fabric. A technique popular in Europe in the late nineteenth century, it is practised today in northern Thailand and Burma.

Spangles

Spangles are small flat discs with one or more holes through which retaining stitches are worked. They are usually made of metal or plastic although nacre embroidery, also known as mother-of-pearl work, requires spangles made of that substance. In some instances seeds, shells, beetles' wings and fishbones can also be attached as spangles.

Spangles have been used by European embroiderers from the fifteenth century. Technically the spangle family includes:

Spangles, circular discs with one central hole.
Sequins, circular discs with one hole at one side.
Paillettes, especially popular with dressmakers during the last 120 years, are often long and narrow, with a variety of outer edge formations, and two holes, one each end.

All forms of the spangle family can be attached to the ground fabric by various methods. Long running stitches can be worked from a hole to the outer edge of the disc, French knots can be executed through the hole, attached to the ground beneath, or a small bead can be held in place above that hole.

Straw

In the main, straw work or straw embroidery implies the use of individual straws, sometimes split, stitched on fabric, usually muslin, and used as costume decoration. Alternatively straw has sometimes been woven into a fabric for embroidery, or three or more straws have been plaited into a braid subsequently applied to a fabric.

In the 1860s, especially in England and America, there was temporarily a craze for another form of straw work. Parallel rows of straws were laid on canvas and densely couched with woollen stitches, rather in the manner of or nué.

Individual straws are difficult to manage and in order to make them pliable they should be damp when being laid on ground fabric.

26. Needlepoint or canvas work

This section is a basic introduction to the main features of needlepoint, a form of needlework which, more than any other, is practised by men and women around the world today. Other chapters relating to the technique include those covering Bargello, chain stitches, crewel embroidery, cross-stitches, Hardanger, Hedebo, lettering, metal-thread work, pulled-thread work, samplers and straight stitches.

Needlepoint, the increasingly popular term for canvas work, also confusingly called 'tapestry', can refer to any needlework executed on canvas, though in Britain, true needlepoint is a hand-made lace. As well as the ubiquitous tent stitch, also known as petit point, literally hundreds of different stitches are worked on canvas and adventurous embroiderers today are perfecting such techniques as chain stitch and Hedebo on a wide-meshed canvas rather than fine-weave ground.

Tent stitch may have originated in the eastern Mediterranean and the art gradually spread west. The earliest surviving English canvas work is the Calthorpe purse, worked in 1540 with about 1,250 silk tent stitches to each square inch of linen canvas. By the latter part of that century professional and amateur needleworkers were embellishing canvas especially in the form of pictures and decorative furnishings.

In America, one of the first records of the technique was in the 1657 Bradford Inventory, although the earliest surviving examples date from the eighteenth century. Sometimes the same design was executed many times. There are, for instance, at least fifty-eight versions of the 'Boston Common' or 'fishing lady' picture showing a lady fishing with views of the Common behind. Various details of the scene differ

'Fishing lady' picture, possibly worked by Mrs Sylvanus Bourne of Barnstable, Massachusetts, in the middle of the eighteenth century (linen canvas embroidered mainly in wool in tent stitch and silk, metal threads and beads, 63 × 128cm [24¼ × 50½in]). It is now thought that the lady herself could have been adapted from an early eighteenth-century English playing card

Mid-nineteenth-century Berlin woolwork sampler (linen worked with wool, silk and silver threads in brick, cross, Florentine, Hungarian and satin stitches, also laid and couched work, and with beads, 3m × 10cm [121¼ × 4in])

from one work to another but the lady herself, now thought to have been copied from a contemporary playing card, is found on each needlework.

During much of the nineteenth century, needleworkers on both sides of the Atlantic were devoted to Berlin woolwork. By 1805 hand-coloured paper graph patterns, first published in Berlin, were available in great numbers. Patterns were copied, typically in a soft worsted known as Berlin, German or zephyr wool, in cross and other stitches on coarse canvas. Beads and ribbons and a wider variety of threads and cruder colours were used by later embroiderers and the technique generally had declined in popularity by about 1880.

Materials

Persian, tapisserie or crewel wools threaded on a tapestry needle are almost universally used today, on one of the many single, double or interlock canvases available (see chapter 18).

Instead of purchasing individual materials, the beginner may prefer to buy a kit. Many different designs are available, especially in needlepoint, with instructions, wools and canvas, sometimes marked with the pattern.

Needlepoint should always be worked with the canvas stretched on a frame as, unless interlock canvas is used, distortion is possible.

Methods of working

All edges of canvas should be bound with tape and the main area of ground marked with the centre. Since needlepoint is a counted-thread technique, all designing should be done consistently by counting threads or pairs of threads (or, if preferred,

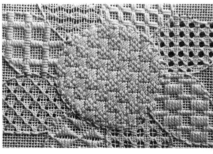

These two photographs illustrate the wide variety of effects that can be obtained by working on canvas. The detail is of a panel designed and worked by Chottie Alderson in which much of the canvas is left exposed. The cushion, designed and worked by Anna Pearson, has all the ground covered with different needlepoint stitches (cushion 30.5 × 39.4cm [12 × 15½in])

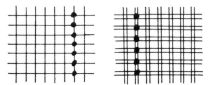
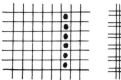

Either threads or holes should
be counted consistently

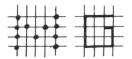
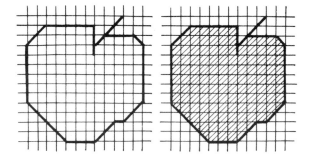

Outlines can be marked by dots at
the intersections of warp and
weft threads or by a continuous
line going through those
intersections.
Marked outlines can, if required,
be filled in with marker,
preferably the same colour as the
embroidery thread

by counting holes between threads of single-weave or main holes between pairs of threads of double-weave canvas).

Here are some of the methods of transposing designs on to canvas:

a The design can be painted with oil paint or non-run fibre marker. Each marker should be tested on each piece of canvas as sometimes the sizing on the latter causes the ink to run or bleed. Either the outline of a design can be drawn on the intersections of the canvas or entire areas of ground fabric can be marked. When dark-coloured thread is to be used on a pale canvas, it is a good idea to mark that area of canvas with the same colour ink to prevent any small bits of canvas colour showing through the finished work.

b The canvas can be laid over an outline drawing on paper. The lines show through the meshes of the canvas and the pattern can be transposed accordingly.

c Double-weave canvas can be trammed. Long straight stitches are worked horizontally between pairs of weft threads, indicating the colours of the tent stitches which are to be worked over them. Tramming provides a padding to the finished stitching.

d Alternatively, a design can simply be worked on to an unmarked canvas, the pattern counted stitch by stitch from a paper graph.

Outlines of motifs are usually stitched before large areas are infilled, and it is a good idea to work test sections of each colour before working large areas to determine how that colour blends into the overall design. In most cases all motifs are worked before reserves are stitched.

Sometimes two pieces of canvas have to be joined, and this can be done in the manner illustrated on p 178.

Stitches

For reasons of clarity, most drawings in this chapter show single-weave canvas except where double-weave is more generally employed.

Drawings are all executed with one *line* representing one *thread* of canvas. Some techniques are illustrated worked in white and shaded yarn to highlight the finished effect.

MARKING A CANVAS

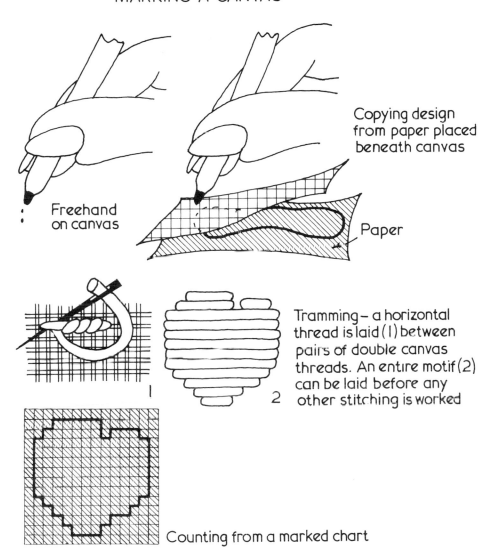

Freehand on canvas

Copying design from paper placed beneath canvas

Paper

Tramming – a horizontal thread is laid (1) between pairs of double canvas threads. An entire motif (2) can be laid before any other stitching is worked

Counting from a marked chart

The fundamental needlepoint stitch is tent stitch, which can be worked in continental or basketweave formation. As already stated, tent stitch is sometimes known as petit point. Cross stitch is covered in chapter 12.

Other needlepoint stitches, predominantly filling stitches, include Aubusson or rep stitch, brick stitch and Byzantine, cashmere, chequer and chevron stitches.

Chottie's plaid stitch, a reversible tent stitch technique with infinite colour and tartan possibilities, is called after its innovator, Chottie Alderson, and is one of the most exciting twentieth-century needlepoint forms.

The list here continues with flat stitch and Gobelin stitch, also known as oblique Gobelin or a form of gros point, with encroaching, plaited and wide variations. Greek stitch is a form of herringbone stitch. Jacquard stitch is diagrammed on p 182, followed by knitting stitch, sometimes called tapestry stitch, and knotted or Persian knot stitch.

Two pieces of canvas can be joined together (embroidered areas are shaded): **1** Two straight edges of canvas are laid together, overlapping one or two warp threads, with weft threads aligned, and joined with straight stitches between weft threads. **2** If two worked pieces of canvas are to be joined, stitching should be worked a few threads back from the edge that will be joined, and rows should end unevenly to give a zigzag formation as illustrated (a). The two pieces of canvas are then joined as at (1), before stitching is executed right across the seam from one piece of canvas to the other (b)

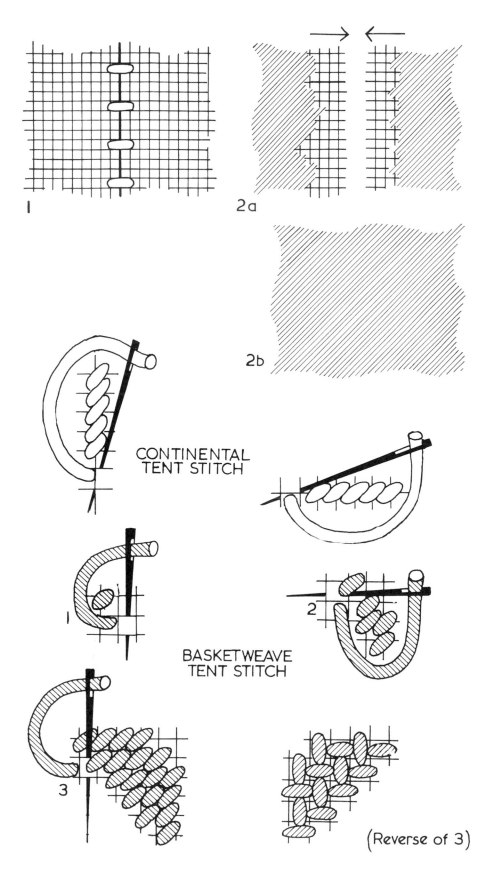

HALF-CROSS STITCH

Half-cross stitch, which can cause some distortion of canvas but requires the least amount of thread

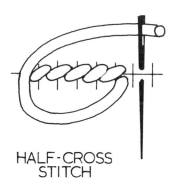

Continental stitch causes most distortion. Worked either vertically or horizontally this is a firm stitch which requires maximum amounts of thread. Basketweave stitch produces an even stitch and, unlike the two forms above, areas worked can be extended at any point without a resulting 'ridge' at the join. Basketweave requires more thread than half-cross stitch but there is no distortion of canvas as, starting from the upper right hand corner of an area to be stitched, rows are formed as illustrated with resulting alternate and opposing 'pulls' of canvas. An interesting basket or woven effect results on the reverse

CONTINENTAL TENT STITCH

BASKETWEAVE TENT STITCH

(Reverse of 3)

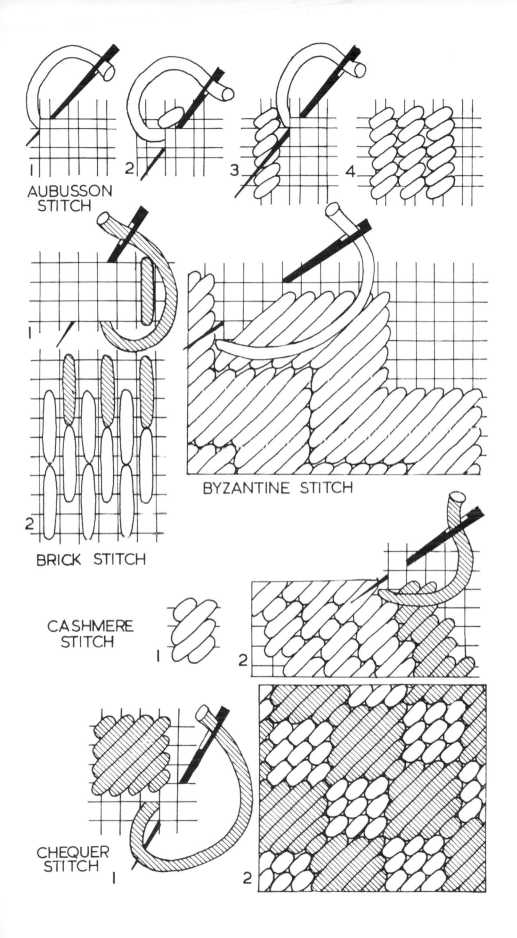

AUBUSSON
STITCH

1 2 3 4

BRICK STITCH

1

2

BYZANTINE STITCH

CASHMERE
STITCH

1

2

CHEQUER
STITCH

1

2

179

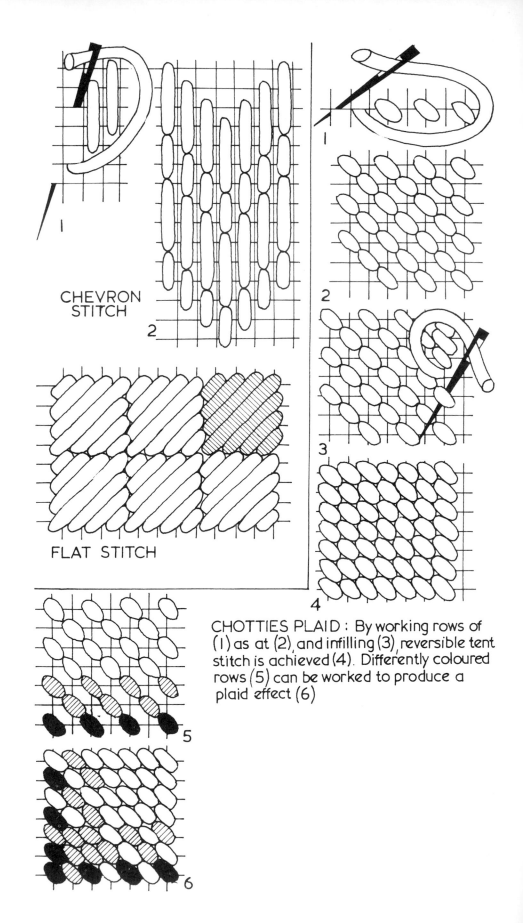

CHEVRON
STITCH

FLAT STITCH

CHOTTIES PLAID : By working rows of
(1) as at (2), and infilling (3), reversible tent
stitch is achieved (4). Differently coloured
rows (5) can be worked to produce a
plaid effect (6)

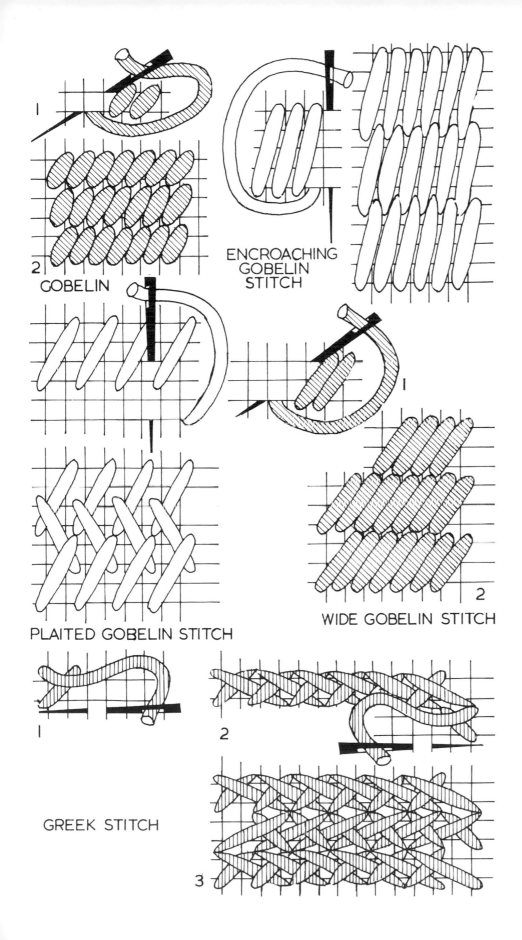

1

2
GOBELIN

ENCROACHING
GOBELIN
STITCH

PLAITED GOBELIN STITCH

1

2
WIDE GOBELIN STITCH

GREEK STITCH

1

2

3

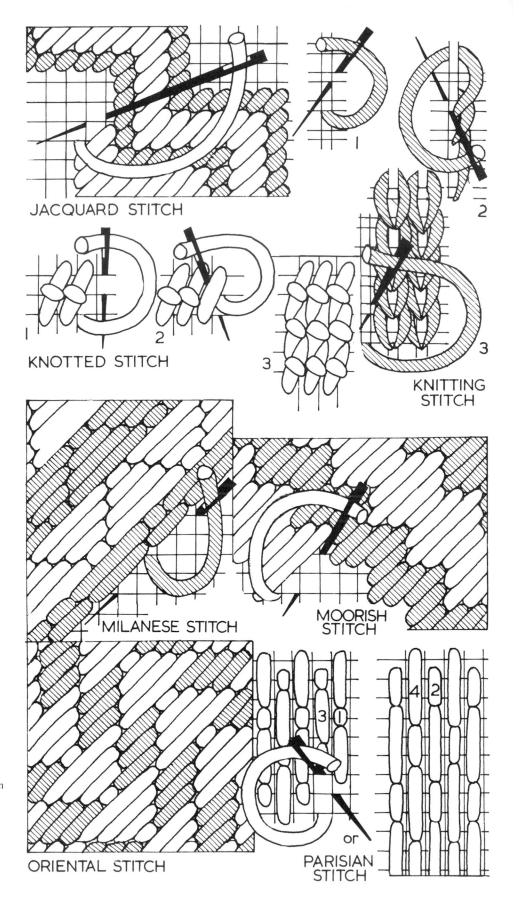

JACQUARD STITCH

KNOTTED STITCH

KNITTING STITCH

MILANESE STITCH

MOORISH STITCH

ORIENTAL STITCH

PARISIAN STITCH

(*Opposite, above*) Embroidery need never be dull! (Anchor stranded cotton display in the Needlewoman Shop in London)

(*Below*) The hill tribes of Northern Thailand are famous for stunning needleworks. This appliqué mat of white cotton hemmed to blue cotton has golden dot stitches added (19cm [7½in] square)

Needleworkers in many parts of the
world execute delightful
autobiographical fabric
pictures. This Colombian scene
is signed Beatriz Jimenez (cotton
decorated with hemmed
appliqué, padded work and
surface stitchery, 152 × 183cm
[60 × 72in])

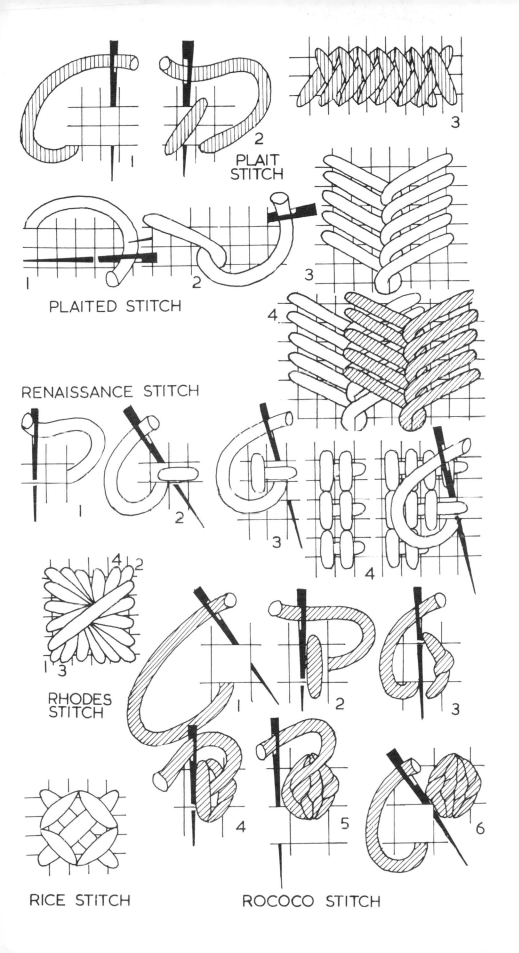

PLAIT
STITCH

PLAITED STITCH

RENAISSANCE STITCH

RHODES
STITCH

RICE STITCH

ROCOCO STITCH

185

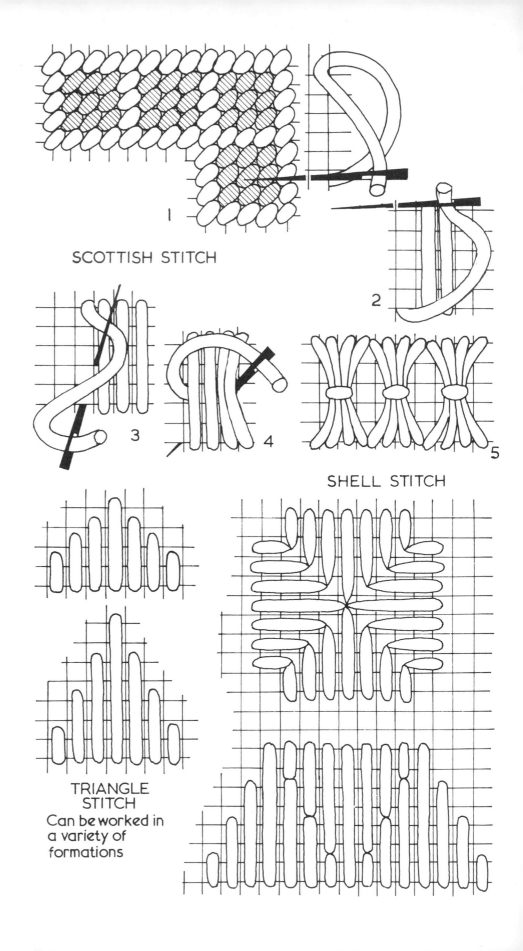

SCOTTISH STITCH

1

2

3

4

5

SHELL STITCH

TRIANGLE
STITCH
Can be worked in
a variety of
formations

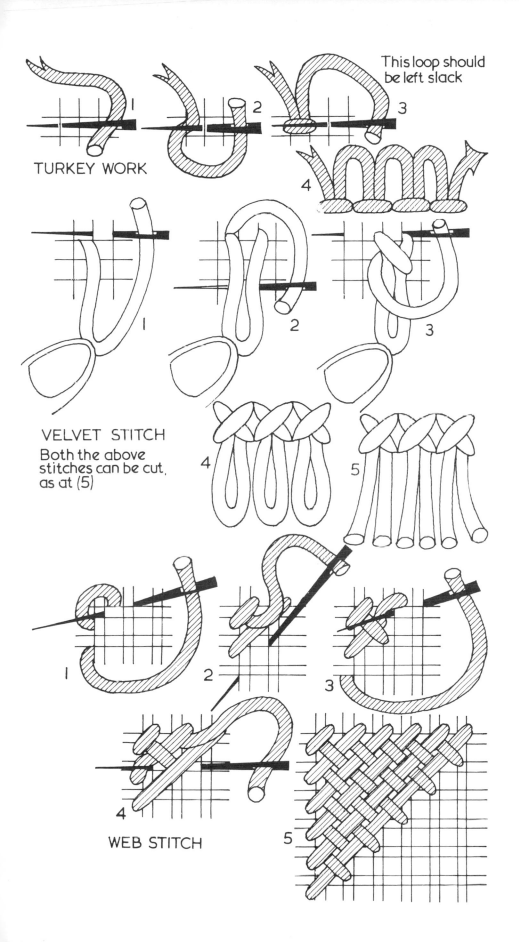

This loop should be left slack

TURKEY WORK

1 2 3

4

VELVET STITCH
Both the above
stitches can be cut,
as at (5)

1 2 3

4 5

WEB STITCH

1 2 3

4 5

SHADING – Lighter areas are
generally inside a motif (1). Strands
of thread can be variegated (2)

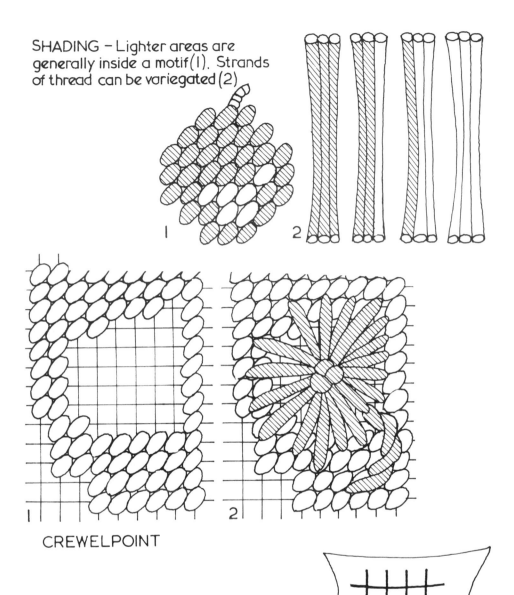

1   2

CREWELPOINT

1   2

NEEDLEPOINT ON
EVENWEAVE

Stitches are worked over waste
canvas which is then removed

1

2

3

Milanese, Moorish and oriental stitches are among the different filling techniques available, and the illustrations continue with Parisian, plait and plaited stitches (pp 182, 185). Renaissance stitch comes next, followed by Rhodes stitch and rice or crossed-corners cross stitch, diagrammed in detail in chapter 12.

Rococo stitch was sometimes in the seventeenth century known as queen's stitch. Scottish, shell and triangle stitches are also illustrated. Turkey work, also known as plush stitch, and velvet or Astrakhan work can either be left with loops or cut as shown. The last of the main stitches shown is web stitch.

(Many other needlepoint stitches can be found in the plentiful supply of specialist books available.)

Shading and blending

There are certain recognized tips to help perfect shading within one area of canvas.

Lighter colours, used to highlight a certain area, are normally worked towards the centre of that area. Similarly, darker colours, implying shade, are usually worked towards the edges of an area. Abrupt colour changes and straight vertical rows at the ends of colour blocks should be avoided wherever possible.

Shading can be achieved by blending together differently coloured strands of wool. Using three strands of Persian yarn blended and worked in the following order:

3 strands of red
2 strands of red and one of yellow
1 strand of red and two of yellow
3 strands of yellow

illustrates this point.

Further needlepoint techniques

Crewelpoint

Tent stitch is often worked for the reserves, or background, of a motif itself executed in stitches not usually associated with needlepoint. In this instance the reserves should be worked first, followed by infilling of motifs with long-and-short and other crewel stitches which overlap the edges of the tent stitches to cover the canvas completely.

Needlepoint on evenweave

This denotes needlepoint stitches worked on evenweave fabric. Embroidery can be worked either straight on to linen with thread count of from 18 to 35 per 2.5cm (1 in), wool, Hardanger or Aida cotton or, alternatively, waste canvas, specially loose-weave canvas with fine threads. An area of this canvas is lightly tacked to the ground fabric and needlepoint is worked through both canvas and fabric, making sure that the needle never pierces canvas threads; stitches should be worked more tightly than usual. When all the embroidery has been worked the individual warp and weft threads of the canvas are carefully withdrawn, leaving aligned stitches on the fabric beneath.

27. Net embroidery

Net embroidery, also known as tulle embroidery, employs darning and running stitches, eyelets, loop and satin stitches and appliqué on a ground of hand- or machine-made open net.

One of the earliest known items of English net embroidery was worked in 1295. Formerly known as lacis, filet darning or spiderwork, net embroidery was worked with linen thread pattern-darned on to hand-made linen net with a square or hexagonal mesh in the manner illustrated.

Many later net embroideries look like lace, which is not surprising as the art of lace-making evolved from cutwork and lacis in the sixteenth century, and since that time embroidered forms have often simulated lace. Embroiderers worked fine patterns on net grounds, copying lace patterns, although especially during the eighteenth century such techniques as Dresden work, pulled thread on muslin, were preferred to net embroidery.

The invention in 1801 of a net-making machine revived interest in net embroidery as large supplies of machine-made net were available. This led to the evolution of some whitework techniques covered in chapter 36.

One specific form of net embroidery was Limerick 'lace', an industry established by Charles Walker in Ireland in 1829 to produce net items embroidered with tamboured chain stitch, darning and running stitches and a variety of filling stitches. This hand-worked 'lace', superseded by machine-made laces, can be compared with Carrickmacross, fully covered in chapter 36.

Section of net embroidery on a needlework sampler worked in 1896

190

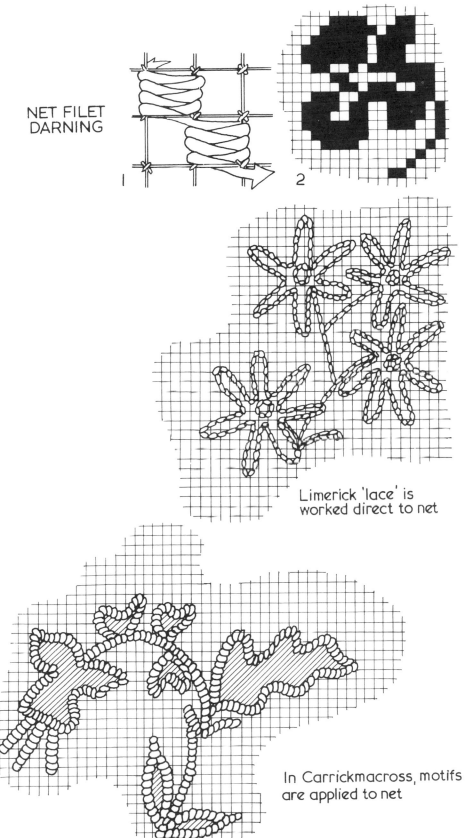

NET FILET DARNING

1

2

Net forms, all illustrated here on square-mesh net. In Limerick 'lace' the design is sometimes tamboured straight on to the net, a different process from Carrickmacross work

Limerick 'lace' is worked direct to net

In Carrickmacross, motifs are applied to net

191

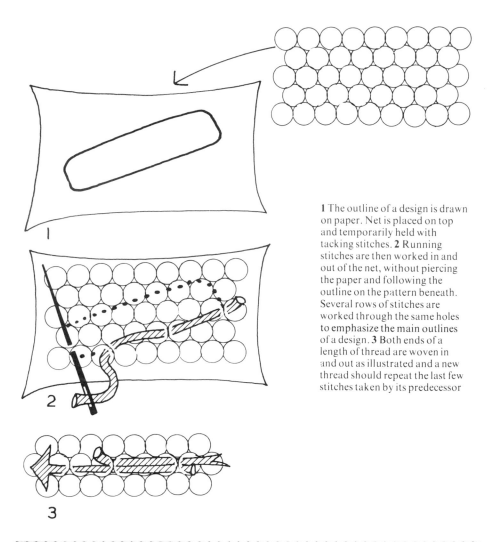

1 The outline of a design is drawn on paper. Net is placed on top and temporarily held with tacking stitches. 2 Running stitches are then worked in and out of the net, without piercing the paper and following the outline on the pattern beneath. Several rows of stitches are worked through the same holes to emphasize the main outlines of a design. 3 Both ends of a length of thread are woven in and out as illustrated and a new thread should repeat the last few stitches taken by its predecessor

Infilling can be worked with running stitches taken in and out of the meshed ground in a variety of formations

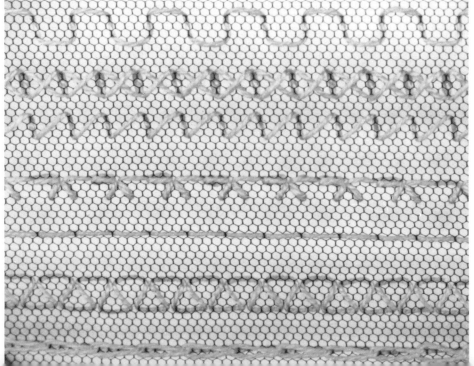

Materials

Net embroidery is today usually worked with white or cream stranded cotton or coton à broder on net the same shade. Hexagonal apertures are easier to work than squares, and to test a fine net which will be less likely to tear during embroidery, a small section should be stretched by inserting a needle. Good-quality net should stretch and not tear. Net embroidery should be worked with a tapestry needle and a frame should always be used.

Methods of working

A required motif should be designed with its area divided into smaller sections, and the outlines drawn on paper which is then tacked beneath the net. Running stitches are worked in and out of the meshes of the net following the outline of the pattern below. No knots or 'bumps' should be formed and each new thread should lie alongside the last few stitches of the previous thread. Several rows of running stitches are worked in and out of the same apertures until all outlines of the sections of the motif are clearly defined.

The paper pattern can then be removed and the sections of the motif embroidered with filling stitches, possibly some of those illustrated here. It is imperative that each new infilling thread should be started from one of the clearly-defined segment outlines, and that it should end at another outline, and thread ends can be unobtrusively secured within the running stitches of those outlines.

Net can also be embellished with the addition of appliqué.

28. Padded and raised work

This section covers embroidery elevated by one means or another to a three-dimensional effect (see colour illustration on p 166).

One of the best-loved forms of padded work is now sometimes called 'stump-work'. Technically known as 'raised work' this implies tiny applied figures and other motifs formed from moulds, padding of cotton wool, wood, wax or ravellings, lengths of thread unpicked from cloth. These figures, sometimes stitched to a linen ground, are decorated with pieces of fabric, parchment, hair, beads, pearls, silk-wrapped wire known as purl and other materials, including embroidery stitches. Then the surplus linen around the edges of the motifs is carefully cut away and they are applied to a main ground fabric, usually white satin and possibly already stamped with an outline design, a feature that may in the past have led to the technique being known as 'on the stamp'. Surface embroidery may be worked direct to the ground fabric and such additions as small pieces of mica are sewn on to simulate windows.

Especially in the third quarter of the seventeenth century, English needlewomen included raised work on pictures with religious themes. This panel shows the Judgement of Solomon, with the king about to decide which of two women can claim a living baby, here being held by the executioner (white satin decorated with raised work and surface embroidery, 33.2 × 44.4cm [13⅛ × 17½in])

From the end of the fourteenth century ecclesiastical vestments were sometimes decorated with metal threads laid over thick linen threads and then couched.

During the Elizabethan era there was a certain amount of metal-thread raised work and buttonhole stitching only partly attached to the ground fabric, but the next main period of padded work was from 1640 to 1680, the apogee of raised work. Panels with religious themes, many taken from the Old Testament, and portraits of Charles I and Charles II were often made into pictures, mirror frames or boxes.

Today padded work, following many seventeenth-century techniques, is enjoying a revival, especially in America. Creative embroiderers also incorporate quilting and other needlework forms with padded work.

Materials and methods of working

Stumpwork

Although white satin is the traditional material, most fabrics other than canvas are suitable for the main ground. A wide variety of small pieces of left-over fabric, assorted wool, cotton, silk and metal threads and spangles, beads and other oddments can be employed for the additional motifs, and muslin takes the place of the linen previously used as their base.

Cotton wool, foam rubber or other wadding is required for the padding, and

'Grey vows', designed and worked by Polly Hope. The figures, formed from men's grey suit linings, are decorated with lamé, silver spangles, ribbons and buttons, machined to a backing and quilted by hand (overall size 3.2m [125in] square and total weight 16 kilos [35lb])

The method of forming a raised work motif: **1** The outline is drawn on muslin. **2** Cotton wool or another padding is laid on the motif and held in place with long stay stitches which must always stay within the outline. Alternatively, padding can be held by another piece of muslin laid on the motif and hemmed to the outline. **3** Pieces of fabric are carefully applied to form 'clothes'. **4** Embroidery is worked to indicate facial and other details, after which the motif is cut out from the muslin about 6mm (¼in) outside the outline. Small snips are made to accommodate curves and the excess is turned under. **5** The motif is then hemmed to a main ground, traditionally white satin, and surface embroidery executed direct to that ground

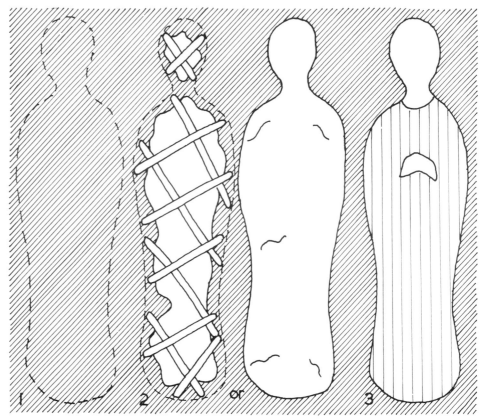

crewel or chenille needles are generally used. As padding makes it difficult to move a small frame from one area of the ground to another a large frame should be set with the entire area of main fabric exposed. The muslin can then be put on to a smaller frame as long as an entire motif is visible at once.

The outline of each motif is drawn on the muslin and then cotton wool or other wadding can be placed within the outline of a motif and held down by long tacking stitches worked from one side of the motif to the other or by another piece of muslin hemmed as illustrated. The shape is then covered decoratively with applied pieces of fabric and stitches (see below).

When the motif is complete, the muslin is cut to about 6mm ($\frac{1}{4}$in) of the outside of

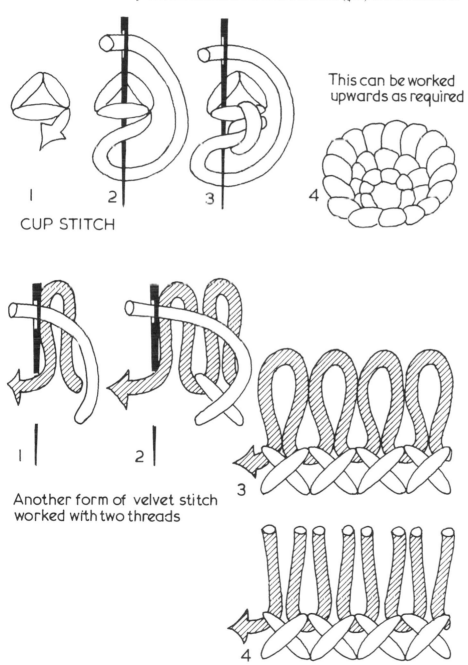

This can be worked upwards as required

1 2 3 4

CUP STITCH

1 2 3

Another form of velvet stitch worked with two threads

4

197

Small areas of needlepoint can be applied to a ground fabric. Excess warp and weft threads of the canvas (1) are taken by plunging (2) through to the reverse of the fabric, leaving needlepoint above the surface (3)

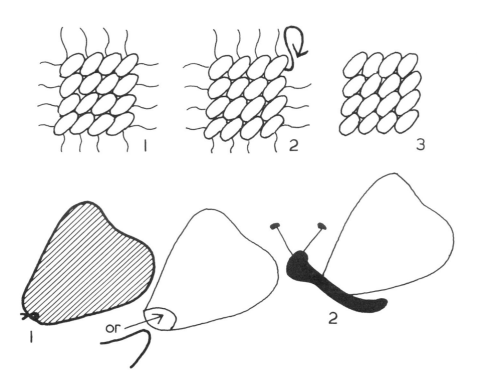

Wire can be used to support three-dimensional motifs. A length of wire is either formed into a frame and buttonhole stitch worked on it or it is inserted between a sandwich of fabric (1) to support a rigid motif (2)

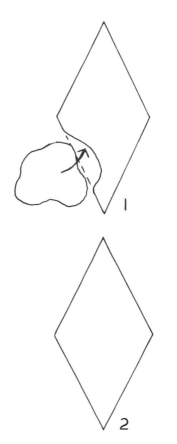

Some embroiderers prefer to apply another piece of fabric direct to the ground. Just before application stitches are finished stuffing is inserted (1) and the gap is closed (2)

the motif. After making small snips to accommodate curves, this excess is turned under and the motif is applied to the main satin or other ground fabric.

Stitches embellishing stumpwork, either worked on motifs or direct to the ground, include general filling stitches (see chapter 10), buttonhole and chain stitches, cup stitch, satin stitch and, especially for figures' faces, split stitch. Turkey work, velvet stitch, bullion and French knots and laid and couched work are also employed.

Other techniques traditionally associated with stumpwork include the application of needlepoint motifs, generally worked with minute tent stitches and sometimes incorporating mica. Narrow wire can also be used to support such fragile shapes as flower petals or butterflies' wings.

Embroiderers today can attach miniature doll or animal figures directly to a ground fabric. Alternatively a flat shape can be applied to the ground with a small gap left through which stuffing is pushed before application stitches are completed.

Other padded work

Although associated primarily with metal-thread work, embroidery over laid strings or pieces of parchment, card, felt or stuff can also be executed with wool, linen, cotton, silk or other threads.

If laid strings are to be used they should be placed in position on the ground fabric and held with stay stitches before the required embroidery is worked over them.

Shapes used for padding can be cut from a sheet of the required material and held in place with tacking stitches or hemming. Contoured padding can be formed in the manner illustrated. Padding is then covered by surface darning or another technique.

One form of padded embroidery, guimped work, implies that a padding shape is laid on the ground fabric and threads, laid in zigzag formation from one side to the other above the padding, are couched at each bend.

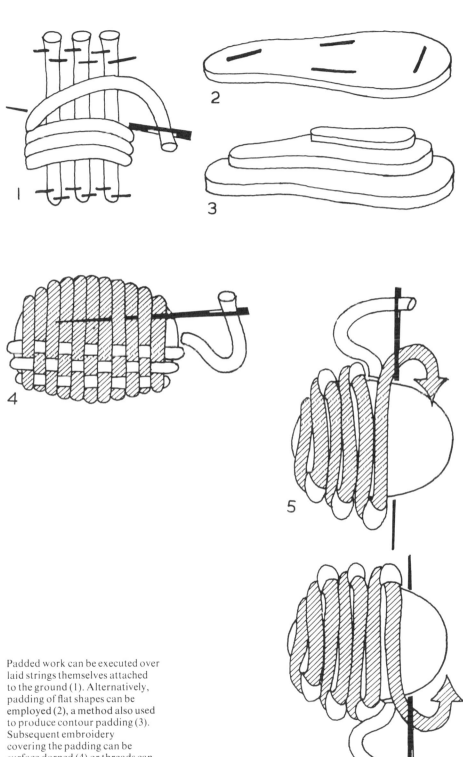

Padded work can be executed over laid strings themselves attached to the ground (1). Alternatively, padding of flat shapes can be employed (2), a method also used to produce contour padding (3). Subsequent embroidery covering the padding can be surface darned (4) or threads can be laid in zigzag formation and couched at each turn (5)

29. Patchwork

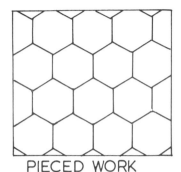

PIECED WORK

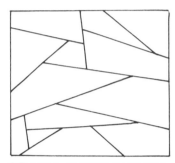

CRAZY PATCHWORK

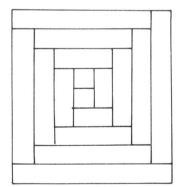

**OVERLAPPING
PATCHWORK**

Patchwork is technically defined as small pieces of fabric sewn together in a planned formation to form a larger area.

The main forms of patchwork are pieced or mosaic work, in which bits of fabric formed over geometric shapes are set one next to the other, crazy or kaleidoscope patchwork, for which irregularly shaped bits of fabric are employed, and overlapping patchwork, sometimes known as log cabin, Canadian or Thai patchwork, in which one shape is sewn overlapping its neighbour. All patchwork variations can be used in conjunction with appliqué and quilting, and machine embroidery.

Section of a crazy quilt made by Jenny Jones, a Welsh lady living in America. Exhibited in a competition in Chicago in 1884, the quilt was later brought back to Wales (quilt composed of nine blocks, each 50.7cm [20in] square, formed from irregularly-shaped patches and with an outer border of dark green velvet with folded ribbon work, overall size 208cm [72in] square)

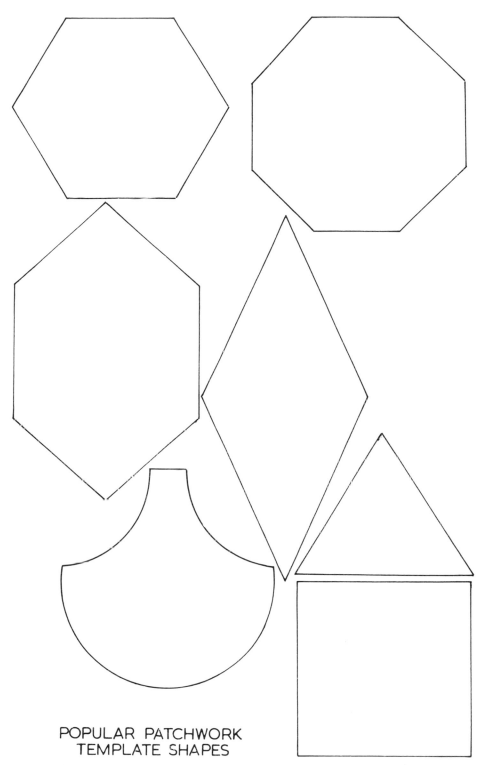

POPULAR PATCHWORK
TEMPLATE SHAPES

The technique of making use of small scraps of fabric has a long history dating back at least as far as the tenth century BC. In more recent times patchwork has been practised by peoples in many parts of the world, especially North America, the Indian sub-continent and south-east Asia. In America from the eighteenth century women used precious scraps of new or left-over fabric to form shapes which were

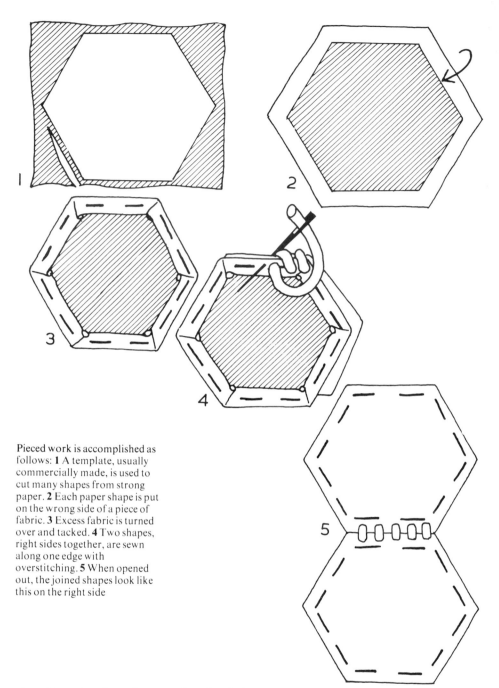

Pieced work is accomplished as follows: **1** A template, usually commercially made, is used to cut many shapes from strong paper. **2** Each paper shape is put on the wrong side of a piece of fabric. **3** Excess fabric is turned over and tacked. **4** Two shapes, right sides together, are sewn along one edge with overstitching. **5** When opened out, the joined shapes look like this on the right side

pieced together in such a way that the designs and colours of the patches sometimes formed 'tumbling block' or 'bear's paw' patterns. Areas of joined patches were made into aprons and other items of clothing, table covers and bed coverlets which were sometimes subsequently quilted.

Materials and methods of working

Pieced work

Materials include a selection of differently coloured pieces of fabric, ideally cotton, and each at least 5cm (2in) square. Sewing cotton and a fine pointed needle, geometric templates and a supply of pencils and paper are required. No form of patchwork is worked on a frame.

A wide variety of exactly proportional hexagonal, diamond, clamshell and other metal or plastic templates is available. Beginners will find hexagons easiest, and curved shapes and those with acute angles more tricky. The template is used as a pattern to cut many shapes from fairly rigid paper (brown wrapping paper is ideal).

Each paper pattern is laid on the wrong side of a piece of fabric with about 6mm

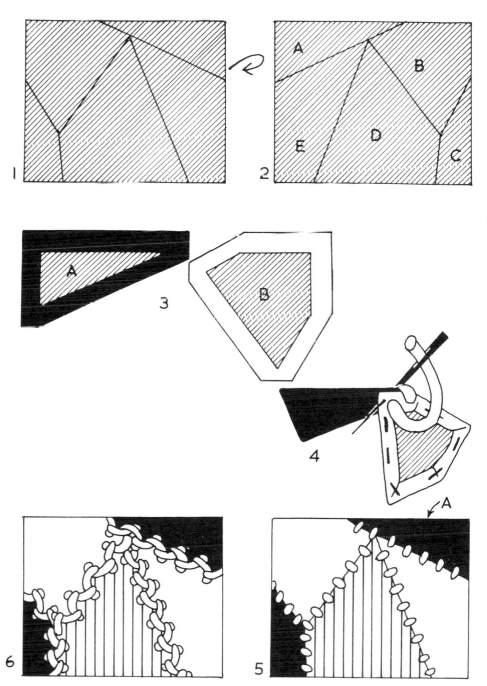

Method of working crazy patchwork: **1** A paper pattern the same size as the intended area of patchwork is divided into segments. **2** Each segment is marked on the reverse. **3** Segments are cut out and each is placed, marked side up, on the wrong side of a bit of fabric. **4** As with pieced work, excess fabric is turned under and tacked in place and, following the original pattern, edges of two adjoining patches are oversewn. When the jigsaw has been put together it is turned to the right side. **5, 6** Seams can be disguised by feather or herringbone stitch

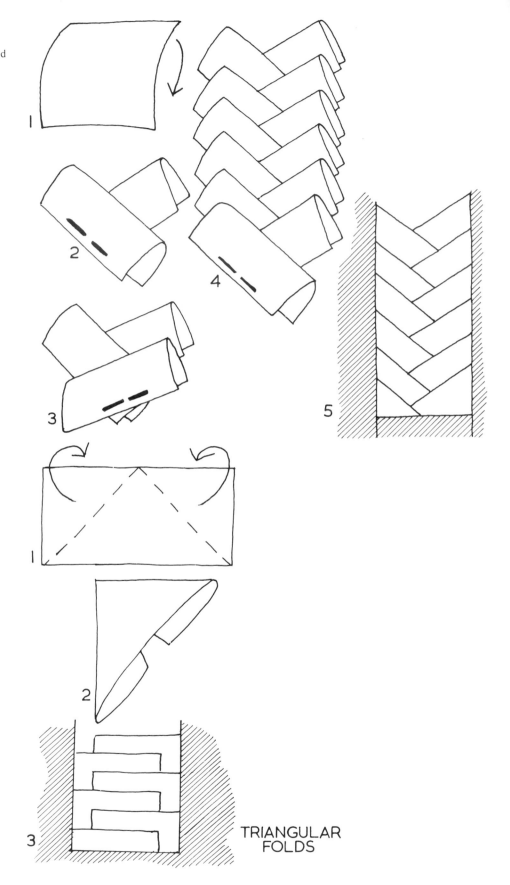

Overlapping patchwork is formed by this method: **1** Rectangular bits of fabric are folded in half. **2** Two folded shapes are placed one on the other, overlapping at a required angle, and sewn through both shapes, away from the folds. **3** A third shape is placed in similar alignment, obscuring the first stitching, and it is itself stitched. **4** A length of overlapping patches is thus built up as illustrated. **5** Untidy edges around the area of overlapping patchwork can be sewn to other pieces of fabric

Overlapping patchwork can be adapted in various ways. Pieces of fabric can be folded into three (1, 2) and sewn together as required (3).

TRIANGULAR FOLDS

($\frac{1}{4}$in) excess all round. This excess is neatly folded over the paper, the corners being pressed well with the fingers to perfect the shape, and temporarily held with tacking.

Adjacent patches are then 'pieced', joined along one edge by being placed right sides together and overstitched along the common edge. The newly joined neighbours can then be opened out.

Each patch must be 'pieced', joined to a neighbour, *along each edge* before the paper shape is removed. Paper shapes around the perimeter of an area of patched fabric should be left in place until the patchwork is hemmed, bound or attached to another area of fabric.

Crazy patchwork

Pieces of fabric of many different patterns and colours are required. Each should be at least 15 × 10cm (6 × 4in), and velvet and other sumptuous materials can be used. Commercial templates are not employed, but other requirements are the same as those for pieced work. Stranded cotton may also be employed.

It is a good idea first to make a paper pattern the same size as the intended area of patched fabric. Pencils and a ruler are used to divide the paper into irregular shapes, each of which should traditionally be less than 12 × 7.5cm (4$\frac{3}{4}$ × 3in). Each shape is numbered or marked on the wrong side to help put the resulting jigsaw back together. The paper is cut out and each shape is placed, marked side up, on the wrong side of a suitable piece of fabric, the excess of which is turned over as in pieced work.

When all the patches have been sewn together with overstitching and the paper shapes removed, the area of patched fabric is turned right side up and feather or herringbone stitches can be worked over the same lines in brightly coloured stranded cotton.

Overlapping patchwork

No paper pattern is necessary for this technique. Rectangular bits of fabric of assorted size, needle and sewing thread are required.

Each fabric bit is folded in half or in triangular formation and two folded bits are

Vogue Paris Original pattern 1653, 2 × 2.5m of mull and scraps of five differently patterned Thai silks were used for this machine-stitched patchwork jacket. Squares and rectangles of silks, smaller bits pieced together, were neatly pressed. Jacket shapes were cut from mull, a silk was placed right side up across the bottom of each shape and tacked on all sides. Another silk was then machined across the top of the first silk, right sides together and through the mull. This 'patch' was opened up, pressed and tacked, and another shape sewn above. When all the mull was covered surplus silk was removed and the jacket made up in the usual way

Pachisi is a popular board game, especially in India

placed one overlapping the other with all folds visible. The two shapes are then stitched together with stitches worked through both shapes as far as possible away from the folds. A third folded shape is then placed, concealing the stitching on the upper shape, to which it is similarly held with stitchery prior to being overlapped by a fourth folded shape, and so on.

Patchwork pachisi design

Pachisi, which may have originated in India before the sixth century, is often called the country's national game. Traditionally played by two, three or four persons, it is alternatively known as India or ludo and is the game from which the simpler western form of ludo derives.

Pachisi is played with counters and dice on a four-armed board which is often easily transportable, made of fabric decorated with laid and couched cord or, as in this instance, of patchwork with subsequent surface stitchery.

Materials

30cm (12in) red cotton fabric 90cm (35½in) wide
30cm (12in) black cotton fabric 90cm (35½in) wide
2 balls Anchor pearl cotton No 8 (here 1 black and 1 yellow No 0290)
Graph paper
Black sewing cotton threaded on a sharp needle
Tacking cotton also threaded on a sharp needle
Piece of black felt 66cm (26in) square, for backing
2 cards of black bias binding (3m, 118in, each card)

Other equipment for playing the game

6 counters for each player
6 'dice', traditionally cowrie shells but thread reels or counters with one marked side will suffice.

Method of making the board

A Following the printed lines of the graph paper, paper squares should be cut so that there are
    96 pieces each 3.8cm (1½in) square
    1 piece 11.4cm (4½in) square.

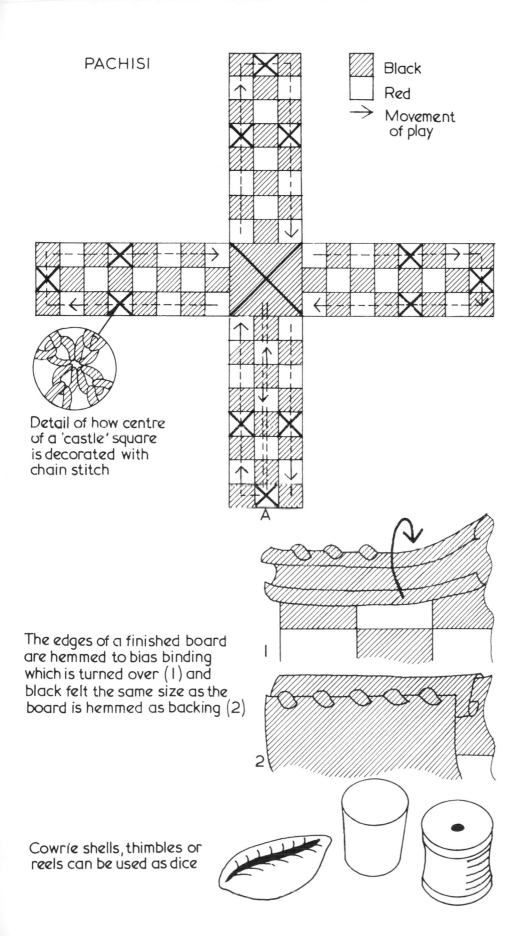

PACHISI

Black
Red
→ Movement of play

Detail of how centre
of a 'castle' square
is decorated with
chain stitch

A

The edges of a finished board
are hemmed to bias binding
which is turned over (1) and
black felt the same size as the
board is hemmed as backing (2)

1

2

Cowrie shells, thimbles or
reels can be used as dice

B The cotton fabric should be cut so that there are

48 pieces red cotton approximately 5cm (2in) square

48 pieces black cotton approximately 5cm (2in) square

1 piece black cotton approximately 12.7cm (5in) square.

C Each piece of cloth should then be tacked, with the excess neatly turned under, to a piece of paper the appropriate size.

D From the wrong side, shapes are then sewn together in the formation illustrated.

E Bias binding is hemmed all around the outside of the finished shape and the paper patterns can be removed.

F Chain stitch is worked on the central square here decorated in yellow pearl cotton, and on twelve other squares, usually in black, as illustrated.

G The bias binding can be turned under and a backing of black felt to fit the board is hemmed to the reverse.

Rules of pachisi

Each player places his counters in the quadrant of the central square (*char-koni*, home) nearest his arm of the board.

Players in turn throw the six 'dice' and the one who achieves the highest number of dice landing mouth or marked side up starts the game, using that number to move one of his counters down the central part (*char*) of his arm.

Thereafter players move in turn, throwing all six 'dice' together and moving as follows:

no 'dice' with marked side up . . . . move 25 points and another throw

1 'dice' with marked side up . . . . move 10 and another throw

2 'dice' with marked sides up . . . . move 2 only

3 'dice' with marked sides up . . . . move 3 only

4 'dice' with marked sides up . . . . move 4 only

5 'dice' with marked sides up . . . . move 5 only

6 'dice' with marked sides up . . . . move 6 only.

Each counter has to make a complete circuit of the entire board in the manner illustrated. When it has returned to A it is taken back up the central *char* to *char-koni*, with the exact number of points required to land at base and retire.

Two or more of one player's counters landing on one square together are thereafter moved around together, thus lessening that player's number of required throws. Except on the castle squares (embroidered with crosses), one player's counter can 'capture' another's and send it back to *char-koni* to start all over again. Any number of different players' counters can rest on one castle square as it is impervious to attack.

30. Pulled-thread work

Pulled-thread work, also known as pulled or drawn fabric embroidery, is a counted-thread technique involving the binding of warp and weft threads to produce holes that form an overall pattern. The difference between this and drawn-thread work (chapter 16) is that in pulled-thread work no threads are actually removed.

Usually filling stitches, pulled-thread stitches are traditionally executed in twisted linen thread on evenweave white or natural cotton or linen fabrics. One of the finest of all types of this technique is Dresden work, typified by flowing floral designs with intricate fillings worked on expecially loosely woven muslin.

The earliest surviving piece of Dresden work is dated 1678 and the technique reached a peak in the middle of the eighteenth century. Although most commonly worked in northern Germany and Scandinavia, it was popular with other

Pulled-thread sampler worked by Rebecke Aasg.n in 1758 (cotton embroidered with linen and silk threads, mainly with pulled-thread techniques with some chain and cross stitches, 33 × 35.5cm [13 × 14in])

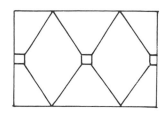

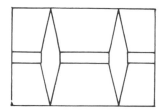

The density of the lace effect is controlled by the tension of the pulling threads

European needlewomen, and it was recorded in Massachusetts as early as 1773. Less expensive than the bobbin lace then in vogue, Dresden work was extensively used for decoration of fichus, aprons, kerchiefs, petticoats and other clothing.

Throughout the western world pulled-thread techniques continued to be employed for adults' and babies' clothes but by the nineteenth century some of the intricacy of Dresden work had been dispensed with. In America the technique was partly superseded by a type of Moravian embroidery as taught by sisters of a religious order from Germany.

In more recent years, pulled-thread work has been a special feature of table linens worked in Scandinavia. A variety of materials, including canvas, is now used particularly in North America.

Materials

Pulled-thread work is traditionally worked with the same coloured fabric and thread, and it is sometimes possible to extract a few threads from the edge of the ground to use as embroidery thread.

Any evenweave fabric and most strong threads can be used, but a possible combination could be Glenshee evenweave linen embroidered with pearl or stranded cottons or coton à border.

For pulled-thread on canvas, a single weave canvas, say 28 per 5cm (2in), would be suitable.

A tapestry needle is required to avoid splitting threads of the ground fabric and a frame is used, partly to facilitate the counting of warp and weft threads.

Methods of working

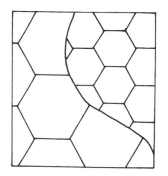

Each stitch within one block should be worked with equal tension, but tension can vary from block to block

Practical instructions in this section refer to fabric (stuff) as well as canvas embroidery. It is helpful, when working areas of different pulled-thread techniques within one design, to follow a pattern already aligned on graph paper. By this means each block of stitching can be carefully centred.

The degree of lace effect of pulled-thread stitches depends on the tension used. The tighter the thread is pulled, the greater the resulting hole. Equal tension should be used for each block within a design, but other blocks on one item can be worked with different tension. It is important to maintain tension at the beginning and end of each line of stitching within a block.

Threads should always be started and finished at the end of a line of stitching. If a new line of stitching, with the same thread, begins in the same hole through which the previous line of stitching ended, a small stitch three threads away should be taken and not pulled tight.

Sometimes long stitches have to be taken across the back of the fabric. As these may show through the finished lacy embroidery, the thread should be darned in and out of the ground fabric as illustrated.

Stitches are drawn here without pull. Many of them are also illustrated, with pull, in the photograph of the eighteenth-century sampler shown at the beginning of the chapter. An embroiderer might like to work his own sampler experimenting with the different effects produced by varying the tension of the stitches diagrammed on the following pages.

Pulled-thread stitches include Algerian stitch, back-stitch rings, basket and cobbler stitches. Faggot stitch is illustrated with double and reversed forms, the latter also known as ground stitch. Festoon stitch is shown, followed by four-sided

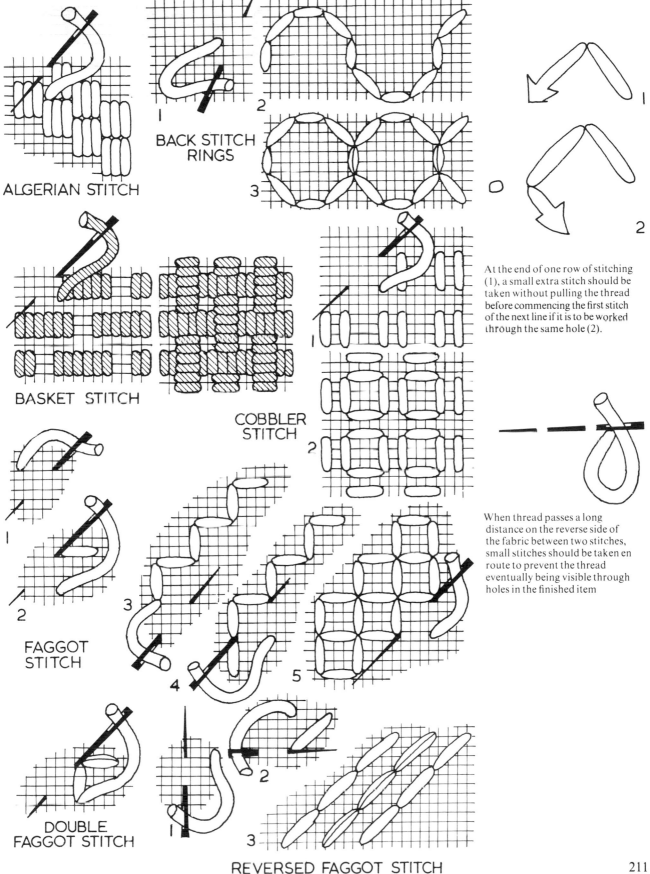

ALGERIAN STITCH

BACK STITCH
RINGS

BASKET STITCH

COBBLER
STITCH

FAGGOT
STITCH

DOUBLE
FAGGOT STITCH

REVERSED FAGGOT STITCH

At the end of one row of stitching (1), a small extra stitch should be taken without pulling the thread before commencing the first stitch of the next line if it is to be worked through the same hole (2).

When thread passes a long distance on the reverse side of the fabric between two stitches, small stitches should be taken en route to prevent the thread eventually being visible through holes in the finished item

211

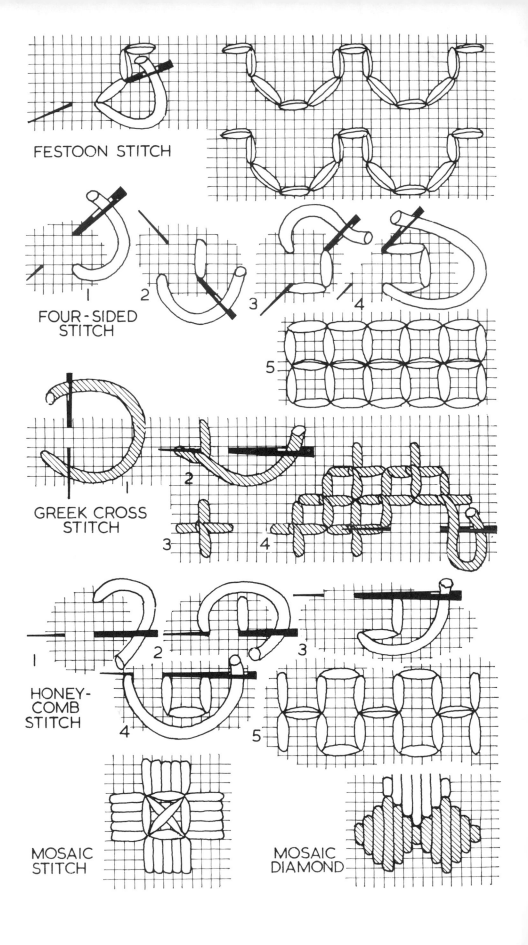

FESTOON STITCH

FOUR-SIDED
STITCH

GREEK CROSS
STITCH

HONEY-
COMB
STITCH

MOSAIC
STITCH

MOSAIC
DIAMOND

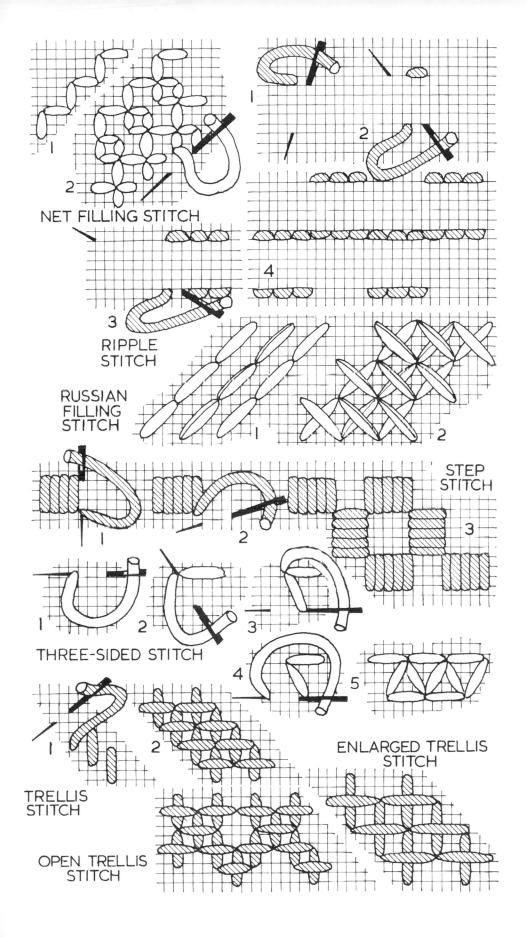

NET FILLING STITCH

RIPPLE
STITCH

RUSSIAN
FILLING
STITCH

STEP
STITCH

THREE-SIDED STITCH

ENLARGED TRELLIS
STITCH

TRELLIS
STITCH

OPEN TRELLIS
STITCH

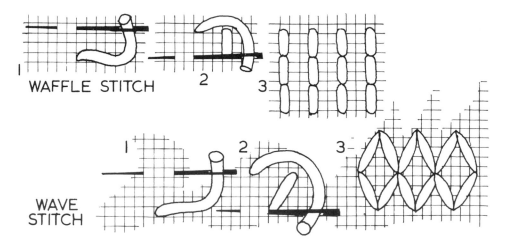

WAFFLE STITCH

WAVE
STITCH

stitch, sometimes called punch stitch, open groundwork or single faggot stitch. Greek cross stitch can alternatively be termed Greek four-sided stitch and honeycomb stitch is also known as net passing stitch.

Other pulled-thread stitches include mosaic and mosaic diamond stitches. Net filling stitch is sometimes called drawn faggot stitch. Ripple stitch is diagrammed followed by Russian filling stitch, step and three-sided stitches, the last also known as Bermuda faggoting, lace and Turkish stitch. Trellis stitch can be called ridge stitch or diagonal or open raised band. The stitches illustrated here end with waffle stitch and wave stitch, the latter alternatively called straight-line stitch or window filling.

Other stitches including eyelets and satin stitch can be sucessfully worked as pulled thread and, on canvas, pulled thread can be combined with tent and other needlepoint stitches.

31. Quilting

Quilting, sometimes called pourpointing, is the art of stitching together two or more layers of fabric, usually with back or running stitches, with padding to provide insulation and protection.

One of the three main universal forms of quilting is generally known as Durham, English or wadded quilting. This consists of equal areas of upper fabric, interlining or padding and main lining of muslin or mull, with stitching worked directly through all three layers.

Cord or Italian quilting, on the other hand, requires only two layers of fabric. An upper layer of silk, satin or similar densely-woven fabric is placed on a lining of butter muslin. The design, typically executed in pairs of parallel lines, is stitched through both layers and, from the reverse, cord is then threaded through the resulting channels. If a thinner fabric is preferred for the upper layer, brightly-coloured cord can subsequently be threaded through the channels to effect what is known as shadow quilting.

The last main technique, trapunto or stuffed quilting, has motifs outlined with single lines and stitched through two layers of cloth, usually silk or linen with muslin lining. Some segments of a design are then carefully padded with bits of cotton wool, prised through from the rear of the item.

False quilting, also known as flat or Queen Anne quilting, was especially popular in England in the eighteenth century, when golden silk back stitch was worked on fabric, possibly with muslin lining but with no extra padding. Another related technique which does not require any sandwiched padding is herringbone quilting, also called cord quilting. Cord laid on the wrong side of fabric is couched with herringbone stitch so that, on the front, parallel lines of running stitch appear giving an effect similar to that of genuine Italian quilting.

It is thought that quilting, one of the oldest embroidery techniques, originated in the east and still today quilted jackets are practical Chinese cold-weather garments. Although the art had long been employed in Europe, quilting became popular in England in the late seventeenth and early eighteenth centuries. White or cream silk or linen petticoats, jackets, waistcoats and coverlets were decoratively quilted, usually in English quilting with a scrolled meandering or vermicular pattern of feathers, fans or scallops, although Italian quilting padded with thick linen cord was sometimes preferred.

In America especially, quilting has long been a communal art. Women needleworkers gather together to work on one item, sometimes with the upper layer formed from patchwork or decorated with appliqué, spread out on a large horizontal frame with two rollers, and such 'quilting bees' continue a tradition started by some of the earliest settlers in North America. Among coverlets worked by more than one embroiderer are special 'marriage' and 'friendship' pieces and those made by friends to celebrate the recipient's coming-of-age.

Quilting continues to be a popular needlework form, both for practical and decorative purposes. As well as traditional quilting, experimental forms of hand quilting and working on domestic sewing machines are now being increasingly employed by creative embroiderers.

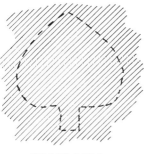

ENGLISH QUILTING

ITALIAN QUILTING

SHADOW QUILTING

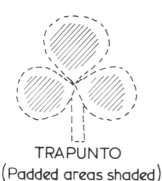

TRAPUNTO
(Padded areas shaded)

215

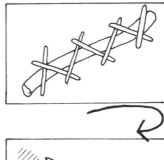

FALSE QUILTING
(No padding)

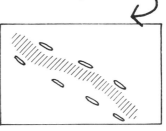

HERRINGBONE
QUILTING

Materials

The upper fabric of a finished quilted item should be soft and pliable and, except in the case of shadow quilting, densely-woven. Pale colours or such lustrous fabrics as silk or velvet show the subsequent padding to the best advantage. Instead of one piece of fabric, an area of patchwork or fabric decorated with applied motifs can be employed. Gauze or another fine material can be used for shadow quilting.

Quilted coverlet worked in 1961 by Mrs Fletcher of Co Durham (white cotton quilted in running stitch, 208 × 147cm [82 × 58in])

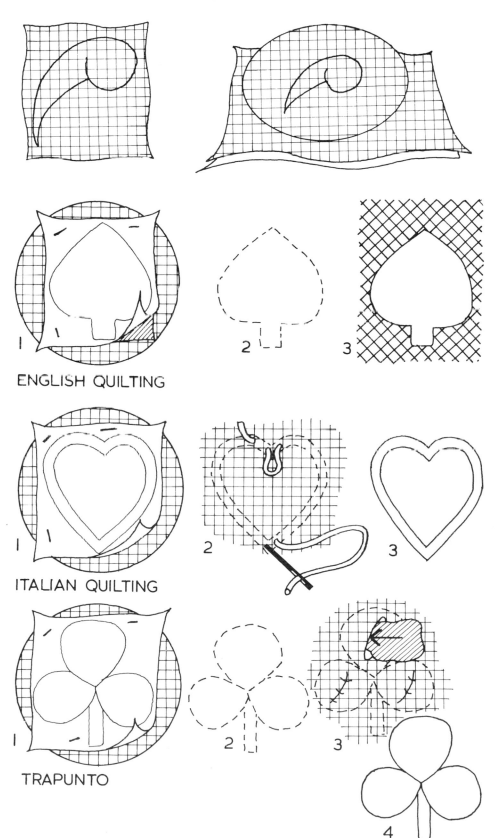

If quilting is to be worked in running stitch the design should be marked on the muslin and the layers of fabric set into the frame muslin uppermost. Embroidery is then worked through all layers. Designs to be worked in back or chain stitches should, on the other hand, be marked and worked from the top layer of the item

Quilting methods are worked as follows:

For English quilting, muslin, wadding and the upper layer of fabric are tacked to a frame (1) and the basic motif worked, either in running stitch from the muslin side or back stitch from the upper layer (2). Reserves can then be decorated with stitches worked in trellis shapes (3).

For Italian quilting, muslin and fabric are placed together (1) and the motif worked in two parallel lines of stitches (2). Then working from the muslin side a length of quilting wool or other piping is threaded through the channels, a loop of thread being left at each angle (2). This produces a raised effect on the front of the item (3).

For trapunto, muslin and fabric are tacked together (1) and the motif outlined with a single line of stitches (2). Working from the muslin side, each segment of the design is then carefully slit so that padding can be inserted and the slit sewn up (3) so that the front of the item shows a design padded segment by segment (4). Reserves can be quilted by another method or decorated with surface stitchery

ENGLISH QUILTING

ITALIAN QUILTING

TRAPUNTO

Threads generally used include pure silk, stranded and pearl cottons and coton à broder. Wool threads are usually too soft.

Other materials required include padding substances:

For English quilting: terylene or cotton wadding, layers of blanket or felt or carded woollen fleece

For Italian quilting: quilting wool (pure wool with little or no twist), piping cord or similar yarn

For trapunto: kapok, cotton (wool) or synthetic wadding.

Muslin is required for lining. Such sharp needles as 'betweens' or 'quilting needles' should be used for the main stitching and a big tapestry or couching needle is required for threading the cord in Italian quilting. All quilting forms should be worked on a frame.

Methods of working

If running stitch is to be used, the design should be marked on the muslin to prevent lines showing on the finished work. The layers of fabric are then placed on the frame, an action known as 'putting in'. Running-stitch designs are put in muslin side uppermost, those subsequently to be worked in back, chain or other stitches are set on the frame with the upper layer of fabric on top.

English quilting

The upper fabric, padding substance and muslin are put in in the manner described above, and the design is stitched in back stitch (working with the upper layer up) or running stitch (working with the muslin lining up), through all three layers. To avoid puckering, it is a good idea to work a design from the centre outwards.

Italian quilting

Upper fabric and muslin are placed on the frame muslin side uppermost and parallel lines of tiny back or running stitches worked around the marked design. Then, still working from the muslin side, a threaded tapestry or couching needle passes through the resulting channels, with small loops of padding yarn left when the needle passes through angles or pronounced curves in the channels.

Trapunto

The design is worked either with back stitch (upper fabric uppermost) or running stitch (muslin uppermost) through the two layers of fabric. Small slits are cut through the muslin of each segment to be padded and wads of cotton wool or another substance are carefully eased into the resulting pockets before the slits are joined with overstitching.

218

32. Samplers

Samplers, occasionally known as sam cloths or examplers are, as their name suggests, pieces of embroidered cloth sometimes worked as test pieces or samples of techniques and patterns. Generally worked by women or young girls, samplers also act as pattern 'records' of stitches. At specific times in history particular types such as map and family-tree samplers have been popular, and the range of samplers is wide.

One of the earliest known pieces that can be termed a sampler, in that motifs were tried out on the cotton ground fabric, was made in Peru in the second century BC. Different bird designs in wool loop and stem stitches may later have been worked many times on another cloth. Ancient sampler fragments have also been found in Egypt and Central Asia.

In the west samplers began to be worked almost as an end in themselves from the sixteenth century. They were treasured possessions, as evidenced by the 1546 will of Margaret Thomson of Dreeston, Lincolnshire, who willed 'Alys Pynchebeck my systers doughter my sawmpler with semes', and Queen Joanna (La Loca) of Spain at one time owned no less than fifty silk and gold examples. Samplers at this time were worked on long pieces of linen, the width usually between 15 and 30cm (6 and 12in), about one third of the height. Running and double-running stitches were the most popular.

The earliest surviving English dated sampler was signed by Jane Bostocke in 1598. Characteristically, many different motifs were crowded on to the precious ground fabric, arranged across it in horizontal bands. Until about 1630, however, items were not often signed and it is sometimes difficult to date them accurately although some identifiable characteristics may help. Cutwork samplers, for instance, date from the second quarter of the seventeenth century, as do motifs of 'boxers' or 'amorini', pairs of nude figures flanking plants. Complete texts were used from the third quarter of the seventeenth century to decorate lettering or alphabet samplers.

By the early eighteenth century foreign sampler fashions meant that English samplers correspondingly tended to be shorter and wider. Tammy wool cloth, known as sampler cloth, became popular and items were often decorated with pictorial motifs inside a main outer border.

Eighteenth-century forms included darning samplers, essentially practical items (see chapter 14), and map and almanack samplers, which both became particularly popular at the end of the century. By this time sampler embroidery was basically a young girls' task and some pieces are signed by five- and six-year-olds. In 1789 Mary Ann Body, then aged nine, worked on her sampler:

'If all Mankind would live in mutual love
This world would much resemble that above' (V & A T.292–1916).

In America, certainly, most surviving examples were worked by schoolgirls, generally in young ladies' schools established in the north-eastern states after 1776. In 1797, for instance, Mrs Susanna Rowson opened an Academy in Boston to instruct 'Young ladies in Reading, Writing, Arithmetic, Geography and needle-work'.

Worked on grounds of linen, linsey-woolsey (linen warp and wool weft) or, occasionally silk, American samplers have distinctive features. Genealogy samplers

Seventeenth-century English samplers were typically long and narrow. Mary Metforde signed and dated her sampler in 1677 (linen embroidered in wools, 71 × 20.2cm [28 × 8in])

Map samplers were handy test-pieces for practising stitch techniques and also provided useful geographical information (linen embroidered in silks, 38cm [15in] high)

have pictures of family trees, often just with the parents and siblings of the young embroiderer. The same family feeling is shown in some mourning samplers, characteristically worked in silk straight stitches and sometimes, as with print work, embroidered in shades of grey and black on a silk ground. Mourning samplers, also known as mourning pictures, have weeping maidens, willow trees, urns and other memorabilia and inscriptions, often to dead parents or brothers and sisters. The same feeling of immediate belonging is shown in other American samplers which have recognizable pictures of local landmarks or scenes, and American map samplers can similarly indicate the heritage of the young embroiderer's family.

Nineteenth-century girls on both sides of the Atlantic put less care into the design and execution of samplers than their predecessors, and schoolgirl samplers were often reduced to basic cross-stitch work. Berlin woolwork, however, provided an opportunity for adults to return to sampler production, and throughout most of the century many needlewomen in England and America, as elsewhere, worked typical brightly-coloured patterns on canvas.

Nowadays old samplers mainly receive the attention of collectors, although embroiderers continue occasionally to work practical test-pieces of stitches and designs.

Samplers still provide unique and personal presents. This 'friendship sampler', worked while travelling through Africa, was formed from 30cm (11¾in) of Glenshee evenweave cotton with thread count of 26 per 2.5cm (1in) and one skein each of Anchor stranded cotton Nos 0382 (dark brown), 0855 (mustard), 0846 (green) and 039 and 027 (pinks) (finished item 34 × 15.5cm [13¼ × 6in])

Other chapters in this book may generate ideas for compiling a sampler, for example using cutwork or darning. And, as with quilting, an article worked for someone, a 'friendship', 'marriage' or 'birth' sampler, provides a unique and personal gift.

33. Shadow work

Shadow embroidery or Etruscan work uses organdie or another sheer fabric decorated on the reverse to give, from the front, a somewhat translucent design.

Often worked with white fabric and threads, shadow embroidery can be produced by various methods. Closed herringbone stitch can be executed on the wrong side of a fabric and, when it is turned over to the right side, areas of criss-crossed threads of the herringbone stitch should be apparent, and the retaining stitches of the herringbone form tiny running stitches bordering the 'shadow' areas.

Alternatively, long zigzag stitches can be worked on the wrong side of the fabric to produce Indian shadow work, or pieces of fabric can be appliéd to the wrong side of a fabric to produce more solid blocks of 'shadow' on the right side. Shadow work is thus combined with appliqué and many other techniques. Shadow quilting, a specific form, is Italian quilting worked on sheer fabrics (see chapter 31).

Shadow work is probably of Indian origin and in the west it has been especially used for lingerie and babies' clothes and for table furnishings and curtains.

Materials

Although traditionally a whitework, shadow embroidery can be effective in coloured fabrics and threads. Such sheer fabrics as organdie, crêpe de chine or fine silk can be sewn with a sharp needle holding stranded cotton, coton à broder or silk. Although it can be hand-held, shadow work is best worked on a frame in order to ensure even tension of each herringbone stitch.

Methods of working

An outline design, traditionally naturalistic, can be carefully marked on the reverse of the chosen ground fabric. This pattern is then generally built up from the reverse by working closed herringbone stitch from side to side of a segment, the lengths of stitches varying to accommodate fluctuations in the shapes of the motif. This results in 'closed running stitches' outlining that motif on the right side of the fabric. Alternatively, long zigzag stitches can be worked as illustrated.

If preferred, other bits of fabric can be applied, neatly hemmed to the main ground. This method results in the backs of the tiny hemming stitches being visible on the right side of the ground.

When the main shadow embroidery is completed, other embroidery can be worked from the right side of the fabric, usually with back or stem stitches.

(*Opposite*) Corner of a shadow-work table napkin worked in Madras at the beginning of the twentieth century (white organdie embroidered with stranded cottons in peppermint green back, buttonhole and closed herringbone stitches and white satin stitch, motif 8.2 × 7.6cm [3¼ × 3in])

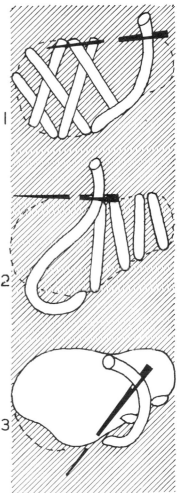

Motifs are usually decorated from the reverse side with herringbone (1) or zigzag stitches (2) or applied fabric (3)

A link twist shadow pattern adapted from a Manx cross design displayed in the Manx Museum, Douglas. After some segments (shaded) have been worked from the rear in closed herringbone stitch, other lines can be formed with stem stitch on the front of the fabric

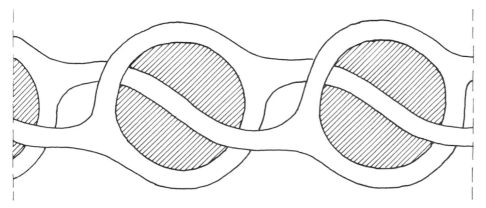

223

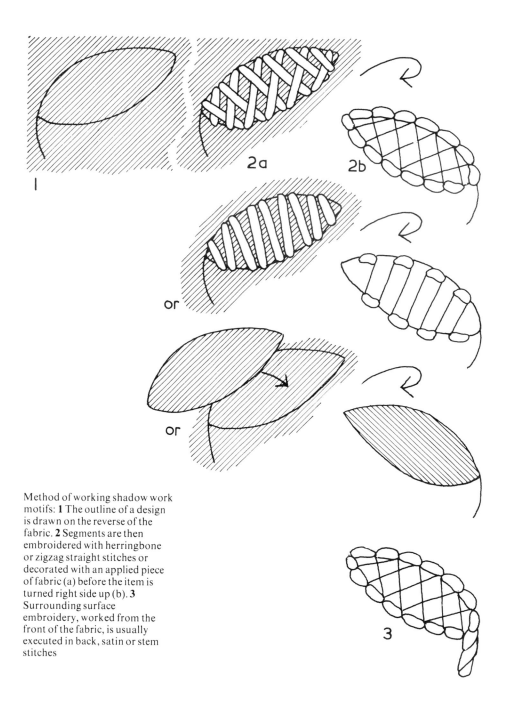

Method of working shadow work motifs: **1** The outline of a design is drawn on the reverse of the fabric. **2** Segments are then embroidered with herringbone or zigzag straight stitches or decorated with an applied piece of fabric (a) before the item is turned right side up (b). **3** Surrounding surface embroidery, worked from the front of the fabric, is usually executed in back, satin or stem stitches

34. Smocking

Smocking consists of fabric gathered into 'tubings', held with versions of stem stitch. Generally the width of the fabric is gathered by temporary running stitches worked at counted or marked regular intervals and, after smocking stitches are accomplished, these running stitches are removed.

An alternative process, American smocking, signifies that no previous gathers are formed and smocking stitches are worked direct on to marked points of the fabric, forming gathers as the embroidery proceeds. Another related technique is Italian pattern shirring, also known as smocked quilting, in which small gathers are made to a planned pattern, the ends of gathering threads are secured and the

A 30cm (11¾in) remnant of scarlet viyella was used to make a smocked dress for this 52cm (20½in) doll. There are tubes of smocking, worked with three strands of white stranded cotton, on the front and back of the dress

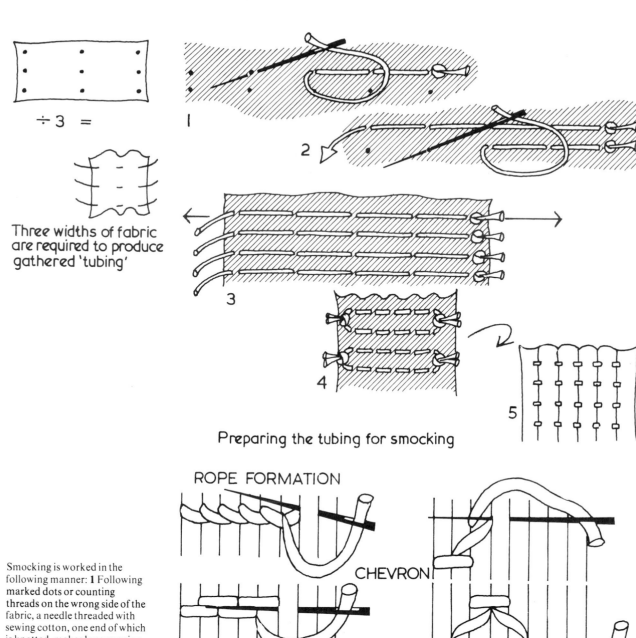

÷ 3 =

Three widths of fabric
are required to produce
gathered 'tubing'

1

2

3

4

Preparing the tubing for smocking

5

Smocking is worked in the
following manner: **1** Following
marked dots or counting
threads on the wrong side of the
fabric, a needle threaded with
sewing cotton, one end of which
is knotted, makes long running
stitches across the fabric as
illustrated. **2** At the end of a line
of stitches the thread is left loose
and another thread is taken
across a horizontal line parallel
to its predecessor. **3** When all the
lines have been worked the loose
ends and knotted ends are pulled
so that the fabric falls into
gathers. **4** Ends of thread are tied
or knotted. **5** The fabric is turned
over so that smocking stitches
can be worked from the right
side. All stem stitch variations
are worked through one gather
of fabric; various smocking
patterns can be executed

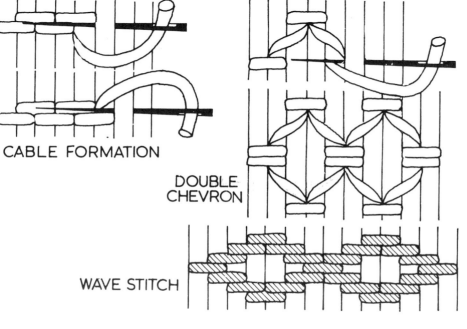

ROPE FORMATION

CHEVRON

CABLE FORMATION

DOUBLE
CHEVRON

WAVE STITCH

gathering stitches therefore form permanent support with no subsequent smocking stitches.

Although smocking had been worked before, it is principally associated with English and Welsh countrymen's overshirts from the eighteenth and early nineteenth centuries. Usually made of white or natural linen fabric embroidered with matching linen thread, these had full fronts and backs tightly gathered and smocked to form decorative chest and back panels, and there was sometimes further gathering and smocking on the upper sleeves and cuffs. Subsequent embroidery was worked direct to an ungathered area such as the collar, yoke panels, shoulders, upper sleeves and cuffs, with motifs sometimes indicating the wearer's profession (a wheel, for instance, could be worked on a wheelwright's smock).

By the end of the nineteenth century, smocks had almost disappeared as men's everyday dress in rural areas. Since then, smocking has been used as decoration for women's and children's dresses, and many smock motifs have been incorporated in Dorset feather stitchery, usually worked in differently coloured stranded cottons in buttonhole, chain and feather stitches and applied zigzag braid on linen or felt, and embellishing aprons, caps and other small items.

Materials

Fabric three times the width of the finished tubes of smocking is usually required, although thicker fabrics produce a looser tension so less fabric is needed.

A wide variety of fabrics can be employed and a beginner might like to work on checked gingham or another material that has points conveniently sited as gathering guides. Traditional smocks can be made from unbleached calico embroidered with pearl cotton, coton à broder or linen thread, or from viyella worked with twisted silk.

Commercially produced dotted transfers are available. Pointed needles and sewing thread for forming gathers are required. Smocking is usually hand-held.

Methods of working

English smocking

Unless the fabric is already checked or otherwise marked, dots should be made, either with a ruler and pencil or ironed on with a commercial transfer, on the *reverse* of the fabric.

Sewing thread, firmly knotted at the end, is used to form tiny running stitches worked through each dot as illustrated. At the end of each row of dots the sewing thread is left and another thread knotted and taken across the line of dots beneath. When all the rows of dots have been worked the loose threads are pulled tight and 'stroked', eased into regular formation, and two or more ends of thread tied together.

The chosen embroidery thread is then used to work stitches on the right side of the fabric, usually from left to right, taking a tiny stitch through the uppermost part of each small gather before passing horizontally or diagonally to the next gather, building up a straight or zigzag pattern as required. Basically, stem stitch rope formation, can be worked with the needle always passing the same side of the thread, or cable or alternating stem stitch can be worked, with the needle alternating from one side to the other. Other possible patterns include chevron or diamond stitch, double chevron stitch and wave or trellis formation.

Detail of a linen smock, probably worked in Dorset at the end of the nineteenth century

When all the smocking stitches are finished, temporary gathering threads are removed and the smocked piece can be made up into a shirt or other item.

American smocking

For this method, dots are made on the front of the fabric. Worked in a horizontal or diagonal line, small stem stitches are executed at each dot, each stitch pulled tight to its predecessor.

Italian pattern shirring

As some of the places otherwise marked would show, spaces should be counted (every fifth thread or so) rather than actually drawn on the fabric.

Working to a paper plan, long running stitches are executed horizontally across the fabric so that when threads are pulled tight a decorative lozenge-shaped pattern appears.

In American smocking, stitches are worked through marked points on the front of the fabric and they form gathers as they are executed.
Italian pattern shirring consists of gathering stitches worked through marked points on the wrong side of the fabric which, when pulled tight, produce a pattern on the right side

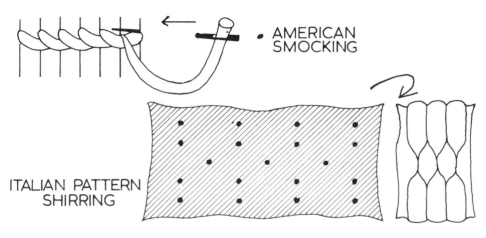

AMERICAN SMOCKING

ITALIAN PATTERN SHIRRING

228

35. Straight stitches

This chapter brings together a number of versions of straight stitches, some of the most practical and simple of all embroidery techniques.

   Known also as single-satin or stroke stitch, straight stitch has many different forms which can be employed in most of the types of needlework covered in other chapters in the book. Crossed straight stitches, known generally as cross stitches, darning stitches, straight filling stitches and tent, Gobelin and other straight needle-point stitches are diagrammed elsewhere.

   Some of the earliest surviving fragments using straight stitches are seventh and eighth century Coptic linen panels embroidered with silk straight stitch forms, satin and split stitches. By the early tenth century the same stitch forms were, with chain stitch, being employed by Mesopotamian embroiderers to work minute kufic texts from the Koran. At the same time, too, split stitch was being worked by English

Straight stitch, one of the most versatile of all needlework techniques, has been used to work most of 'The death of Uriah'. This seventeenth-century English needlework shows one episode from the story of David and Bathsheba (II Samuel ll). At David's command, Uriah the Hittite, Bathsheba's husband, was set in the forefront of the hottest battle so that he was killed (detail of a white satin panel 54.4 × 54cm [21½ × 21¼in])

embroiderers to form the lettering on St Cuthbert's stole and maniple, and since then many different straight-stitch forms have been used by embroiderers in most countries of the world.

Materials

Straight stitches can be worked on any ground, including canvas, evenweave, felt, card and leather. Except in needlepoint and counted thread forms which require that the threads of the fabric are not split, pointed needles are generally employed. A frame is not usually essential, other than for needlepoint.

Methods of working

Some of the most popular straight techniques illustrated here are back stitches. Basic back stitch is complemented by double back stitch, also known as crossed back or shadow stitch. Laced back stitch can alternatively be called Pekinese or the forbidden or blind stitch as Chinese embroiderers have been known to work it with as many as forty minute back stitches per 2.5cm (1in). Pueblo back stitch is followed by ringed back stitch, sometimes termed festoon stitch, and threaded, double threaded, trellis, triple trellis and triple closed back stitches. Whipped and zigzag back stitches complete the list.

Chevron stitch comes next, with closed, half and whipped forms, the last alternatively called Astypalea stitch. A variety of eyelets, including Algerian eye, are shown, as are fern stitch, Japanese stitch, Kerman stitch and long-and-short stitch, variously known as embroidery, feather, plumage or shading stitch.

The list continues with Macedonian stitch, and members of the satin stitch group. This includes a basic satin stitch, with alternating, encroaching and knotted versions, the last also known as rope stitch. Padded satin stitch comes next, followed by surface satin stitch, sometimes called New England economy or one-sided satin stitch. Two-sided, voided and whipped satin stitches are also diagrammed.

Slanting Slav stitch is shown in three different forms. Split stitch, one of the most versatile of all straight techniques, is sometimes called Kensington or Opus Anglicanum stitch; and a basic stem stitch, itself known variously as French filling or stalk stitch, is illustrated with alternating and Portuguese knotted versions.

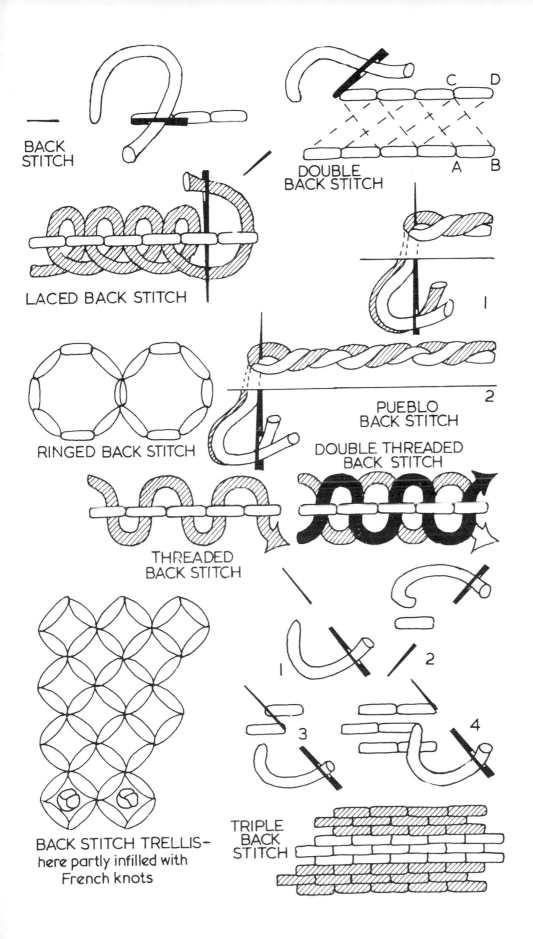

BACK
STITCH

DOUBLE
BACK STITCH

C   D

A   B

LACED BACK STITCH

1

2

PUEBLO
BACK STITCH

RINGED BACK STITCH

DOUBLE THREADED
BACK STITCH

THREADED
BACK STITCH

1

2

3

4

BACK STITCH TRELLIS—
here partly infilled with
French knots

TRIPLE
BACK
STITCH

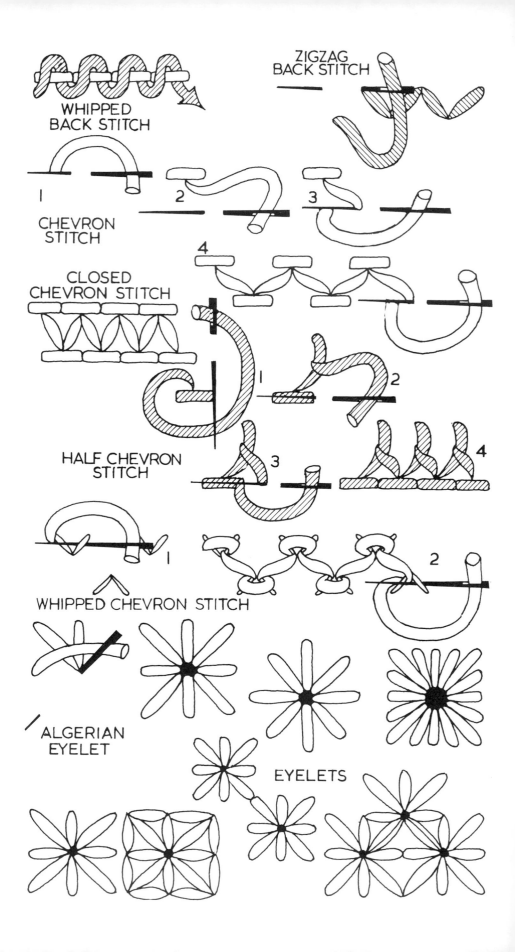

WHIPPED
BACK STITCH

ZIGZAG
BACK STITCH

CHEVRON
STITCH

1   2   3

CLOSED
CHEVRON STITCH

4

HALF CHEVRON
STITCH

1   2   3   4

WHIPPED CHEVRON STITCH

1   2

ALGERIAN
EYELET

EYELETS

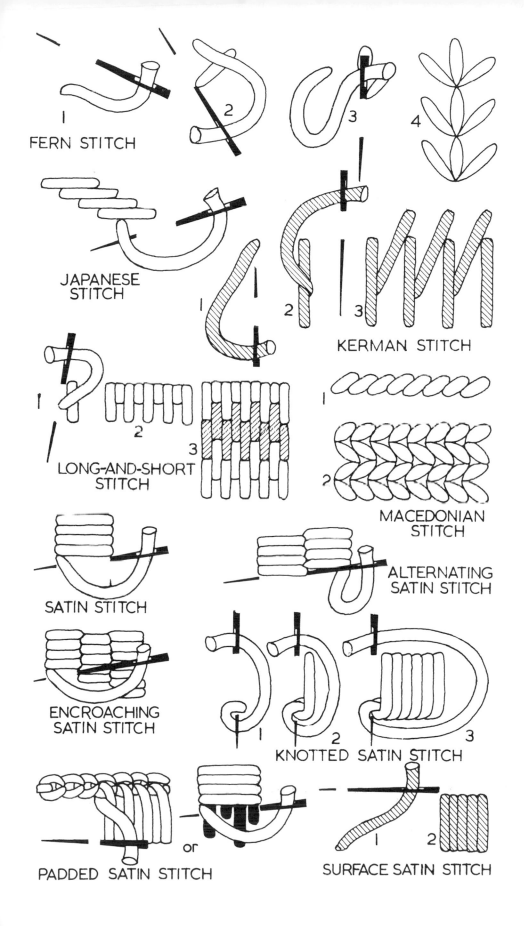

FERN STITCH

1   2   3   4

JAPANESE
STITCH

KERMAN STITCH

1   2   3

LONG-AND-SHORT
STITCH

1   2   3

MACEDONIAN
STITCH

1   2

SATIN STITCH

ALTERNATING
SATIN STITCH

ENCROACHING
SATIN STITCH

KNOTTED SATIN STITCH

1   2   3

PADDED SATIN STITCH

or

SURFACE SATIN STITCH

1   2

233

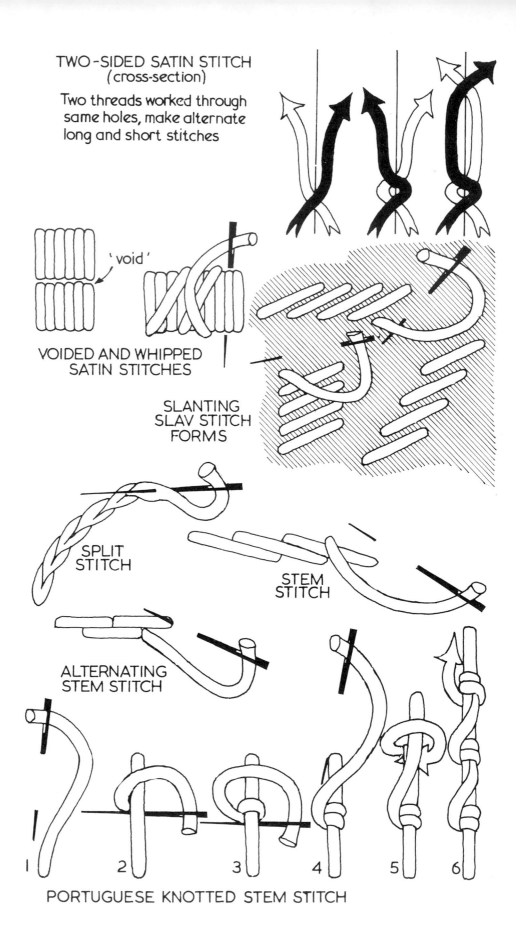

TWO-SIDED SATIN STITCH
(cross-section)

Two threads worked through
same holes, make alternate
long and short stitches

'void'

VOIDED AND WHIPPED
SATIN STITCHES

SLANTING
SLAV STITCH
FORMS

SPLIT
STITCH

STEM
STITCH

ALTERNATING
STEM STITCH

1   2   3   4   5   6

PORTUGUESE KNOTTED STEM STITCH

36. Whitework

Although whitework can be any white fabric embroidered with white thread the term is generally reserved for fine embroidery on white muslin. The technique co-ordinates with many other needlework forms and whitework is also found as broderie anglaise and other cutworks, net embroidery, some pulled-thread work and shadow embroidery. This chapter ties up whitework forms primarily connected with local areas of Britain and Ireland, namely Ayrshire, Carrickmacross, Coggeshall and Mountmellick.

Some of the earliest surviving fragments of whitework were found in Coptic tombs. By the Middle Ages heavy white linen fabric embroidered with white thread was being employed, especially in Switzerland and Germany, to form altar frontals and other hangings. In Italy intricate examples of cutwork forms worked in white on white linen eventually led to the separate art of lace making referred to in chapter 13.

With the development of trade with India, Indian whitework embroideries worked on fine cotton muslin with downy nap were imported to Europe. European embroiderers themselves worked on delicate cotton fabrics brought from India and, later, on locally-produced materials. This availability of supplies helped give rise to some individual forms of whitework.

Ayrshire work

Known as sewed muslin or flooerin', this developed in Scotland from earlier Dresden work (see chapter 29).

Characterized by cotton fabric, firmer than that used for Dresden, decorated with white cotton thread, Ayrshire work has large cutwork holes partly infilled. There is surrounding satin stitch, sometimes padded, and stem stitch, also veining or beading, small ladders formed from close holes pierced with a stiletto and subsequently bound.

This panel, worked *c* 1912 by Lady Evelyn Stuart Murray (1868–1940), youngest daughter of the seventh Duke of Atholl, is undoubtedly one of the finest examples of whitework (white cambric embroidered with cotton, satin and stem stitches and pulled-thread filling stitches, 55.8 × 63.5cm [22⅞ × 25in] overall)

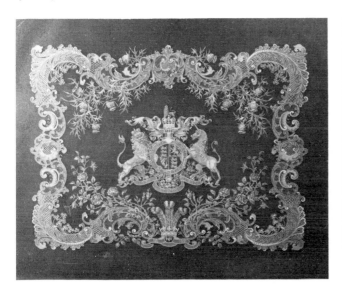

In the earlier Dresden work, sheer fabric was tacked to a board printed with an outline design. Ayrshire work was executed from a design already stamped on to fabric. Satin and padded satin stitches and pulled-thread techniques were employed, as was 'veining', formed with closely-spaced small holes made, as in broderie anglaise, with a stiletto (1), and the edges subsequently overcast (2)

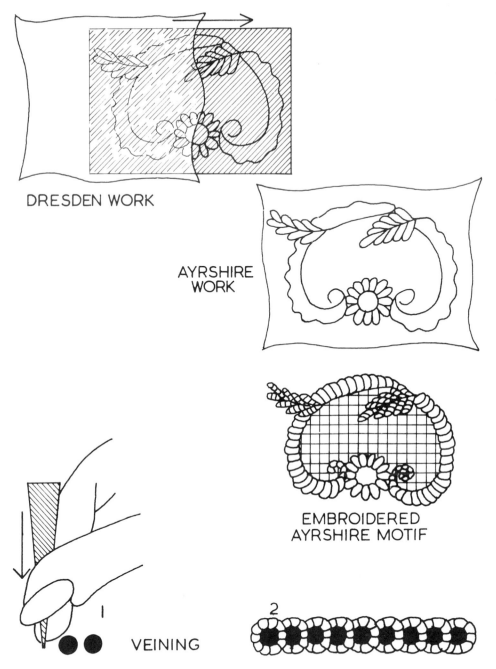

DRESDEN WORK

AYRSHIRE WORK

EMBROIDERED AYRSHIRE MOTIF

VEINING

The first Scottish mill working with raw cotton from the southern states of America had been built in Rothesay in 1775, and although local embroiderers copied imported Dresden examples it was not until about 1814 that an Ayrshire agent, Mrs Jamieson, adapted designs from a French christening robe. These were stamped direct on to fabric, which obviated the need for the cumbersome patterns used for Dresden work.

Ayrshire work was extensively produced, mostly by women outworkers, and sold especially as christening robes or other baby clothes. Its main lifetime lasted until the effects of the American Civil War restricted the supply of cotton to the Scottish mills.

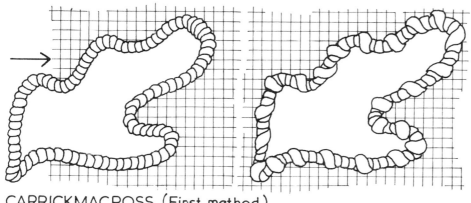

CARRICKMACROSS (First method)

Carrickmacross can be worked by two methods. A linen motif bound with overcasting is applied, possibly by hemming, to a ground of net. Alternatively, a piece of linen is placed direct on the net and the outline worked in running stitch before the reserves of the motif are carefully cut away and the raw edges covered, possibly with chain stitch

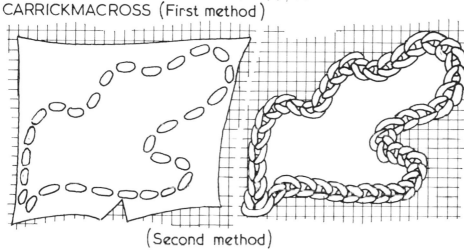

(Second method)

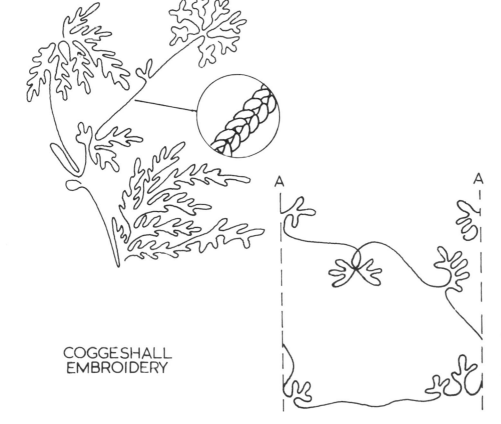

COGGESHALL EMBROIDERY

Coggeshall embroidery, worked in tamboured chain stitch, is typified by wild flower and repeating scroll designs

Carrickmacross

This is an Irish whitework form that can also be termed appliqué and net embroidery.

Two main methods are used in its making. Motifs, generally drawn on white cambric, can be cut out, bound with overcasting and applied to white net with hemming or needlework bars. Alternatively a marked piece of muslin is tacked to the net and the design outlined in running stitches. The reserves of muslin are cut away and the raw edges of the motif bound with overcasting or covered with tamboured chain stitch. The surrounding net can be further decorated with pulled work and chain or running stitches.

This technique, named after a market town in Co Monaghan, was established as a home industry in the 1820s and it was later revived after the famine of 1846.

Some Carrickmacross is still commercially produced, decorating handkerchiefs, collars and cuffs and wedding veils. Reticella cutwork executed on white linen is also sometimes known as Carrickmacross.

Coggeshall embroidery

This English whitework has tamboured designs of honeysuckle, cow parsley and other wild flowers trailing over a wide area of sheer muslin shawls, flounces, capes and other costume items.

In about 1823 a French immigrant living in this Essex town employed young embroiderers in a factory, and older outworkers, all copying designs from card patterns either propped up behind the embroidery or placed underneath it so that the design showed through.

Coggeshall embroidery was regularly sold until 1939 and some thirty years later the same designs began to be worked again by embroiderers for their own enjoyment.

Characteristic Mountmellick designs include corn husks formed from long bullion knots and blackberries worked with French knots. Other fruits and petals can be worked with padded satin stitch, leaves bordered with satin stitch and infilled with French knots, and further details executed in stem stitch

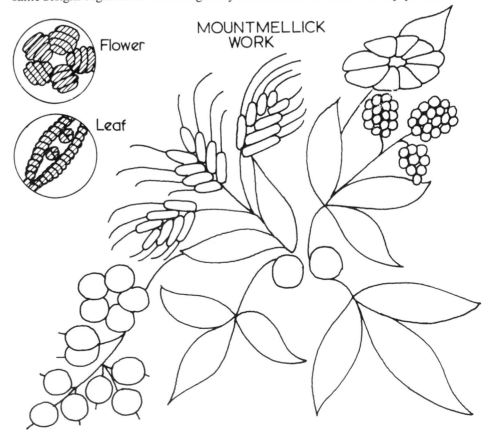

A piece of paper temporarily placed, possibly tacked, over a half-finished embroidery prevents whitework becoming dirty.

Mountmellick work

Worked in soft unmercerized cotton, sometimes known as knitting cotton, on a ground of shiny satin-like cotton jean, Mountmellick work is heavier in effect than other whitework techniques mentioned here.

Taking its name from a rural district in central Ireland, Mountmellick work is characterized by designs of blackberries worked with French knots, passion flowers made with bullion knots, sometimes known locally as worms, and snail's trail, formed from alternating straight stitches and French knots. Some Mountmellick pieces, including nightdress cases and pillow shams, are sub-sequently bordered with heavy white fringes.

From about 1825 Mountmellick work was commercially produced by out-workers but later it became an amateur embroiderers' pastime.

Materials for whitework

With the exception of Mountmellick, all the techniques mentioned here can be worked on any sheer fine white fabric such as organdie, lawn, batiste or muslin. Stranded cotton or coton à broder are popular threads, worked with a pointed needle.

Mountmellick work can be worked with satin stitched with coton à broder. All forms of whitework are best worked on a frame.

Working tips

Any whitework embroidery requires absolute cleanliness. Perspiration from the embroiderer's hands can stain threads, especially on a hot day.

Hands can be kept dry with powdered French chalk. Chalk is placed in the centre of a square of muslin, the corners of which are then tied tightly together to form a ball which can be used to freshen hands as required.

And, as in metal thread work, another centuries-old tip is to cover areas of fabric already embroidered, using acid-free tissue paper temporarily tacked over the stitching.

Coats products and publications

(available in 1978)

Embroidery Articles

4636 Clarks Anchor Stranded Cotton, 8m (9yd) skeins, 250 shades

4375 Clarks Anchor Coton à Broder, No 18, 114 shades; No 25, 29 shades

4334 Clarks Anchor Soft Embroidery, 9m (10yd) skeins, 149 shades

4591 Clarks Anchor Pearl Cotton, 10g (0.35oz) balls, 5's and 8's, 45 shades

4504 Clarks Anchor Machine Embroidery, 30's 53 shades, 50's 56 shades

4230 Coats Anchor Tapisserie Wool, 13.7m (15yd) skeins, 220 shades

4225 Coats Anchor Tapisserie Grounding Wool, 28.4g (1oz) hanks, 35 shades

Milwards Crewel Needles, Sizes 4–10, Assortments 3/9: 5/10

Milwards Heavy Embroidery Needles

H2132 Plastic Embroidery Hoops, 10cm (4in), (H2133, 15cm [6in], H2134, 20cm [8in]; H2135, 25cm [10in]); H2136, oval, 11.4 × 23cm (4½ × 9in)

H497 Wooden Embroidery Hoops, 10cm (4in), 15cm (6in), 20cm (8in), 25cm (10in)

H2153 Needlecraft Scissor, stainless steel, plastic handle, 14cm (5½in)

H1618 Embroidery Scissor, stainless steel, 9cm (3½in)

Embroidery Publications

441	Cross Stitch Embroidery
570	Cross Stitch European Designs
592	Binca Embroidery
614	Coloured Hardanger Motifs
650	Drawn Thread Embroidery
755	Modern Spanish Blackwork
837	Sunshine Cross Stitch from the Mediterranean
882	Flowers & Leaves in Embroidery
925	Cut-work Embroidery
935	Petit Point Embroidery
1007	Anchor Needlework Tapestry
1040	Shadow Work Embroidery
1046	17 Counted Thread Designs
1047	20 Multi-Impression Embroidery Transfers
1055	20 Multi-Impression Embroidery Transfers
1056	Jacobean Embroidery in Modern Style
1058	Church Kneelers
1066	Hardanger for Today
1067	32 Embroidery Stitches Book No. 1
1069	Florentine Embroidery
1070	100 Embroidery Stitches
1083	32 Embroidery Stitches Book No. 2
1085	Drawn Fabric Embroidery
1094	Around the World in Cross Stitch
1098	Norweave Embroidery
1101	20 Multi-Impression Transfers
1114	Canvas Embroidery
1135	Cross Stitch for the 70s
1145	Zodiac Signs Embroidery
1154	Norweave Designs
1169	Embroidery Panels
1176	Embroidery on Canvas
1177	6 Alphabets and Numerals
1184	Mix and Match
1186	Leaf Embroidery
1198	Canvas Embroidery Patterns
1199	Smocking and Quilting
1204	Children's Motifs
1206	Embroidery in Fashion
1214	The Bargello Embroidery Book
1218	50 Canvas Embroidery Stitches
1220	Panels in Embroidery
1225	Ravenna Mosaics in Embroidery
1229	Top Ten in Embroidery
1243	50 Free Style Embroidery Stitches
1244	Wall Decor in Embroidery
1245	50 Counted Thread Embroidery Stitches
1256	Checkweave Canvas Embroidery
1257	Mixed Canvas Stitches
1258	Countryside Embroidery

Further Reading

Mary Gostelow's other books illustrating embroidery techniques are:

A World of Embroidery (Mills & Boon, London, 1975).

Blackwork (Batsford, London, 1976).

*Embroidery: traditional designs, techniques and patterns from all over the world (Marshall Cavendish Editions, London, 1977).

General

Anchor manual of needlework (Batsford, London, 1958).

Clabburn, Pamela. *The needleworker's dictionary* (Macmillan, London, 1976).

Dillmont, Thérèse de. *Encyclopedia of needlework* (DMC, 1886).

Enthoven, Jacqueline. *The stitches of creative embroidery* (Van Nostrand Reinhold, Wokingham, 1964).

Gostelow, Mary. *A World of Embroidery* (Mills & Boon, London, 1975).

———. *Embroidery: Traditional designs, techniques and patterns from all over the world* (Marshall Cavendish Editions, London, 1977).

Petersen, Grete (with Elsie Svennås). *Handbook of stitches* (Batsford, London, 1970).

Phillpott, Pat. *The craft of embroidery* (Stanley Paul, London, 1976).

Snook, Barbara. *Embroidery stitches* (Batsford, London, 1963).

Thomas, Mary. *Mary Thomas's dictionary of embroidery stitches* (Hodder & Stoughton, Sevenoaks, 1934).

———. *Mary Thomas's embroidery book* (Hodder & Stoughton, Sevenoaks, 1936).

Wilson, Erica. *Erica Wilson's embroidery book* (Faber, London, 1975).

As well as the books listed above, there are specific publications covering some of the techniques described in this book. These include:

Appliqué

Mann, Kathleen. *Appliqué design and method* (Black, London, 1937).

Assisi

Cornelius, Rosemary (with Peg Doffek and Sue Hardy). *Exploring Assisi* (Sinbad, New York, 1976).

DMC. *Assisi embroideries.*

Bargello

Fischer, Pauline (with Anabel Lasker). *Bargello magic: how to design your own* (Dent, London, 1972).

Hall, Nancy (with Jean Riley). *Bargello borders* (Edwards, New York, 1974).

Kaestner, Dorothy. *Four-way Bargello* (Scribner's, New York, 1973).

———. *Needlepoint Bargello* (Scribner's, New York, 1974).

Rome, Carol Cheyney. *A new look at Bargello: the florentine needlepoint stitch book* (Crown, New York, 1973).

Snook, Barbara. *The craft of Florentine embroidery* (Scribners, New York, 1971; Mills & Boon, London, 1974).

Stevens, Gigs. *Free-form Bargello* (Scribner's, New York, 1977).

Williams, Elsa. *Bargello: Florentine canvas work* (Van Nostrand Reinhold, New York, 1967).

Blackwork

Drysdale, Rosemary. *The art of blackwork embroidery* (Mills & Boon, London, 1975).

Geddes, Elisabeth (with Moyra McNeill). *Blackwork embroidery* (Mills & Boon, 1965).

Gostelow, Mary. *Blackwork* (Batsford, London, 1976).

Scoular, Marion. *Blackwork* (Leisure Arts [US], 1976).

White, A.V. *Blackwork embroidery of today* (Mills & Boon, London, 1955).

Wilson, Erica. *The craft of blackwork and whitework* (Scribner's, New York, 1973).

Blocking and mounting

Burchette, Dorothy. *Needlework blocking and finishing* (Scribner's, New York, 1974).

Ireys, Katharine. *Finishing and mounting your needlepoint pieces* (Crowell, New York, 1973).

Conservation

Finch, Karen (with Greta Putnam). *Caring for textiles* (Barrie & Jenkins, London, 1977).

Crewel embroidery

Davis, Mildred. *The art of crewel embroidery* (Crown, New York, 1962).

Hedlund, Catherine. *A primer of New England crewel embroidery* (Old Sturbridge Village, Mass., 1971).

Jones, Mary Eirwen. *English crewel designs* (Macdonald, London, 1974).

Edwards, Joan. *Crewel embroidery in England* (Batsford, London, 1975).

Wilson, Erica. *The craft of crewel embroidery* (Faber, London, 1977).

Cross stitches

Gierl, Irmgard. *Cross stitch patterns* (Batsford, London, 1977).

Kinmond, Jean. *Counted thread embroidery* (Batsford, London, 1973).

Nye, Thelma N (ed). *Cross stitch patterns* (Van Nostrand Reinhold, New York, 1973).

Thompson, Ginnie. *Teach yourself counted cross stitch* (Leisure Arts, [US], 1975). 1975).

Cutwork

Cave, Oenone. *Linen cut-work* (Vista Books, 1963).

Designing

Howard, Constance. *Embroidery and colour* (Batsford, London, 1976).

——. *Inspiration for embroidery* (Batsford, London, 1966).

Whyte, Kathleen. *Design in embroidery* (Batsford, London, 1969).

Drawn-thread work

DMC. *Drawn thread work* (series I and II).
Melen, Lisa. *Drawn threadwork* (Van Nostrand Reinhold, London, 1972).

Lettering

Cirker, Blanche (Ed). *Needlework alphabets and designs* (Dover, 1975).
DMC. *Monograms and alphabets for combination*
Russell, Pat. *Lettering for embroidery* (Batsford, London, 1972).
Weiss, Rita (Ed). *Victorian alphabets, monograms and names for needleworkers* (Dover, 1974).

Machine embroidery

Butler, Anne. *Machine stitches* (Batsford, London, 1976).
Clucas, Joy. *Your machine for embroidery* (Bell, London, 1973).
Gray, Jennifer. *Machine embroidery: technique and design* (Batsford, London, 1973).

Metal-thread work

Dawson, Barbara. *Metal thread embroidery* (Batsford, London, 1968).
Zimmerman, Jane. *Techniques of metal thread embroidery* (Zimmerman, [US], 1977)

Needlepoint or canvas work

Ambuter, Carolyn. *Carolyn Ambuter's complete book of needlepoint* (Crowell, New York, 1972)
Beincecke, Mary Ann. *Basic needlery stitches on mesh fabrics* (Dover, 1973).
Donnelly, Barbara (with Karl Gullers). *The crewel needlepoint world* (Gullers, New York, 1973).
Grafton, Carol Belanger. *Geometric needlepoint designs* (Dover, 1975).
Gray, Jennifer. *Canvas work* (Batsford, London, 1974).
Green, Sylvia. *Canvas embroidery for beginners* (Studio Vista, London, 1970).
Hanley, Hope. *Needlepoint* (Scribner's, New York, 1964).
——. *New methods in needlepoint* (Scribner's, New York, 1966).
——. *Patterns for needlepoint* (Scribner's, New York, 1976).
House, Jody. *Designs for needlepoint boxes* (Leisure Arts, [US], 1976).
Lane, Maggie. *Needlepoint by design* (Scribner's, New York, 1972).
Lantz, Sherlee. *Trianglepoint: from Persian pavilions to Op Art with one stitch* (Viking, New York, 1976).
——. (with Maggie Lane). *A pageant of pattern for needlepoint canvas* (Deutsch, London, 1974).
Needlepoint stitches on fabric (evenweave embroidery) (Leisure Arts, [US], 1976).
Perrone, Lisbeth. *The new world of needlepoint* (Random House, New York, 1972).
Rhodes, Mary. *Ideas for canvas work* (Batsford, London, 1970).
——. *Needlepoint: the art of canvas embroidery* (Octopus, London, 1974).
Rome, Carol Cheyney. *A new look at needlepoint* (Allen & Unwin, London, 1973).
Springall, Diana. *Canvas embroidery* (Batsford, London, 1969).

Patchwork

Colby, Averil. *Patchwork* (Batsford, London, 1976).
——. *Patchwork quilts* (Batsford, London, 1965).

Mahler, Celine. *Once upon a quilt: patchwork design and technique* (Van Nostrand Reinhold, New York, 1973).
McKim, Ruby. *101 patchwork patterns* (Dover, 1962).

Pulled-thread work

McNeill, Moyra. *Pulled thread* (Mills & Boon, London, 1971).
Meyer, Ann. *Pulled thread on canvas* (Leisure Arts, New York, 1976).

Quilting

Ickis, Marguerite. *The standard book of quilt making* (Dover, 1959).
McNeill, Moyra. *Quilting for today* (Mills & Boon, London, 1975).

Samplers

Bolton, Ethel (with Eva Coe). *American samplers* (Dover, 1973).
Colby, Averil. *Samplers yesterday and today* (Batsford, London, 1964).
Dreesmann, Cécile. *Samplers for today* (Van Nostrand Reinhold, New York, 1972).
Huish, Marcus. *Samplers and tapestry embroideries* (Dover, 1970).
Meulenbelt-Nieuwburg, Albarta. *Embroidery motifs from Dutch samplers* (Batsford, London, 1974).
Samplers (HMSO, 1960).
The story of samplers (Philadelphia Museum of Art, 1971).

Whitework

Boyle, Elizabeth. *The Irish flowerers* (Ulster Folk Museum and the Institute of Irish Studies, 1971).
Swain, M. H. *The flowerers: the origins and history of Ayrshire needlework* (Chambers, Edinburgh, 1955).
Wilson, Erica. *The craft of blackwork and whitework* (Scribner's, New York, 1973).

Index

This is a practical index focusing mainly on stitches and techniques which are listed under their main reference. Main (chapter) entries are indicated in **bold** type; diagrams in *italics*.

246